Emergent Literacy

Studies in Written Language and Literacy

A multi-disciplinary series presenting studies on written language, with special emphasis on its uses in different social and cultural settings. The series combines sociolinguistic and psycholinguistic accounts of the acquisition and transmission of literacy and brings together insights from linguistics, psychology, sociology, education, anthropology and philosophy.

For an overview of all books published in this series, please see *http://benjamins.com/catalog/swll*

Volume 13

Emergent Literacy. Children's books from 0 to 3
Edited by Bettina Kümmerling-Meibauer

Emergent Literacy

Children's books from 0 to 3

Edited by

Bettina Kümmerling-Meibauer
University of Tübingen

John Benjamins Publishing Company
Amsterdam / Philadelphia

The paper used in this publication meets the minimum requirements of American National Standard for Information Sciences – Permanence of Paper for Printed Library Materials, ANSI Z39.48-1984.

Library of Congress Cataloging-in-Publication Data

Emergent literacy : children's books from 0 to 3 / edited by Bettina Kümmerling-Meibauer.
p. cm. (Studies in Written Language and Literacy, ISSN 0929-7324 ; v. 13)
Includes bibliographical references and index.
1. Reading (Preschool) 2. Toddlers--Books and reading. I. Kümmerling-Meibauer, Bettina.
LB1140.5.R4E43 2011
372.4--dc23 2011032908
ISBN 978 90 272 1808 7 (Hb ; alk. paper)
ISBN 978 90 272 8323 8 (Eb)

John Benjamins Publishing Co. · P.O. Box 36224 · 1020 ME Amsterdam · The Netherlands
John Benjamins North America · P.O. Box 27519 · Philadelphia PA 19118-0519 · USA

Table of contents

CHAPTER 1

Emergent literacy and children's literatu

Bettina Kümmerling-Meibauer

This volume touches upon issues at the heart of emergent literacy studies: how do we know what very young children aged from 10 months to three years – at least in Western countries – learn by joint looking at pictures in picturebooks or by intensively listening to a children's book story? What are the mental prerequisites that enable such learning processes? The process usually starts when children aged 10 to 12 months first encounter picturebooks. Since young children at this age do not know what to do with a picturebook, they first have to learn the "rules of book-behaviour" (Lewis 2001:78) in interaction with an adult mediator. This includes sitting still, turning the pages, holding the book in the correct position, and looking carefully at the pictures. In fact, young children's first actions might consist in scratching at the paper and pointing at the pictures, and their first utterances might be gurgles and sounds of joy and surprise before they start to name the depicted objects. However, involvement with picturebooks at this early age is mainly determined by joint looking at the images, usually with parents and other carers. These first encounters with picturebooks exert a great influence on the child's developing sense of literacy, as has been demonstrated by scholars such as Jones (1996), Kress & van Leeuwen (1996), Kümmerling-Meibauer & Meibauer (2005), Lowe (2007), Nikolajeva (2003), Ninio (1983), Snow & Goldfield (1983) and Whitehead (2004).

Despite this, studies in emergent literacy research dealing with the impact of picturebooks on children under three are extremely rare – White (1954), Butler (1979; 1980) and Crago & Crago (1983) were among the first academics to take book sharing with infants and toddlers seriously. Indeed, the majority of early literacy projects and studies refer to the cognitive, emotional and aesthetic input of picturebooks and other children's books on kindergarten children and preschool children, i.e. children aged four to six (Braun 1995; Dickinson & Neuman 2007; Goswami 1998; Hall et al. 2003; McCartney & Philips 2006; Marsh & Hallet 2008; Tucker 1990).

There are various reasons for neglecting the study of emergent literacy in the first two to three years of life. Firstly, picturebooks published for this target group are deceptively simple: they do not contain any text, or include only short texts denoting the depicted objects or describing the scenes in the pictures. They lack the complex text-picture relationship typical of picturebooks for older children. Secondly, it is exceptionally difficult to work with children under three and with books addressed to this audience, since an empirical researcher has limited possibilities of eliciting and interpreting reader responses to books because of young children's restricted vocabulary and general knowledge. This means it is not easy to design questionnaires for investigating young children's understanding of picturebooks. They have not yet fully acquired the ability to communicate their feelings, impressions and comprehension problems verbally, let alone to answer complex questions. Thirdly, the neglect of children's books for very young children in the academic world subtly influences the situation – even today, the majority of scholars, educationalists and other caretakers underestimate the fundamental impact of these first picturebooks on the young child's emerging sense of literacy. Academics working in the realm of children's literature research do not consider these first picturebooks as an essential part of their field of study, since these books usually lack written text. This has led to the assumption that the books are not basic contributions to literature in a general sense, but are seen rather as "learning toys," as Apseloff (1987) has suggested. Although picturebooks for children under three years of age introduce children to the book format and a variety of topics and illustrations, stimulate their imagination, initiate verbalization and create intimacy between adult mediator and child, they are still underrated and their investigation is not regarded as a serious enterprise.

Given this, the following essay will discuss the actual nature of books for children under three, why they are so important for research in the realm of language acquisition, literacy studies and cognitive studies, and how they might contribute fresh insights into young children's cognitive, linguistic, and aesthetic development.

Children's books from 0 to 3

There is no consensus on how to classify books for children aged under three. These types of book are generally subsumed under the heading of "baby books"; yet this term is far too broad as it covers all the books written and published for children aged from approximately 10 months to two or three years. Moreover, this label applies to a whole range of both fictional and nonfictional works, including early-concept books, picture dictionaries, movable books, pop-up books, toy books, song books, coloring books and books to read aloud. These books always have illustrations to catch the eye of the small child, while many have only a short text or no text at all. There is still no concise classification of these books and their different functions (see Kümmerling-Meibauer 2006b and Kümmerling-Meibauer & Meibauer in the present volume). It is clear, however, that the books appear to encourage language acquisition, visual literacy, and acquisition of general knowledge on topics such as food, hygiene, nature, animals, colors, etc. (Ganea et al. 2008; Ganea et al. 2011; Siegal 2008).

To appeal to very young children, picturebooks are often disguised as playthings. Some offer the possibility of lifting up flaps on the pages; others combine picturebook and stuffed animal or puzzle, stimulating the child to use the picturebook as a tool. Other kinds of picturebook contain inserts of fluffy clothes and sparkling surfaces that invite the child to touch the pages and clothes. There are also picturebooks that make animal noises when the child turns the pages or pushes buttons. Some picturebooks are shaped like a car, a ball, a cube or an animal, previewing the book's general content. These types stress the picturebook's materiality on the one hand, and its synesthetic quality on the other. They encourage the young child to make use of different senses in looking at the pictures, listening to the sounds, and touching the different materials. The variety of forms and materials mean that people are sometimes puzzled as to how to classify these products. Are they still books, or are they toys? Or a hybrid of book and toy? The impact of these picturebook-objects on the young child's book concept has not been investigated yet, and remains a desirable topic for future study.

Children typically encounter the first wordless picturebooks when they are about one year old. One reason for the dawning interest in picturebooks is that children start to master their first words at this age. This is the beginning of the acquisition of the early lexicon consisting of approx. 50 words (Clark 2003). The first picturebooks depict objects from the young child's surroundings, which have been coined "early-concept books" (Kümmerling-Meibauer & Meibauer 2005). It is clear that many picturebooks are arranged according to conceptual classes or domains, i.e. toys, animals, vehicles, food, and even abstract conceptual classes, such as letters, numbers, and sizes. All this supports the young child's acquisition of concepts (Murphy 2002). Another type of book depicts scenes and locations such as shopping at the market, eating breakfast in the kitchen, or life and work on a farm, stimulating the acquisition of cognitive scripts and schemata. One specific type of wordless picturebook is the "wimmelbook" ("busy book"), a neologism coined by German publishers to describe the fact that the images are crammed with figures and scenes. Wimmelbooks stimulate the young child to look carefully at the pictures and to narrate the events depicted in the images (see the chapter by Remí in the present volume). The wimmelbook demands high standards of visual literacy, and presents a kind of threshold to picturebooks containing a story or narrative (with or without text). Even the

"I Spy" books share some elements with the wimmelbook, since they encourage the child to look for objects on the pictures, which may be hidden behind flaps that have to be lifted.

Although books for very young children rarely feature a progressive narrative, short, simple texts are found in illustrated books that either contain rhymes and poems for children or tell a short story. These books with traditional jingles, finger plays, lullabies, riddles or nursery rhymes, often supplemented by musical scores, form the young child's first poetry experience and give her aesthetic pleasure (Foy 2003; Scott in the present volume). Their brevity and strongly accentuated rhymes and rhythm foster memorability. Such verses can also be regarded as concise narratives of four to six lines that prepare the listening child for longer, more complex texts (see Ahrens in the present volume). At about three years of age children are normally accustomed to a simple concept of story such as Eric Carle's *The Very Hungry Caterpillar* (1969), which has an episodic structure centered on one main figure.

These picturebook narratives presuppose that the child has already acquired the ability to understand a simple story, either told orally or read aloud by an adult mediator. Moreover, as several scholars have demonstrated, children aged three are usually able to tell a short, simple story, building a bridge between the child's ability to understand a story and the child's capacity to narrate a story herself (Bamberg 1997; Boueke et al. 1995). However, while picturebook narratives are considered a seminal step towards the acquisition of literacy, we are still in the fledgling stage as regards analysis of the impact of images in general on the young child's developing concepts of "literature" and "story," and particularly of the effect of wordless picturebooks for young children such as early-concept books or wimmelbooks.

Research on emergent literacy

In an ever increasing range of cultural settings, current research reveals the variety and importance of the pre-school experiences and knowledge that children gain from early acquaintance with stories and books. The more we have learned about children's first approaches to literacy, the more we have been confronted with evidence of the topic's historical, social, linguistic and psychological complexities (Kümmerling-Meibauer 2006a; Snow 2006). Nevertheless, studies in early literacy usually focus on children over three years old and neglect the impact of children's books on small children, even infants and toddlers. Although children's literature research is a rapidly expanding field and picturebook research is especially prominent and dynamic, scholars working in these research areas are usually not involved in investigating children's books targeted at children under three years of age.

There are a fair number of seminal studies on young children's language acquisition (for example, Bloom 2000; Clark 2003; Tracy 2007), their color preferences (Koerber 2007; Werner in the present volume) and the impact of young children's drawings on their conceptual knowledge about pictures (Golomb 2011; Lancaster 2003; Lancaster 2007). However, there are hardly any investigations on the mutual relationship between language acquisition, emergent literacy, cognitive development and children's literature, especially in relation to picturebooks for the very young. Moreover, a thorough analysis of young children's developing understanding of forms, colors, schemata, and artistic styles – features that determine picturebooks for young children – and the analysis of the influence of wordless picturebooks on the young child's increasing narrative competence would certainly cross-fertilize child psychology, cognitive linguistics, pedagogy, and children's literature research.

While detailed study of children's development dates back to the end of the 18th century, some of the most interesting studies were carried out in the 19th and 20th century. The discovery of small children as a serious audience goes back to Romanticism, especially to Johann Gottfried Herder's concept of early childhood as a lifespan that reflects earlier stages of human development. Interest in the earliest years of the child's development increased during the first half of the 19th century. The educationalists Friedrich Fröbel and Johann Heinrich Pestalozzi claimed that books played a crucial role in early learning by providing accessible images of the world (see the chapter by Deppner in the present volume). In order to spread his newly developed educational theory, Fröbel edited the volume *Mutter und Koselieder* (Mother's Songs, Games, and Stories, 1844), which demonstrates the connection between play and language acquisition and the affection between mother and young child. At the same time, the first picturebooks and movable books for very young children were published (see Kümmerling-Meibauer & Linsmann 2009). Growing interest in the cognitive and psychological development of the young child led to the establishment of child psychology as a new area of research in the 1880s. The German researcher Friedrich Dietrich Tiedemann, who kept a diary about his newborn son at the end of the 18th century, is regarded as a pioneer. The book based on this diary, entitled *Beobachtung über die Entwicklung der Sehfähigkeiten bei Kindern* (Observation on the Development of Children's Visual Faculties), was posthumously published in 1895 and greatly influenced scholars such as Berthold Sigismund, James Sully and W.B. Drummond, who pointed to the remarkable interest of one-year-old children in pictures. Anticipating recent research in child psychology, they discovered that young children prefer pictures with primary colors that depict single objects from the child's surroundings. Sully also observed that children try to grasp the pictured object from the book page and concluded that they are not yet able to distinguish between real objects and their illustration. The research results were published in newly founded scholarly journals, such as *Babyland* (1876ff.) and *Babyhood* (1883ff.), in order to alert academics and carers to the astonishing cognitive, emotional and aesthetic development of infants and toddlers (Kümmerling-Meibauer & Linsmann 2009). Further research was undertaken during the first half of the 20th century, and gradually accumulated after 1945. By now the distribution of picturebooks for children aged 1 to 3 on the international book market has rapidly increased. A remarkable range of book types for small children has been established. It emphasizes the importance of the preschool years for learning and stimulates the child's knowledge of words, images and concepts. These trends coincide with the growing interest in emergent literacy since the 1980s. Studies in linguistics, cognitive psychology, educational theory and children's literature showed that children's books are fundamental to language acquisition, visual literacy and literary literacy. For example, analysis of joint picturebook reading of parents and small children has demonstrated that it encourages verbal interaction. It also stresses the connection between early book usage and later skills in reading and writing (Hall 1987; Newman & Dickinson 2003; Whitehead 2002).

Since the mid-1980s there has been a revolution in our knowledge of infant cognition: new techniques for exploring what young children know within the first three years of life have revealed striking early abilities in the understanding of both the physical world and abstract concepts like number or sizes, as well as in the development of an awareness of self (Blatt 2007; Nodelman 2010). Over a similar period there have been parallel changes in the study of language acquisition. Both areas – the study of cognitive development and the study of language acquisition – are rich in innovative ideas about what might constitute adequate new theories to cover the fresh ground. For historical reasons these strands of investigations have often grown apart. One reason, perhaps, is that methods of investigation sometimes diverge. Another reason is that, despite many attempts to relate significant stages, there is still a lack of interdisciplinary projects that coordinate these different strands, including literacy studies.

The importance of emergent literacy has also been stressed by the Bookstart Project, initiated in 1993 at the University of Birmingham and designed to investigate book sharing among families with small children. Many similar projects have since been set up throughout the United Kingdom, the United States, Germany, Belgium, Japan, and other countries.

Since these mechanisms seem far from being properly understood, new interdisciplinary approaches that attempted to link up linguistics, narratology, semiotics, cognitive psychology and picture theory were established in the 1990s. They demonstrate the close relation between language acquisition, child psychology, visual perception and education. For instance, some studies revealed the impact of theory of mind (TOM) and relative cognitive concepts, such as second order belief, on young children's emotional development (Astingston 1994; Wellman 1990). To grasp the multi-dimensional character of this approach, a new theoretical framework was established that attempts to connect the different strands of literacy studies: multimodality or multimodal literacy (Jewitt & Kress 2003; Kress & van Leeuwen 1996; Kress 1997). Multimodality starts from the theoretical position that treats all modes as equally significant for meaning and communication, although societies and specific communities may prefer certain modes to others. However, multimodality refers to complex relationships such as those between image and text, image and writing, and image and oral storytelling. This is based on the assumption that different modes have potentials that make them better for certain tasks than others. The shift between different modes (for example the interplay between image and sound) might stimulate the ability to develop narratives. While multimodality was applied to case studies dealing with literacy acquisition of children aged three to four and older, there are hardly any investigations that take the multimodal aspects of emergent literacy into consideration.

To demonstrate that a multimodal approach is relevant for the analysis of young children's understanding and reception of books, pictures, and stories, I shall now highlight some aspects of processes that create underlying meaning.

To begin with, the assumption that visual images are easier to interpret than verbal texts has been contradicted by Goldsmith (1984), Kiefer (1995), Kress & van Leeuwen (1996), Nikolajeva & Scott (2001) and Nodelman (1988). Their seminal studies indicate that children have to learn to understand pictures just as they learn to read written texts (Arizpe & Styles 2003; Stewig 1975). Looking closer, we can see that even pictures such as those in early-concept books that show objects from the child's surroundings are quite challenging, since they require the young child to acquire rather complex strategies such as the distinction between figure and ground, the recognition of a three-dimensional object on a two-dimensional surface, and awareness that colors, shapes, and lines are essential parts of illustrated objects. These "picture book conventions" (Nodelman 1988: 35) are not innate, but have to be learned in a lengthy process. Kress and van Leeuwen (1996) have shown that even the seemingly plain images in picturebooks for small children disclose "visual codes." Children generally acquire these codes through concentrated looking at pictures in picturebooks. This is ideally supported by adults encouraging the child to focus on the images and verbalize her experiences, which fosters a process of "dialogic reading." This concept emphasizes that visual literacy is strongly connected with language acquisition, since picturebooks for young children obviously contribute to enlarging the child's early lexicon; but it is also linked to syntactic and pragmatic knowledge (Hofbauer-Horn 2008; Klein & Meibauer 2011; Meibauer 2006; Rhyner 2009). Case studies by Fletcher & Reese (2005), Ezell & Justice (2005), Ninio (1983), Snow & Goldfield (1983), Valdez-Menchaca & Whitehurst (1992) and Whitehurst et al. (1988) have demonstrated that the "dialogic reading" of picturebooks has a question-answer-structure. The adult asks a question, such as, "What is this?" (pointing to a pictured object) or "Where is the ball?" (prompting the child to point at the respective object in the picturebook). Besides the pointing game, the child is encouraged to answer the question by naming the object. If the answer is correct, the adult may confirm this by repeating the child's answer. If the answer is wrong, the adult will certainly correct the child and get her to repeat the right answer (Bloom 2000: 67). It is possible to vary and extend this schema, for instance by imitating noises typical of the pictured object. Patterns of this kind have been consistently investigated (Bus 2003; De Temple & Snow 2003; Galda & Liang 2007; Jones 1996; Ninio & Bruner 1978; Moerk 1985; Smiley & Huttenlocher 1995). For example, when pictures display actions done with objects, the question-answer procedure might lead to simple sentences composed of a combination of nouns and verbs (Kümmerling-Meibauer & Meibauer in this volume). As the child grows older, the syntactic structure of the utterances may become more complex, supporting the young child's acquisition of sentence structures, such as the structure of "wh" – questions (Blewitt et al. 2009). Moreover, the interaction between adults and children while looking at picturebooks together facilitates the young child's acquisition of pragmatic capacities, for example the ability to understand that a question elicits an answer, and that gestures and questions are clues to starting a communication process (Nachtigäller & Rohlfing 2011; Nachtigäller & Rohlfing in this volume). Children then practice taking their turn in a typical question-answer-format.

The appreciation of rhymes is somewhat different, being overtly connected with the development of phonological awareness (Casalis 2000; Foy 2003). The exploration of rhymes supports young children's developing sense of metalinguistic awareness, i.e. the ability to reflect upon language (Gombert 1992). Some scholars even stress that children benefit from early advancement of phonological awareness, since this capacity facilitates the acquisition of functional literacy, i.e. the ability to read and write. As for other metalinguistic devices, such as metaphor and irony, it is evident that they are fully acquired by the time children are over three years old (Kümmerling-Meibauer 1999; Winner 1988). Some academic specialists claim that metaphors already occur in picturebooks for young children, and that one may distinguish between visual and linguistic metaphors (Rau 2007; see the chapter by Rau in the present volume).

Given these facts, we may assume that any scholar interested in the impact of picturebooks and children's story books on very young children should certainly be keen to know how these books and the related child-adult discussions have the potential to enhance children's understanding of how visual images and the accompanying text manifest meaning. Moreover, for anyone dealing with young children, parents, educationalists, kindergarten teachers, parents and preschool teachers, being able to comprehend the codes and conventions of visual images and narrative strategies will assist understanding of the actual developmental stages of young children, enabling adults to provide learning experiences that can build upon young children's current knowledge and skills.

Consequently, we need many different lines of inquiry to comprehend the relevant processes and investigate how young children come to terms with the great variety of different pursuits.

Main topics in this volume

The chapters in the present collection are revised versions of papers presented at an international conference held at the Picturebook Museum "Burg Wissem" in Troisdorf nearby Cologne, Germany, in March 2009. The conference was funded by the Fritz Thyssen Stiftung (Cologne). This offered the rare opportunity to bring together scholars from different countries and different fields, i.e. children's literature research, picturebook theory, art history, linguistics, cognitive psychology and pedagogy; all the participants are pursuing different lines of investigation in this field. This was also the first conference to focus on multidisciplinary approaches, stressing the strong relationship between early literacy and children's books for young readers under three years of age. While there are a number of works on educational and pragmatic aspects of emergent literacy and early literacy, including the use of books, the specific focus of this collection with its mix of approaches and disciplines is intended to fill a gap. We hope it will make a significant contribution to the field and prove useful for scholars as well as practitioners. What is unusual about the present volume is that it constitutes the first serious, sustained examination of the study of children's books for children aged from 0 to 3 with contributions by scholars working in different domains and attempting to assess the recognition of the role and influence of children's literature on the cognitive, linguistic and aesthetic development of young children.

One aim of the collection is to achieve a balance between theoretical, empirical, historical and cross-cultural approaches. The chapters in this volume are linked by many intersecting themes. While a linear structure cannot do justice to this, the chapters are organized into three sections.

Part One addresses fundamental issues about the premises of early literacy, such as the impact of children's drawings on their developing sense of fictionality, the development of color perception in young children and its significance for the recognition and appreciation of colors in picturebooks, and the mutual influence of pedagogical theory, picturebook art and basic design in modern art forms, for example, minimal art and concept art.

Part Two examines the broad range of picturebooks for children under three years of age, ranging from early-concept books through wimmelbooks and ABC books for small children to picturebooks that support the young child's acquisition of behavioral norms. Aspects covered in this section include the use of visual and verbal metaphors in picturebooks for young children, the cognitive challenges of concept acquisition in relation to language acquisition, visual literacy and literary literacy, and the consideration of the aesthetic qualities of picturebooks targeted at this age group. These chapters also acknowledge the interaction between the child and the adult mediator during the process of joint reading.

This provides a natural transition to the third part, which examines questions about the child-book interaction based on meticulous case studies, covering the impact of picturebooks on the emotional and linguistic development of monolingual and bilingual children, the importance of children's play and talk in understanding and developing creative acquaintance with stories, and the influence of the way mothers talk about objects and actions on the young child's awareness of picturebooks displaying objects from the child's surroundings.

Although many of the chapters are closely interconnected, they may be read independently. The reader is invited to follow the trail according to her interests. The principal aim of this collection is to offer fresh insights into the mutual relationship between emergent literacy and children's books targeted at children under three, and to explore what this relationship reveals about young children's developing sense of books, stories, pictures, and their understanding of the world. The contributors to this volume draw on detailed analysis, observations and case studies of children in the age range from ten months to three years to develop theoretical insights that challenge traditional accounts of emergent literacy. A key theme of the collection is that concise understanding of emergent literacy has to be an interdisciplinary endeavor if it is to do justice to the complex, multi-modal and essential nature of the developing ability of young children to grasp pictures and stories in children's books.

A second thread running through the collection is the argument that it is important to study the cognitive, emotional, aesthetic, and linguistic processes that occur when children are immersed in the activity of joint picturebook reading. Many of the contributors to the present volume offer detailed and careful interpretive analyses of these processes, drawing on recent research in this area. Some contributors adopt a case study approach to back up this argument, drawing on observation of individual children, or pairs and groups of children.

To sum up, the present volume offers the reader a range of new approaches to the epistemological question that opened this introduction, and new perspectives on this question. What we are presenting here is a relatively new field of investigation that is rapidly evolving. It is a subject worth watching for every linguist, cognitive scientist and scholar working in the field of children's studies and children's literature.

References

Apseloff, M. 1987. Books for babies: Learning toys or pre-literature? *Children's Literature Association Quarterly* 12: 63–6.

Arizpe, E. & Styles, M. 2003. *Children Reading Pictures. Interpreting Visual Texts.* London: Routledge.

Astington, J. W. 1994. *The Child's Discovery of the Mind.* London: Fontana.

Bamberg, M. (ed.). 1997. *Narrative Development – Six Approaches.* Mahwah NJ: Lawrence Erlbaum Associates.

Blatt, J. 2007. A father's role in supporting his son's developing awareness of self. *Infant Observation* 10(2): 173–182.

Blewitt, P., Rump, K. M., Shealy, S. E. & Cook, S. A. 2009. Shared book reading: When and how questions affect young children's word learning. *Journal of Educational Psychology* 101(2): 294–304.

Bloom, P. 2000. *How Children Learn the Meanings of Words.* Cambridge MA: The MIT Press.

Boueke, D. et al. 1995. *Wie Kinder erzählen. Untersuchungen zur Erzähltheorie und zur Entwicklung narrativer Fähigkeiten.* Munich: Fink.

Bus, A. G. 2003. Joint caregiver-child storybook reading. A route to literacy development. In *Handbook of Early Literacy Research,* S. B. Neuman & D. K. Dickinson (eds), 179–191. New York NY: Guilford Press.

Braun, B. 1995. *Vorläufer der literarischen Sozialisation in der frühen Kindheit – eine entwicklungspsychologische Fallstudie.* Frankfurt: Peter Lang.

Butler, D. 1979. *Cushla and her Books.* Auckland: Hodder & Stoughton.

Butler, D. 1980. *Babies Need Books.* London: Penguin Books.

Casalis, S. 2000. Morphological awareness and phonological awareness in the onset of literacy. *Research on Child Language Acquisition* 1: 208–222.

Clark, E. V. 2003. *First Language Acquisition.* Cambridge MA: The MIT Press.

Crago, M. & Crago, H. 1983. *Prelude to Literacy: A Preschool Child's Encounter with Picture and Story.* Carbondale IL: Southern Illinois University Press.

De Temple, J. & Snow, C. 2003. Learning words from books. In *On Reading Books to Children: Parents and Teachers,* A. van Kleeck, S. A. Stahl & E. B. Bauer (eds), 16–36. Mahwah NJ: Lawrence Erlbaum Associates.

Dickinson, D. K. & Neuman, S.B. (eds). 2007. *Handbook of Early Literacy Research,* Vol. II. New York NY: The Guildford Press.

Ezell, H. K. & Justice, L. M. 2005. *Shared Storybook Reading: Building Young Children's Language & Emergent Literacy Skills.* Baltimore MD: Brookes.

Fletcher, K. & Reese, E. 2005. Picture book reading with young children: A conceptual framework. *Developmental Review* 25: 64–103.

Foy, J. 2003. Home literacy environment and phonological awareness in preschool children: Differential effects for rhyme and phoneme awareness. *Applied Psycholinguistics* 24: 59–88.

Galda, L. & Liang, L. A. 2007. Reading aloud with young children. In *Literacy for the New Millenium,* Vol. 1: *Early Literacy,* B. J. Guzzetti (ed.), 129–140. Westport CT: Praeger.

Ganea, P., Pickard, M. & DeLoache, J. 2008. Transfer between picture books and the real world by very young children. *Journal of Cognition and Development* 9: 46–66.

Ganea, P., Mar, L. & DeLoache, J. 2011. Young children's learning and transfer of biological information from picture books to real animals. *Child Development* 82: 1421–1433.

Goldsmith, E. 1984. *Research into Illustration.* Cambridge: CUP.

Golomb, C. 2011. *The Creation of Imaginary Worlds. The Role of Art, Magic and Dreams in Child Development.* London: Jessica Kingsley Publishers.

Gombert, J. 1992. *Metalinguistic Development.* New York NY: Harvester Wheatsheaf.

Goswami, U. 1998. *Cognition in Children.* London: Psychology Press.

Hall, N. 1987. *The Emergence of Literacy.* London: Hodder & Stoughton.

Hall, N., Larson, J. & Marsh, J. (eds). 2003. *Handbook of Early Childhood Literacy.* Thousand Oaks CA: Sage.

Hofbauer-Horn, M. 2008. Linguistische Betrachtung von Büchern für Kleinkinder. *Zeitschrift für Literaturwissenschaft und Linguistik* (Lili) 152: 140–155.

Jewitt, C. & Kress, G. (eds). 2003. *Multimodal Literacy.* Frankfurt: Peter Lang.

Jones, R. 1996. *Emerging Patterns of Literacy. A Multidisciplinary Perspective.* London: Routledge.

Kiefer, B. 1995. *The Potential of Picturebooks: From Visual Literacy to Aesthetic Understanding.* Englewood Cliffs NJ: Merrill.

Klein, W. & Meibauer, J. (eds). 2011. *Spracherwerb und Kinderliteratur.* Special issue of the Journal *Zeitschrift für Literaturwissenschaft und Linguistik* (LiLi) 162.

Koerber, S. 2007. Welche Rolle spielt das Bildersehen des Kindes aus Sicht der Entwicklungspsychologie? In *Neue Impulse der Bilderbuchforschung,* J. Thiele (ed.), 31–47. Baltmannsweiler: Schneider Verlag Hohengehren.

Kress, G. 1997. *Before Writing. Rethinking the Paths to Literacy.* London: Routledge.

Kress, G. & van Leeuwen, T. 1996. *Reading Images. The Grammar of Visual Design.* London, New York: Routledge.

Kümmerling-Meibauer, B. 1999. Metalinguistic awareness and the child's developing sense of irony: The relationship between pictures and text in ironic picture books. *The Lion and the Unicorn* 23: 157–183.

Kümmerling-Meibauer, B. 2006a. Literacy. In *The Oxford Encyclopedia of Children's Literature,* Vol. 3, J. Zipes et al. (eds), 453. Oxford: OUP.

Kümmerling-Meibauer, B. 2006b. Preschool books. In *The Oxford Encyclopedia of Children's Literature,* Vol. 3, J. Zipes et al. (eds), 288–291.Oxford: OUP.

Kümmerling-Meibauer, B. & Linsmann, M. (eds). 2009. *Literatur im Laufstall. Bilderbücher für die ganz Kleinen.* Troisdorf: Bilderbuchmuseum Burg Wissem.

Kümmerling-Meibauer, B. & Meibauer, J. 2005. First pictures, early concepts: Early concept books. *The Lion and the Unicorn* 29: 324–347.

Lancaster, L. 2003. Moving into literacy: How it all begins. In *Handbook of Early Childhood Literacy*, N. Hall, J. Larson & J. Marsh (eds), 145–153. Thousand Oaks CA: Sage.

Lancaster, L. 2007. Representing the ways of the world: How children under three start to use syntax in graphic signs. *Journal of Early Childhood Literacy* 7(2): 123–154.

Lewis, D. 2001. *Reading Contemporary Picturebooks. Picturing Text.* London: Routledge Falmer.

Lowe, V. 2007: *Stories, Pictures and Reality. Two Children Tell.* London: Routledge.

McCartney, K. & Philips, D. (eds). 2006. *Blackwell Handbook of Early Childhood Development.* Oxford: Blackwell.

Marsh, J. & Hallet, E. (eds). 2008. *Desirable Literacies. Approaches to Language & Literacy in the Early Years.* London: Sage.

Meibauer, J. 2006. Language acquisition and children's literature. In *The Oxford Encyclopedia of Children's Literature*, Vol. 2, J. Zipes et al. (eds), 400–401. Oxford: OUP.

Moerk, E. L. 1985. Picture-book reading by mothers and young children and its impact upon language development. *Journal of Pragmatics* 9: 547–566.

Murphy, G. L. 2002. *The Big Book of Concepts.* Cambridge MA: The MIT Press.

Nachtigäller, K. & Rohlfing, K. J. 2011. Einfluss von erlebten und vorgestellten Ereignissen auf die Erzählweise in kindgerichteter Sprache. In *Spracherwerb und Kinderliteratur*, W. Klein & J. Meibauer (eds). Special Issue of the journal *Zeitschrift für Literaturwissenschaft und Linguistik* 162: 139–155.

Newman, S. B. & Dickinson, D. K. (eds). 2003. *The Handbook of Early Literacy Research*, Vol. I. New York NY: The Guildford Press.

Nikolajeva, M. 2003. Verbal and visual literacy: The role of picturebooks in the reading experience of young children. In *Handbook of Early Childhood Literacy*, N. Hall, J. Larson & J. Marsh (eds), 235–248. Thousand Oaks CA: Sage.

Nikolajeva, M. & Scott, C. 2001. *How Picturebooks Work.* New York: Garland Publishing.

Ninio, A. 1983. Joint book reading as a multiple vocabulary acquisition device. *Developmental Psychology* 19: 445–451.

Ninio, A. & Bruner, J. 1978. The achievement and antecedents of labelling. *Journal of Child Language* 5: 1–15.

Nodelman, P. 1988. *Words About Pictures.* Athens GA: University of Georgia Press.

Nodelman, P. 2010. The mirror staged. Images of babies in baby books. *Jeunesse: Young People, Texts, Cultures* 2(2): 13–38.

Rau, M. L. 2007. *Literacy. Vom ersten Bilderbuch zum Erzählen, Lesen und Schreiben.* Berne: Haupt.

Rhyner, P. (ed). 2009. *Emergent Literacy and Language Development. Promoting Learning in Early Childhood.* New York NY: Guildford.

Siegal, M. 2008. *Marvelous Minds. The Discovery of What Children Know.* Oxford: OUP.

Smiley, P. & Huttenlocher, J. 1995. Conceptual development and the child's early words for events, objects, and persons. In *Beyond Names for Things. Young Children's Acquisition of Verbs*, M. Tomasello & W. Merriman (eds), 21–61. Hillsdale NJ: Lawrence Erlbaum Associates.

Snow, C. E. 2006. What counts as literacy in early childhood? In *Blackwell Handbook of Early Childhood Development*, K. McCartney & D. Philips (eds), 274–294. Oxford: Blackwell.

Snow, C. & Goldfield, B. 1983. Turn the page please: Situation-specific language acquisition. *Journal of Child Language* 10: 551–569.

Stewig, J. W. 1975. Assessing visual elements preferred in pictures by young children. *Reading Improvement* (Summer 1975): 94–97.

Tracy, R. 2007. *Wie Kinder Sprachen lernen. Und wie wir sie dabei unterstützen können*. Tübingen: Francke.

Tucker, N. 1990. *The Child and the Book: A Psychological and Literary Exploration*. Cambridge: CUP.

Valdez-Menchaca, M. C. & Whitehurst, G. J. 1992. Accelerating language development through picture book reading: A systematic extension to Mexican day care. *Developmental Psychology* 28(6): 1106–1114.

Wellman, H. M. 1990. *The Child's Theory of Mind*. Cambridge MA: The MIT Press.

White, D. N. 1954. *Books Before Five*. Oxford: OUP.

Whitehead, M. 2002. Dylan's routes to literacy: The first three years with picturebooks. *Journal of Early Childhood Literacy* 2(3): 269–289.

Whitehead, M. R. 2004. *Language and Literacy in the Early Years*, 3rd edn. Thousand Oaks CA: Sage.

Whitehurst, G. J., Falco, F. L., Lonigan, C. J., Fischel, J. E., DeBaryshe, B. D., Valdez-Menchaca, M. C. & Caulfield, M. 1988. Accelerating language development through picture book reading. *Developmental Psychology* 24(4): 552–559.

Winner, E. 1988. *The Point of Words: Children's Understanding of Metaphor and Irony*. Cambridge MA: The MIT Press.

PART I

Premises of early literacy

CHAPTER 2

The dragon in the cave

Textual representations of fictional and everyday events by children under three

Lesley Lancaster

This chapter looks at how children first start to engage with the material representation of cultural meanings, including stories in different modes and media, and the structure of inscriptional systems such as writing. It suggests there is a continuum of representational activity that starts from early infancy, and that rather than being driven primarily by language is a multimodal process driven by cultural and psychological histories, and the social interactions between child and adult sign-makers. It considers evidence that children under the age of three already understand much about the generic underpinnings of texts, and have extensive semiotic repertoires. It examines the relationship between conventional, practically-lived, and appraising texts through a discussion of the findings of a study that examines the mark-making of children under the age of three, and the kinds of textual interpretations and structures that they work with at this age. This is exemplified through an extended discussion of the textual activity generated between a 2-year-old subject and her mother, involving a family visit to Disneyland. The paper presents a micro, multimodal analysis of ways in which the child recognizes and acknowledges distinct generic forms and textual structures in her mark-making.

Introduction

Until very recently there has been little said on the subject of how children first start to unravel the complexities of the various systems of representing meaning, on which human societies are becoming increasingly dependent. The general affective and cognitive benefit of sharing stories and picturebooks with infants and children under the age of three is universally accepted. How they interpret the complex arrays of drawn, written, numerical, and even musical signs and inscriptions that are presented to them on the page or screen, and what this might inform them about the textual structures and symbolic systems used in their representation is much less clearly understood. In the case of writing systems and textual structures, the question of what infants and children under the age of three understand about them is one that many scholars concerned with early child development often consider not worth asking. The difficulty of answering of these questions lies in establishing not just what it is that young children understand and know, but also what is knowable for them at this age. One way of engaging with the problem is to look at it from the other end, and to consider how an examination of the marks, signs, and early texts produced by such young children, and the social and bodily processes involved, might provide insights into early understandings of textual and systemic structures.

One reason for the very limited research in this area lies in the commonly held opinion that meaning resides principally in language. The enduring view that writing is about the transcription of speech follows from this (Havelock 1976), and continues to be reflected in an extensive emphasis on the structured teaching of grapho-phonic relationships in many early reading programmes (Strauss and Altwerger 2007). Language is considered to be a necessary prerequisite for learning about writing, and until children are able to speak reasonable fluently, the argument goes, there is not much that they are able to understand about it. Similarly, texts are seen as predominately written documents, with the ability to produce them following from the ability to write. This position is also associated with certain philosophical and psychological approaches to the relationship between language and meaning, where the two are considered for all intents and purposes to be synonymous: without language, there is no meaning. Meaning, according to Jerome Bruner, is a 'culturally mediated phenomenon that depends on the existence of a shared symbol system.' (1990: 69). Young humans, he suggests, are not able to 'enter into' the arena of shared cultural meaning from the outset, but have to wait until they are able to use language.

This position begs a lot of questions, not just about what writing is, and what texts do, but also about how we judge the point at which children are ready and able to enter into meaning, and participate in the symbol systems of their cultures, and what happens, representationally speaking, during this apparent meaning-making interregnum. Most importantly, it makes no contribution to answering the fundamental question that underlies any account of learning to write or produce texts (or indeed to produce other representational systems): namely, how an understanding of systems that have evolved and developed to high levels of complexity over six thousand years (Fischer 2001) can be conflated into a period of approximately seven years, and by the youngest and least experienced members of human societies. In this chapter I want to look at some of the processes involved in young children's earliest representation of personal, social, and textual events by means of graphic marks and signs: in other words, the extent to which they are makers as well as 'readers' of texts. In doing this, I shall draw on some of the findings of a study[1] whose starting point was an interest in this question, and that looks at the mark-making of children under three years old, examining how everyday social, bodily, and material experiences and interactions are used by children of this age to evolve their own textual structures.

A continuum of meaning

Trevarthen (2004) takes a different view of the symbolic participation of very young children. Young infants are able to demonstrate many behaviours that are for the purposeful communication of their mental states with the mental states of others, he suggests. In other words, they have the capacity to intentionally represent meaning long before they develop the ability to use language and speak. A newborn baby can seek communication with an adult, showing intentional expressive and receptive states (4). Trevarthen shows evidence of newborns participating in imitation games, putting out a tongue, or lifting fingers in response to adult actions, for example. At around six months babies can be observed demonstrating such actions and mannerisms to others, sharing meanings socially through use of a culturally agreed sign system. Signs and objects become part of an 'act of meaning' (17) where they can be made to represent things other than themselves.

The studies discussed by Trevarthen provide evidence that point to a continuum of representational activity starting from birth, and scholars researching the early stages of graphic sign[2] and text-making also cite evidence that points to the logic of this position. Wolf and Perry (1988) in a study of children's development of drawing systems between the ages of one and three, show how 'children exhibit an almost "rampant" exploration of symbolisation.' (19). Kress's (1997) 'rethinking' of children's paths into literacy starts from a similar position, pointing to the 'absolute plethora of ways, with an absolute plethora of means,' (xvii) that children use to make meaning; and Lancaster (2003) suggests that it would be surprising if 'from an apparent position of no serious engagement with print at all, children are suddenly able to explode into the type of rampant, creative, independent and reasoned relationship with the medium' (145) that is typical of the graphic activity of children under the age of three.

1. Economic and Social Research Council RES-000-22-0599 *Grammaticisation in Early Mark Making: a Multimodal Investigation.*

2. The 'Grammaticisation' project uses the term 'graphic sign' to describe meaningful marks, and groups of marks made by children under three. The term 'sign' is derived from the work of Ferdinand de Saussure.

If language is not the prime driver of the move into writing and text production, or at least not at the kind of systemic level that the proponents of early phonics teaching suggest that it is, then we need to look more closely at what characterises the 'plethora' of means that children use to make meaning, and how these relate to the material and structural features of graphic modes. Writing (and drawing) are in essence visual, spatial modes, and according to Tisseron (1994) the genesis of texts involving these modes of representing meaning lies in the spatial play that is staged by the hand (whether using conventional or digital media), and the relationship between the hand and its 'tracings' (Naginski 2000). In other words, the starting point for the physical production of a graphic text derives from human patterns of bodily movement, perceptual interactions, and manipulation of objects (Johnson 1987). For very young children their physical and embodied relationship to spatial structures and to objects are a matter of conscious daily interest and concern. This transfers to symbolic space; the very emptiness of a blank piece of paper, for example, signifies possibilities, and raises questions about location, placement, containment, and direction, as well as about pattern, size, shape, analogy.

Wolf and Perry show that children's development of drawing skills at the age of two involves a process of generating a repertoire of visual languages, and acquiring a keen sensitivity to when each is appropriate. There is recognition that they are characterised by different rules depending on the kinds of information to be recorded, and the most apt and powerful ways to do this. This all happens well before children are able to produce 'lookalike forms' (19), and in this Wolf and Perry point to the assumption of a similar interregnum in meaning making in the case of drawing as well as writing, with a belief that no significant representation can take place until the desired end of 'realistic picturing' is achieved (this is particularly ironic in the light of the huge range of illustrative genres evident in picturebooks for the youngest children). Children can already 'read' differences between different systems of inscription such as writing, drawing, and number by the age of eighteen months (Karmiloff-Smith 1992). This applies equally to children in cultures using alphabetic and those using logographic scripts (Wu 2009). Lancaster (2007) considers evidence showing that the repertoire of graphic languages used by children of this age also distinguishes between the production of marking systems that are moving towards drawing, and those that are moving towards writing. Children will use mark types with iconic, drawing-like, affordances when they want to represent a whole physical entity, for example, but will use non-iconic, arbitrary marks or mark systems with writing-like affordances for the purposes of simply representing locational relationships between things.

There are, in other words, foundational questions about the purpose and structure of the various representational systems used by human cultures that need to be addressed by children (Rowe 2008a) before the fine detail of these operating systems can be fully appreciated and understood. Far from there being any kind of cognitive interregnum, children are actively engaged in addressing these questions from the beginning. Their day-to-day social and cultural experiences, and their interactions with people, objects, and texts form the basis of their early cognition and interrogation of representative processes; and their bodily engagement with the physical world provides them with resources that help them account for aspects of the spatial structure and design of graphic systems. Tisseron points out that writing and drawing systems exist temporally as well as spatially, not simply in terms of the time taken to move the eye around or across the page, but also in the variety of ways and means that are deployed to represent the duration and sequence of events, and the passing of time. From the initial moment of tracing or inscribing, 'an original notion, an idea, an inspiration', which has 'neither extension nor duration' (30) is given both by the action of making marks. The mark becomes a visual and material reality, and therefore available for reflection, and for development and change. For young children, this is the essence of graphic representation, whatever representative system is involved.

Practically lived texts

The visual signs and inscriptions that children create prior to producing conventional systems such as drawing and writing are not random 'scribbles' (Lancaster 2003), but demonstrate consistent semiotic intention (Rowe 2008b). Early graphic productions often show evidence of purposeful design, with strategic location and juxtaposition of marks being used to generate specific meanings, representing spatial, affective, and numerical associations, for example: a case in point is a child marking a long line close and adjacent to a shorter line, to represent two people, a parent and child (Ferreiro and Teberosky 1983). Another way of putting this is that children under the age of three intentionally produce not just marks and signs, but also texts, where the construction of such texts is informed at a systemic level by the child's knowledge of social and bodily relationships and events. As has already been suggested, the traditional view of text is a linguistic one, concerned with the arrangement of spoken or written wordings (Halliday 1978). Kress and Van Leeuwen (2001) however, point to major changes in the ways in which meaning-making is viewed, partly through the development of social semiotic theory over the last twenty years. According to this theory, it is the social, cultural, and psychological histories of sign-makers that drive the process of sign making. It is a process that involves the use of diverse modes of representation by human societies, of which language is only one of the socially agreed ways and means of representing and communicating meaning (45).

This multimodal approach to meaning-making opens up theoretical views of what a text is in ways that make it easier to start to understand children's liking for often complex and abstract picturebooks, and the process of children's early sign-making. Accordingly, all meaning-making resources available within a culture need to be considered as having equal value, and operating in complementary relationships, rather than a hierarchical one with language as the prime mode. It is an inclusive rather than an exclusive definition of text, and one that can accommodate the multimodal and idiosyncratic approaches to sign-making that characterise the productions of very young children. Kress and Van Leeuwen use the term 'practically lived texts', to encompass the semiotic import of the everyday practices of ordinary people, which exist alongside conventionally text-like objects such as picturebooks, TV programmes, and videos (24). For example, they discuss 'a house' as a complex, material sign and text that signals the social relations and value systems of those who live there (39). The term can be usefully extended to take account of the events, activities, and interactions that are associated with the house and its inhabitants.

For young children, these events and activities are frequently revisited in new texts that are created through their interactions with adults: yesterday's day out might be recollected and appraised in a conversation, or by sharing and looking at a book, toy, or video associated with the occasion, and further texts generated through play, making, marking, or just imagining, and creating new visual and material realities. Language plays a significant role in the process of reflecting and remembering, but again only a partial one. Antonio Damasio considers how we engender images of things that involve complex, multimodal ensembles of meaning. Images are recalled that include not just the objects concerned, but attributes of these objects, and also past reactions and feelings associated with them:

> By *object* I mean entities as diverse as a person, a place, a melody, a toothache, a state of bliss; by *image* I mean a mental pattern in any of the sensory modalities, e.g., a sound image, a tactile image, the image of a state of well-being. Such images convey aspects of the physical characteristics of the object and they may also convey the reaction of like or dislike one may have for an object, the plans one may formulate for it, or the web of relationships of that object among other objects.' (Damasio 1999: 9)

I would agree that there are three kinds of 'text' that provide some of the bases for children's earliest understanding of systems of representing meaning, and that inform their 'reading' and production of texts: conventional texts, in different modes, genres and media, that depend on the use of systems of communication and inscription agreed within cultures; practically-lived texts that take account of the semiotic relationships between designed environments and social actions; and appraising texts, that materialise memories and reflections of past events and social actions.

I want now to examine some aspects of the process by which these different kinds of textual experience are associated by young children, and the transformative impact that making these connections can have on their developing understanding of textual and systemic structures. To clarify the process, I shall first discuss an early experience of my own in which these associations can be clearly traced (although the outcome in this case was not a graphic one); I shall then move on to discuss the *Early Mark Making* project, and to review some of its findings, extending the discussion of the process in relation to a child's own text production using one episode from the data as exemplification.

The wolf in the cave

When I was just over the age of three, my parents took me to visit a friend of theirs, a male colleague of my father's who shared a house with a friend in a small village a few miles from where we lived. Our house was large and rambling, with big, light rooms, and high ceilings; the house we visited by contrast was a small, dark, damp cottage, with low, beamed ceilings, and was quite unfamiliar to me in all these respects. It was a social occasion with food and alcohol on offer for the adults, but in those far less child-centred days, there was nothing taken along or provided for me to play with. Our hosts must have taken pity on me however, and went to see what they could find for my entertainment. The only thing they came across in the house was a copy of *Struwwelpeter*[3], and having been reassured by my parents that I liked looking at books, they settled me down on a cushion in the corner and handed it over. Of course I could not read at that time, so spent my time looking at the pictures, and I suspect, given what happened later, mainly looking at the pictures that illustrated *The Story of Cruel Frederick*. Whilst the house and the occasion I can recollect to this day, the details of the book I remember less clearly, and these were filled in some years later, enabling me to piece together subsequent events.

3. *Struwwelpeter* was written in 1845 by Heinrich Hoffman, a German doctor, for his three year old son. It relates in pictures and verses the unfortunate consequences that befall children that misbehave.

That night, back at home, I had my first nightmare, or at least my first remembered nightmare. In my dream I was back in the cottage, but this time I was completely alone. I was aware of how dark it was in there, and as I looked at the walls, they seemed suddenly to be made of rock, and to be wet and mossy. The room gradually transformed, and I realised that I was now in a cave, and where the door had once been there was now just an opening in the rock. Standing still and silent in that entrance at the end of the cave, and looking towards me was an animal that I recognised as a wolf. At that point, I woke up, terrified, suffering from the outcome of a terrible collision of textual events.

At this point I need to backtrack a little. My grandmother was a great storyteller, particularly of traditional fairy tales, and she enjoyed embellishing them, and introducing a bit of sensationalism here and there. The end of *Little Red Riding Hood* in particular lent itself to the development of further lurid detail, which I encouraged with lots of questions about *how* the wolf ate the grandmother, and how fierce wolves were, and what glittering red eyes they had. The Little Red Riding Hood wolf was definitely fictional territory, and so those discussions could be safely had, but I knew too that wolves were real creatures, and that the boundaries between fiction and reality were not securely drawn. I must have had some idea of what a wolf looked like, and I know that I sometimes wondered about them, and that the wolf became a 'recallable' image that I would frequently refer to, and that was available to bring to mind at the time I was introduced to *Struwwelpeter*. The first story in the book is about Frederick, who is cruel to his dog, amongst other creatures. On the second page the illustrations show an odd looking boy, and a dog-like animal in a number of confrontational situations; the physical background of the picture consists of some kind of countryside or grand estate, including what looks like a rocky cliff-side, covered with mossy grass.

Since no one read the story to me, the illustrations were the only clues available at the time to help me work out what might be going on. Without the written text, the semantic intention of the images is unclear, and the relationship between dog and boy is ambiguous; I had to draw on my existing repertoire of visual images and textual resources to make some sense of it. My assumption, I am sure, when I looked at the image was that the animal was a wolf, since I knew nothing about dogs, but did know about wolves, and about the uncertain and ambiguous relationship that appeared to exist between wolves and children. The familiar, 'told' story of Red Riding Hood was used as means of interpreting what was happening in the other, unfamiliar story text. Both of these 'conventional' texts supported my creative interpretation of the physical environment in which I found myself: an unfamiliar 'practically-lived' text. This collision of images and events was materialised in my dream, an 'appraising' text in which spoken and visual narratives combined with fictional, real, affective, and kinaesthetic interpretations of objects, events, and environments. There are three representations of Frederick and his dog on the page, with each having a spatial composition suggesting threat and proximity. My association with the wolf from *Little Red Riding Hood* underwent one transformation when it was used as a means of interpreting events on the page in *Struwwelpeter.* A further set of transformations provided the content of my dream: the dark, low-ceilinged cottage that I had visited with my parents, became visually associated with the grassy rocks illustrated on the page, and changed into a cave; and the fictional wolf, mediated by my visual interrogation of the uncertain relationship between Frederick and his dog, transformed into a very real wolf, confronting me in strange territory.

The reminiscence I have just described shows the powerful and transformative relationship that can develop between 'conventional' fictional texts, and practically lived texts in the minds of very young children. It also illustrates the need to acknowledge the complexity, and multimodality of meaning-making resources if we are to understand how young children start to make sense of texts and symbolic systems of meaning; images, and illustrations, for example, are far from transparent, and are as much part of a system requiring interpretation as are inscriptive systems; the apparent simplicity of picturebooks for young children belie the complexity of their construction. Language, particularly the story telling of my grandmother played a significant role in what happened, but was at several removes from the final, 'appraising' text of my dream. It also demonstrates some of the practical difficulties associated with researching the early stages of children's textual understanding; this was an isolated, albeit serendipitous childhood memory from which useful insights were gleaned, but which could not in any sense be deemed a rigorous environment for research. The *Early Mark Making* project worked at developing strategies that approached the interpretation of very young children's textual insights in systematic ways, accommodating the bodily and multimodal qualities of their interpretation and production of texts.

The *Early Mark Making* project

This project (see Lancaster and Roberts 2006, Lancaster 2007) was also concerned with the kinds of textual interpretations and structures that children work with when they are first presented with conventional texts. It aimed to consider what very young children know and understand about signs and texts by describing and analysing the processes that are involved in their own early mark-making and text production. It investigated whether children under three years of age intentionally represented objects and experiences in the world around them by means of graphic marks, and whether the marks they make can be considered to be meaningful signs and texts, as opposed to 'random scribbling'. It sought to describe the different categories of experience that the children represented in their marking, and the strategies they used in doing this. The researchers were particularly interested in exploring whether children this young showed any understanding of features and structures that are typically associated with systems of writing and text production. To this end it looked for any evidence of regularity in those structures and systems which the children used in arranging and organising marks and signs on the page, since such regularities can be considered a significant feature of writing and textual systems. It also considered the extent to which such regularities reflected structures present in their social, bodily, and material experiences.

Participants

The participants in the study were ten children, four boys and six girls, aged between eighteen and thirty-six months, and their families. The adults involved were in most cases the mothers of the children, but several fathers, one grandmother, and one child's aunt took part, and two older siblings also participated. The adults were asked to introduce mark-making activities to the children in ways that were familiar to them, and encouraged to proceed in as normal a way as possible. The nature of the activity to be undertaken was generally left open for the child and adult to negotiate. All the children except one were familiar with making marks on paper, and enjoyed doing it. They were also familiar with other representational and digital media, including phones, games, and computers and were particularly interested in film versions of favourite stories.

Collecting and analysing data

The collection of data had two phases, separated by a six-month gap. The data were of three different kinds: background information about each of the children and their families, including informal unstructured observations and interviews with the adults made during data collection sessions; children's graphic productions, produced over the course of the project, which were collected and digitally scanned; and video-recordings of the process of the children's mark-making and related activity, inclusive of the interactions with the adults and any other activity that may have been going on at the time. This generated a significant amount of data, from which key parts were selected to create a set of episodes averaging around 1–2 minutes in length, which were then transcribed.

As has already been noted, taking account of what very young children know in more than a very general way is not easy. Children of this age are still developing as language users, and so simply asking them about things is not necessarily a reliable option. Even if it was, part of what they are doing is likely to involve non-conscious processes, which are not readily accessible to conscious discussion. Furthermore, there is the added difficulty of establishing common ground between adults and young children with respect to the symbolic representation of meaning; a shift of consciousness occurs once we learn to draw, read and write that makes it hard to recapture an earlier, pre-iconic, pre-literate state. One solution commonly used within educational practice is to extrapolate intention from the products of children's marking activity, avoiding the often very practical difficulties of describing the processes involved in their production. However, this project started from the position that we learn about children's thinking by seeing these processes as an integral part of the product. It took the view that all bodily and semiotic modes involved in communicative and productive processes carry meaning, and so need to be taken into account. Incorporating these as an integral part of the transcriptive process makes for a much more refined and delicate description on which to base interpretations of young children's graphic activity. To this end, all gaze, language, action, and gesture was transcribed, in order to describe the communicative process as fully as possible, and to provide a firm basis for interpretations of the child's intentions in each episode. This also further extended the concept of the 'practically-lived' text to incorporate bodily actions into accounts of semiotic relationships between social actions and designed environments.

Transcription and analysis

Digital viewing and editing software made the data accessible to repeated viewings and analyses, and provided a basis for multimodal transcriptions that tracked activity second by second, revealing how bodily activity and social and interpersonal events were drawn on directly in the children's construction of marks, signs, and texts. Intentionality[4] became much more evident and describable by close viewing and micro-transcription, and the ways that the children were thinking about things became clearer, even if the process was at times difficult and time-consuming.

4. The children in the study were, without exception, intentional in their marking, in the sense that they indicated what each of their marks or signs meant. This was sometimes done prior to marking, and sometimes following the production of a mark or sign.

Digital editing provided a frame-by-frame analysis of the process of marking signs, showing a step-by-step construction, and identifying some of the different ways in which children interpreted the marks they made as they went along.

Findings

Two findings of the study have a particular contribution to make to an understanding of how children first learn to comprehend and construct texts. The first of these indicates that children under the age of three are able to construct 'graphic signs' which, whilst not fully identifiable with conventional systems, are communicative in their own right, and have some discernable characteristics associated with these systems. There was repeated evidence of systematic representation of different categories of personal experience involving people, animals, actions, and attributes, and regularities in how marks were used and arranged. In doing this, the children drew strongly on bodily experiences, on social experiences involving friends and family, and on textual characters and events; in other words, on both 'practically-lived', and 'conventional' texts. All the children enjoyed picturebooks, including retellings of traditional stories in Disney cartoons. Two-year-old Ruby, for example, looked at the Disney version of *Beauty and the Beast* with great regularity, and during the same marking episode she represents the heroine, Belle in two quite distinct ways: firstly as a physical entity, in which body parts and features are represented iconically, in realistic, 'drawing-like' spatial relationships to each other; and secondly as a relational entity, using a single, non-iconic 'writing-like' zigzag mark to show Belle's physical, and locative relationship to the boundary of the castle she has marked. In both cases, the marks are made in the context of a more extended, appraising text. This suggests that long before they reach their third birthday, children are capable of actively and independently exploring the kinds of representative principles that underpin symbolic systems in general, as well as looking at the operation of specific systems.

The second of these findings concerns the organisational principles and design that children use. The children used a number of consistent organisational strategies in their representations, depending on the informational purpose of the production. They were able to link and organise signs in systematic ways, showing some evidence of an understanding of certain kinds of generic organisation, particularly those typical of diagrammatic genres that combine writing and visual display. In doing this, they drew on structuring principles associated with bodily activity, and with social events and visits in which they had participated. These included 'settings' and 'mappings', which showed graphic representations of places in which events took place. Elements were located according to consistent principles, such as the representation of distance between two objects by placing them on distant parts of the page, and the signifying of a semantic or affective association by locating them close together. In the case of 'mappings', routes or paths between places or elements of the setting were also shown. Children also produced 'inventories' of people attending events. These were constructed dialogically, with the listing taking place in the course of a discussion with a parent. No notational distinction was made between the type of mark used to represent the various items on the list, and marks were arranged in some kind of linear order. Amy, for example, uses a set of single, parallel lines along the bottom of the page to represent a group of her friends (Figure 1); and Jamie produces a linear sequence of discrete signs, using looped marks, to identify friends and family who attended an Halloween party with him. In both cases, it is the listing of people, and their affective relationship to the marker that drives the choice of notation, and the organisational structures used. These appear to combine 'practically-lived' texts, in their attention to the relationship between physical environments and social actions, and appraising texts in their reviewing and materialising of previous events.

Figure 1. Friends
Reprinted by permission of Lesley Lancaster

Generic frameworks

The use of generic frameworks of this kind appears to be the driver that enables very young children to generate symbolic associations between personal and bodily experience, and purposeful forms and arrangements of graphic marks. In other words, this process is supported by the use of super-ordinate, socially driven frameworks derived from children's familiar, day-to-day experiences. Deacon's explanation of how children learn language provides a parallel explanation for their ability to engage with the symbolic principles underlying writing and other inscriptional systems at such an early age (1997). He suggests that the difficulties that infants and young children initially have with comprehending the details of language structure may actually provide an advantage. Learning any kind of symbol system, he suggests, requires an approach that allows attention to seemingly obvious associations to be set aside in order that the overarching, combinatorial patterns of relationships between symbols can be noticed, allowing 'the relevant large-scale logic of language' to "pop-out" of a background of other details 'too variable for them to follow'. At first they cannot 'tell the trees apart', but 'can see the forest' (135).

The early generic texts that children construct are derived from their observations of patterns of social, affective, and material relationships in their own lives, as well as picturebooks and other texts with which they are familiar: the super-ordinate frameworks that exist in their personal worlds, in other words. Dunn (1988) discusses ways in which children first learn to participate and play a role in 'family drama', where these patterns are learned in the course of day-to-day activity. This is part of an ongoing narrative that generates different genres of communicating and representing meaning. Bruner points to the role of narrative in organizing experience: it involves a unique sequence of events, mental states, and happenings, he suggests (equivalent in many respects to Damasio's images), which are given meaning by their place in 'its plot or *fabula*' (43). The props of childhood and family drama also involve the inner chambers of the mind, which may also involve fear and struggle (Miller 1987). Dunn describes the part played by the child as a protagonist in everyday dramas: as an agent, victim or accomplice. Importantly, she also points to the way in which children frequently hear accounts and reviews of the parts they play in these dramas given by parents or siblings. Hence, the child is a participant, but also has the opportunity to view and reflect on this version of events as an independent text from a distant standpoint. This lays the ground for the process of appraisal, and for kind of transformative movement between lived texts and fictional texts that I described in my discussion of the 'wolf' dream. I shall now consider how such transformations are represented graphically by one of the project children, Ruby.

Ruby and Disneyland

Ruby was two years and eight months at the time that the following episode was filmed. Shortly before this she had visited Euro Disney with her parents and older brother. Like many of the project children, Ruby accessed a great deal of fictional narrative by repeated viewings of Disney cartoons, and an associated Disney picturebook, her particular favourite being *Beauty and the Beast.* In spite of their popularity with children, Disney's interpretations of fairy tales are not without their critics. Giroux (1995) suggests that Disney deploys a reductive and trivialising approach to history and narrative, presenting a closed and anodyne world of enchantment, where threats are contained or rendered harmless. Wonderly (2009) suggests that children are not fooled by this simplification, and have a greatly underestimated capacity for critical and moral deliberation. Zipes (1982) points to the continuing power of fairy tales to confront dilemmas, however packaged. Ruby talks extensively about the characters in the videos she watches, incorporating them into her own texts, and accommodating and transforming them in the process.

In this episode however, it is the Euro Disney dragon that is the focus of her interest. The Disneyland theme park extends the concept of the closed world of fantasy to the entire physical landscape in which the characters are encountered, creating a seamless fantasy space (Yoshimoto 1994), and a designed environment whose semiotic impact is fictional, but whose material structure is 'real'. The dragon is an audio-animatronic creation, measuring 27 metres from head to tail. It is chained up in a cave in the theme park, close to Sleeping Beauty's castle:

> As soon as you walk through the cavernous cave entrances, the atmosphere of the place is dark and foreboding. Take a minute to listen to the sound effects (dripping, screeches etc.) and look out for the blinking red eyes in the blackness. Then you come face to scaly face with a giant, moving, breathing dragon! Almost everything moves, from its fiery eyes to its clawed talons, and now it even breathes real smoke!
> (www. dlrpmagic.com/reviews/attractions/la taniere-du-dragon)

During the filming of the 'dragon' episodes, Ruby is sitting at the kitchen table next to her mother, Anna. She marks using a red felt-tipped pen on a sheet of pink coloured paper. On the right hand side of the page are representations of 'Daddy', 'Mummy', and her older brother who were with her on the visit. The dragon had already been discussed during a previous episode, and Ruby had produced her first dragon image at that point (Figure 2). This first dragon sign foregrounds the location of the dragon: a heavily over-marked green image (the dragon), encircled by a containing red mark (the castle). Like the wolf, the dragon is regarded as a dangerous and destructive animal (Bettelheim 1976), a fact that Ruby acknowledges by enclosing it within the walls of a castle, and thereby securing the safety of herself and her family from any threat it may pose. In the next episode, the researcher raises the subject of the dragon again, asking where it was while 'mummy and daddy were looking at it'. The subject is then picked up by Ruby and her mother, and during the dialogue that follows, Ruby makes sequences of large dots with a red felt-tipped pen in three phases generating distinct, but related textual representations of the creature.

Figure 2. The dragon in the castle
Reprinted by permission of Lesley Lancaster

The dragon in the cave

Phase 1

Ruby responds to the researcher saying that that the dragon is 'in the castle'. As in the case of the wolf, there is an ambiguity to the 'reality' status of this creature. The Euro Disney dragon (and its location) is of course very real in the material sense of being a physical object viewed by Ruby and her family. At the same time it is a highly engineered 'text', representing an entirely fictional creature. In this part of the episode, the reference is to the 'real' Euro Disney dragon, even though its ambiguous status remains an underlying issue throughout the construction of the text. Anna responds by making a deictic gesture, pointing to the left, directing Ruby's attention to the unmarked side of the paper, and the researcher asks whether the dragon is 'on the different page'. Ruby then simultaneously turns her gaze to this side of the page and makes a large red dot halfway up and in the centre of this section. She then over-marks the dot with a short line, giving emphasis to its significance as the subject of the text.

This is the first of a sequence of dots whose purpose is to record certain attributes of the dragon. This first dot records the existential quality of the dragon 'being there'. Thereafter, Ruby produces three more dots, spacing them out around the original 'dragon' mark. These dots provides a graphic record of different attributes of the dragon, which are spoken in turn by Ruby and Anna, with the marking of each dot synchronised with the vocal listing. The second attribute is spoken by Ruby, 'he's got big eyes', with her gaze directed at the researcher in acknowledgement of the continuation of the discourse about the dragon, before returning it to the page in preparation for recording the 'big eyes' attribute with a mark. She then places the dot a little way below and to the left of the first mark. Anna then describes two more features of the dragon, 'and he breathed fire [pause] smoke', and Ruby responds by placing a single dot to represent both these features a little distance away and to the right of the dragon mark. She then decides to give what is to her the more salient of these attributes an individual mark. Turning her gaze to Anna, she repeats what Anna said, 'and he breathed fire', before returning her gaze to the page and placing a dot a little distance above the previous mark. At the end of this first phase of marking, Robyn has produced a text that records the existence of the 'real' dragon as seen, and has listed a number of his attributes. It 'appraises' and materialises features of the family visit to Disneyland, and structurally has much in common with the inventories previously discussed, using a consistent, non-iconic mark for each attribute marked.

Phase 2

The start of the second phase is marked by Anna introducing a generic shift in the text, bringing to the fore the ambivalent, 'fictional or real' status of the dragon. The Euro Disney dragon's real physical attributes represent a considerable feat of engineering, and its very technological effectiveness means that minimal suspension of disbelief is required for it to appear as a real and consequently terrifying creature to a young child. Alternatively, if it is understood as fictional construct, it can still be terrifying, much as the wolf was for me, having the potential to induce 'estrangement or separation from a familiar world ... which is both frightening and comforting.' (Zipes 1982: 309). The fictional arena is opened up still further in Anna's next contribution about the dragon, 'yea but he had a big wall around him so he couldn't get us and we weren't scared mummy and daddy were we'. The implication that the dragon might somehow 'get them' is of course entirely fictional, given that the dragon is not a 'real' creature, but at the same time, Anna's statement embodies Zipes' fear and comfort: the fictional dragon was potentially dangerous and destructive through its imaginative impact, but they were protected from the fictional threat by the 'real' wall, and by the adults' real but fictional lack of fear. The boundary between the 'conventional', fictional text, and the material environment of the 'practically-lived' text is very permeable here.

Ruby continues to negotiate this complex network of living and fictional textual elements in her marking. She makes four dots in total, which mirror the number of points that Anna makes in support of her line of reasoning about how well they were protected from the potential danger of the dragon. Whilst Anna is talking, Ruby continues dotting at a measured pace, still spacing the dots, but without synchronising them with Anna's listing in the exact way that she previously did, or moving her gaze from the page. This section of the text is now transformed from an inventory of 'real' attributes to a numerical record of Anna's listing of 'fictional' arguments. Throughout this stage, however, her gaze remains fixed on the page, instead of shifting from page to person, and her locating of the dots becomes more patterned. She continues marking up the page, covering the top half by means of a diagonal movement, placing one dot up and to the right, the next dot up and to the left, and so on. Both this patterning, and her intent and concentrated gaze signify a shift in the focus of her interest and attention to the visual and spatial effects of her marking as it emerges on the page.

Phase 3

Phase 3 starts with brief return to a synchrony between what Anna says, and the final dot in the phase two sequence made by Ruby (Figure 3). Anna refers to a chain that secures the dragon, 'a big chain'. This completes her set of 'fictional' arguments for the safety of the dragon: in addition to everything else, it is secured by means of a big chain. Almost simultaneously Ruby makes a large dot in the top left corner of the page. Anna ascribes the meaning of this mark linguistically, 'you want to draw his big chain', maintaining the fictional genre, 'so he can't fly away'. This provides Ruby with a timely semiotic resource. She continues to concentrate on the visual and spatial effects that she has created on the top half of the page, but now identifies a new pattern that give a visual and semantic coherence to all the dots that she has made. This insight leads to the final textual transformation in this episode. The line of evenly spaced dots that spread up and across the page now have an iconic affordance, resembling as they do the links in the long, heavy chain that tethers the dragon. Her gaze moves back down the page, and using a deictic gesture, she indicates a dot at the bottom left of the page, 'that's his chains', and then continues pointing at the dots, moving back up the page, identifying the visual attributes of the sequence of marks, 'all his chains', and ending back at the initial 'chain' mark at the top of the page. The text is now transformed to a visual, iconic image of the dragon's chains that arguably also plays a 'fictional' role in maintaining the 'safety' of her family. The iconicity is derived from Ruby's visual memory of the chain that secures the 'real' dragon in its Euro Disney cave. Ruby's final text is a complex amalgam of three 'appraising' texts that relate to her understanding of the fictional-but-real dragon in its fictional-but-real cave. Each of the texts represents a distinct generic form: an inventory of the dragon's 'real', material attributes; an inventory of arguments for the safety of the dragon in a fictional context; and a visual, iconic representation of the dragon's chains based on a 'recalled image' of a real object in a fictional space.

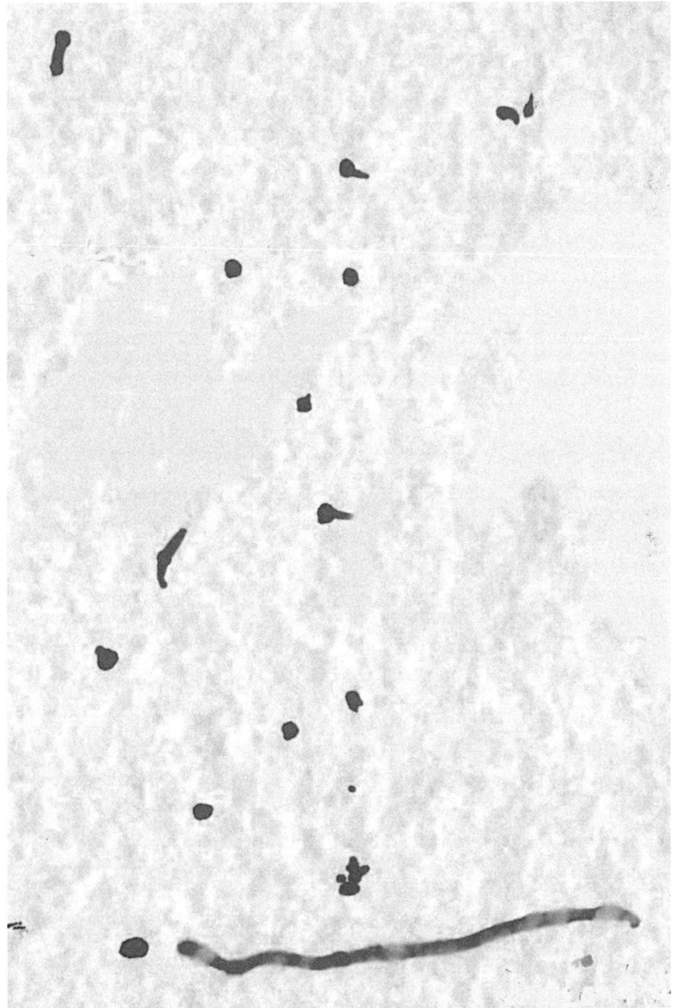

Figure 3. Chains
Reprinted by permission of Lesley Lancaster

Conclusion

The view that children cannot participate in the creation of cultural meanings until they are competent language users belies the evidence from observation and research. Far from there being some sort of representational interregnum prior to the development of language, children use available resources in multiple modes to communicate and represent graphic meanings from early infancy; they are both interpreters and producers of texts. The research discussed in this chapter, in its examination of children's early text production, shows how children under three already understand much about the complex textual and inscriptional structures that are deployed in picturebooks and other texts produced for very young children. Not only that, but they are able to draw on these texts transformatively, in terms of both meaning and structure, to devise and produce new texts of their own.

The graphic signs, which children of this age create already have some features that can be associated with conventional systems of drawing, writing, and number, whilst not yet being identifiable with any individual system. They are both multimodal and multifunctional, and children use marks to create signs and texts in diverse and creative ways. Children also have an early understanding of design and genre, and use this to extend and enhance the communicative possibilities of their productions. Picturebooks are also highly eclectic semiotically speaking, using design strategically and skilfully, and like young children deploy a plethora of means and modes to communicate their meanings. In this sense, there is sympathy of semiotic intent, and a productive relationship between the creators of many picturebooks, and young children as creators of original and purposeful texts.

Finally, both the 'reading' of picturebooks, and the production of children's own early texts are activities that both commonly take place in the context of close interpersonal communication and interaction between adults and young children. Whilst the importance of this has long been recognised as a means of supporting early reading development, it is less clearly recognised as also being of great significance in the development of children's early writing and text production.

References

Bettelheim, B. 1976. *The Uses of Enchantment: The Meaning and Importance of Fairy Tales*. London: Penguin Books.

Bruner, J. 1990. *Acts of Meaning*. Cambridge MA: Harvard University Press.

Damasio, A. 1999. *The Feeling of What Happens: Body, Emotion and the Making of Consciousness*. London: Vantage.

Deacon, T. 1997. *The Symbolic Species*. New York NY: W. W. Norton & Co.

Dunn, J. 1988. *The Beginnings of Social Understanding*. Cambridge MA: Harvard University Press.

Ferreiro, E. & Teborosky, A. 1983. *Literacy Before Schooling*. Exeter: Heinemann Educational Press.
Fischer, S. R. 2001. *A History of Writing*. London: Reaktion.
Giroux, H. A. 1995. Memory and pedagogy in the "Wonderful World of Disney": beyond the politics of innocence. In *From Mouse to Mermaid*, E. Bell, L. Haas & L. Sells (eds), 43–61. Bloomington IN: Indiana University Press.
Halliday, M. A. K. 1978. *Language as a Social Semiotic*. London: Edward Arnold.
Havelock, E. A. 1976. *Origins of Western Literacy*. Toronto: OISE.
Johnson, M. 1987. *The Body in the Mind: The Bodily Basis of Meaning, Imagination, and Reason*. Chicago IL: University of Chicago Press.
Karmiloff-Smith, A. 1992. *Beyond Modularity: A developmental Perspective on Cognitive Science*. Cambridge MA: The MIT Press.
Kress, G. 1997. *Before Writing: Rethinking the Paths to Literacy*. London: Routledge.
Kress, G. & van Leeuwen, T. 2001. *Multimodal Discourse*. London: Arnold.
Lancaster, L. 2007. Representing the ways of the world: How children under three start to use syntax in graphic signs. *Journal of Early Childhood Literacy* 7(2): 123–154.
Lancaster, L. 2003. Moving into literacy: How it all begins. In *Handbook of Early Childhood Literacy*, N. Hall, J. Larson & J. Marsh (eds), 145–154. London: Sage.
Lancaster, L. & Roberts, M. 2006. *Grammaticisation in Early Mark Making: A Multimodal Investigation*, End of Award Report: RES-000-22-0599.
Miller, A. 1987. *The Drama of Being a Child*. London: Virago.
Naginski, E. 2000. Drawing at the crossroads. *Representations* 72: 64–81.
Rowe, D. W. 2008a. Social contracts for writing: Negotiating shared understandings about text in the preschool years. *Reading Research Quarterly* 43(1): 66–95.
Rowe, D. W. 2008b. The social construction of intentionality. *Research in the Teaching of English* 42(4): 387–434.
Strauss, S. L. & Altwerger, B. 2007. The logographic nature of English alphabetics and the fallacy of direct intensive phonics instruction. *Journal of Early Childhood Literacy* 7(3): 299–319.
Tisseron, S. 1994. All writing is drawing: the spatial development of the manuscript. *YFS* 84: 29–42.
Trevarthen, C. 2004. Learning about ourselves from children: Why a growing human brain needs interesting companions. Edinburgh: Perception-in-Action Publications.
Wolf, D. & Perry, M. D. 1988. From endpoints to repertoires: Some new conclusions about drawing development. *Journal of Aesthetic Education* 22(1): 17–34.
Wonderly, M. 2009. Children's film as an instrument of moral education. *Journal of Moral Education* 38(1) 1–15.
Wu, L. 2009. Children's graphical representations and emergent writing: Evidence from children's drawings. *Early Child Development and Care* 179(1): 69–79.
Yoshimoto, M. 1994. Images of empire: Tokyo Disneyland and Japanese cultural imperialism. In *Disney Discourse: Producing the Magic Kingdom*, E. Smoodin (ed.), 181–199. London: Routledge.
Zipes, J. 1982. The potential of liberating fairy tales for children. *New Literary History* 13(2): 309–325.

CHAPTER 3

Color perception in infants and young children

The significance of color in picturebooks

Annette Werner

From early childhood on, color is an important aspect of our visual experience. Already one month old infants spontaneously prefer colored pictures over gray stimuli (Adams 1987). Not surprisingly, therefore, color plays an important role in picturebooks. However, when born, an infant's visual system is still immature and needs to develop. In this chapter I will consider the significance of color in picturebooks, and how colored pictures may be perceived by infants and young children up to three years of age, given the development of color vision in this age group. Possible consequences for the choice of colors in picturebooks are discussed.

Introduction

From early childhood on, color is an important aspect of our visual experience. Already one month old infants spontaneously prefer colored pictures over gray stimuli (Adams 1987). Not surprisingly, therefore, color plays an important role in picturebooks. However, when born, an infant's visual system is still immature and needs to develop. In this chapter I will consider the significance of color in picturebooks, and how colored pictures may be perceived by infants and young children up to three years of age, given the development of color vision in this age group. Possible consequences for the choice of colors in picturebooks are discussed.

Significance of color in picturebooks

The role of illustrations in picturebooks is distinct from that in other books, where the pictures or figures mainly serve to illustrate particular aspects of a story, and enhance motivation. In picturebooks, illustrations have an additional strong narrative function, and are essential for the understanding of the story. Being "windows to the world", they support not only the perceptual but also the cognitive and emotional development of children.

The importance of color in picturebooks has been widely recognized (e.g. Bang 1991; Kress & van Leeuwen 2002, 2006; Moebius 1990; Nodelman 1988; Painter 2007, 2008). In fact, color serves a whole range of purposes: first of all, color has a strong aesthetical value, making pictures more beautiful to look at. Children spontaneously prefer looking at colored pictures, compared to black and white pictures, and therefore color has a high impact on the attractiveness of a book.

In general, color is a salient feature of children's visual perception and more impressive than shapes or numbers (Odom & Guzman 1972). Also, children classify objects and develop concepts better when based on color than when using form or function (Lee 1965; Tomikawa & Dodd 1980). Furthermore, color clearly supports the recognition and identification of objects, as well as enhances memory: by adults, too, colored objects are better remembered than those shown only in black and white (Hansen et al. 2006; Vernon & Lloyed-Jones 2003). Color is also an important tool for communication, whose symbolic meaning is immediately understood. Take for example color signals used in traffic lights (red for "stop", and green for "go"), or the warning colors of some animals, i.e. the combination of yellow/red or yellow/black, used by amphibians (frogs), reptiles (snakes) and insects (wasps, bees) to indicate "beware – I am poisonous!". The symbolic meaning of color may therefore serve as a tool for non-verbal communication in picturebooks.

In addition to these values, further aspects of color in picturebooks can be identified, with color being part of a "visual grammar" (Kress & van Leeuwen 2002, 2006). According to Painter (2008), the different functions of color in picturebooks can be understood in terms of three so called "metafunctions" (after Halliday & Matthiesen 2004): hereby, the "ideational function" refers to the support of the content of a story, by providing additional information about the appearance of objects, animals etc. The second, "textual function" refers to the support of the organisation of a story by highlighting important aspects by the choice of color for particular elements of a picture.

Finally, the "interpersonal function" refers to relations and feelings expressed in the narrative; this is perhaps the most important aspect of color in narratives, since colors evoke emotions, and create an emotional atmosphere or "ambience" (Painter 2008). For example, bright, radiant colors transport a feeling of vividness and happiness, whereas sadness may be indicated by dull, dark colors and greys. Icy, blue colors may evoke a feeling of coldness, whereas red, brown and orange give a sense of warmth and coziness. Accordingly, Painter (2008) classified three main features of color in creating "ambience", namely "vibrancy", "warmth" and "familiarity". She proposed that vibrancy, realized by highly saturated and bright colors, will create an ambience of excitement, and energy and – transferring to another sensory quality – even loudness. Dull, unsaturated colors, on the other hand, will create a quieter feeling. By using warm colors (e.g. red, orange) or cold colors (blue), the warmth in a picture represents the subjective feeling in a situation, location or the relation between the actors of a story. The third category, familiarity, is equally important in creating an emotional ambience: Realistic colors, i.e. those which correspond to the true colors of real objects, will create a sense of familiar situation, whereas unrealistic colors, like for example a blue strawberry, may indicate an artificial or unreal environment, like for example that of dreams or illusions.

Thus, taken together, colors compliment the story told by the book on an additional, non-verbal level, where the emotional content is interpreted. To fully appreciate the role of colors in picturebooks and their significance, it is helpful to understand the nature of color, and, in particular, how color vision develops in infants and young children.

What is color?

Different from most people's understanding, color is not an intrinsic and physical property of objects; instead, it is a perception which is constructed by our brain. This has been pointed out already by Goethe in his *Farbenlehre* (Science of Colors; Goethe 1810), based on his observations on phenomena of color contrast. For example, a grey spot appears reddish if surrounded by green, but greenish, if surrounded by red. Similarly, after looking for 30 seconds at a bright red object and then at a white wall, a so called afterimage of an emerald green patch will appear. In Figure 1 an illusion can be appreciated where non-existing black dots appear at the crossing sections of a black and white grid (a particular version of the well known *Hermann Gitter)* when viewed peripherally; if fixated, the spots disappear immediately. Such effects demonstrate the influence of the spatial and temporal context, respectively, on our visual perception.

Figure 1. Scintillating grid illusion (also known as Lingelbach illusion; Schrauf, M. et al. 1995). Illusory black dots appear at the cross sections of the grey lines when viewed in the periphery, but disappear immediately if one tries to fixate them

Perceptually, color is often described by three terms, i.e. hue, saturation and lightness or brightness (also known as Helmholtz' coordinates of color; v. Helmholtz 1866). *Hue* refers to the experience of e. g. red, blue, green, yellow, purple etc. *Saturation* describes the perceived purity of a color, for example, pink is the less saturated or pure version of red, as obtained by adding white light or paint to a mixture. *Lightness* and *brightness*, on the other hand, describe how light or dark a paper/light appears, respectively.

The construction of color in our visual system

How is color derived in our visual system? The retina in our eyes contains four types of photoreceptors, which detect light: so called rods detect objects at low light intensity, for example at dawn or in the night. Though highly sensitive, rods only allow vision with low acuity and in shades of grey. In daylight, we see with another class of photoreceptors, the cones. These receptors provide high acuity vision (e.g. for reading) and their three subtypes are a prerequisite for color vision: because their spectral sensitivity differs, each cone type absorbs light particularly well in a different part of the spectrum, accordingly named short (blue)-, middle (green)- and long (red)- wavelength receptors (Figure 2). The cones generate neural signals, which are then processed along the visual pathway in several stages from the retina to the visual cortex in order to construct the full range of colors which we finally perceive.

Most importantly, our visual system constructs a *stable* color percept: to fully appreciate this performance, one has to consider that the light which reaches our eyes, changes considerably over the course of the day, whether we see an object in full sunlight or in the shadow, or whether indoors or outdoors (outdoor illumination typically has a higher content of blue light). Therefore, one might expect that the color of surfaces change accordingly – which they do not. This phenomenon, i.e. to perceive the colors of objects nearly unchanged despite changes of their illumination, is called color constancy. This is important, because it ensures that we recognize objects under a large range of viewing conditions.

Most importantly, color perception is not only constructed from sensory input alone Rather it is also strongly influenced by our memory and experiences: in our memory, colors are often more saturated than really are (Hansen et al. 2006) and it is well known that professional photos are often presented at high saturation.

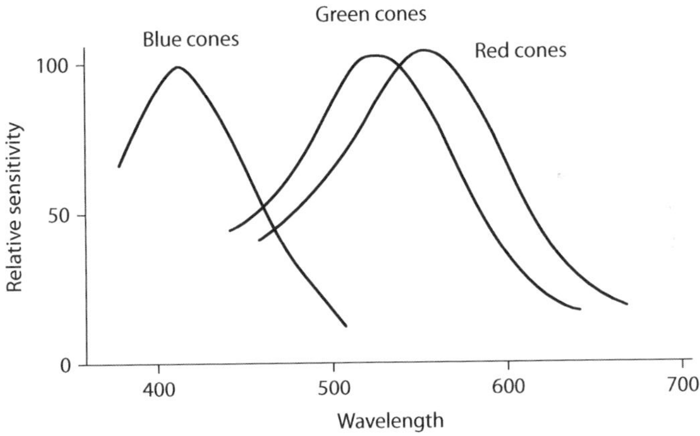

Figure 2. Spectral sensitivity of short- , middle-, and long-wavelength cones in the human eye

How is color vision tested in infants and preschool children?

Humans with normal color vision can discriminate up to 6 million different colors. This requires a full set of three types of cones (trichromacy) with normal spectral sensitivities. However, genetic variations can cause color vision deficits, and this occurs relatively often in the male population (in Europe, approximately

8% of men, and 0.5% of women are affected). These color vision deficits most often concern red/green color discrimination, but rarely the discrimination of blue versus yellow colors. It needs to be emphasized that this does not mean that red and green or blue and yellow, respectively, are not perceived by these people; rather, depending on the exact deficit, colors are perceived differently and discrimination of certain colors will be reduced, depending on the severity of the defect. A total loss of color vision (achromatopsia) is extremely rare and may be caused by damages to specific color regions of the brain.

However, because of the importance of color vision in our daily life, one should be aware of color vision deficits. Color vision in adults is often tested using Ishihara plates (or their modern versions on a Monitor screen) or color ordering tests, like for example the Farnsworth Munsell 100 hue test (FM100). Ishihara plates contain numbers made up from colored dots, which are presented on a background of differently colored dots. The colors are chosen in such a way, that the numbers can only be read by means of their chromatic difference against the background. Obviously, the Ishihara Test cannot be used reliably by preschool children and therefore versions of this test have been developed which use representations of animals or other objects, which are familiar to children. However, the problem remains that the results of these tests are confounded with the cognitive abilities of the observers. In particular, very young infants cannot be tested with these methods.

Instead, an alternative method has been developed, which tests young infant's visual performance behaviorally using a forced-choice preferential looking paradigm (Fantz et al. 1962; Teller 1979): this method avoids the cognitive factor by using a child's spontaneous looking behavior when presented with a new (i.e. interesting) stimulus. The child is typically presented with two large stimuli on cards or on a monitor screen, one containing the test-stimulus and the other a control stimulus. The researcher, usually hidden from the infant, then records the direction of the child's first look, the amount of time spent looking at a target and the number of looks. By those means, the visual performance of a young infant can be quantified. Even when testing older children, it is often desired to use non-verbal responses like pointing in the direction of the detected stimulus, in order to make the results comparable over a wider range of ages. Other techniques to test visual responses include the measurement of visually evoked cortical potentials (VEPS) and optokinetic nystagmus (OKN). In the first method, changes in electrical potentials correlating with the viewing of a stimulus are recorded from the surface of the head; in the latter method, a slowly moving drifting stimulus is presented which prompts the eyes of the child to follow (optokinetic nystagmus).

The development of color vision

In the next paragraph I will describe the development of color vision, under two aspects: (1) the sensory ability to discriminate and recognize colors; (2) the categorization of colors and the learning of color names.

1. Sensory development of color vision

Although functional cones are present by four or eight weeks the latest (Bieber et al. 1998), the visual system at this age is still very immature: this concerns the optics of the eye, the control of eye movements, as well as morphology and physiology of the retina: foveal cones of infants are extremely short and less densely packed (Yuodelis & Hendrickson 1986) than those of adults. This has consequences for visual performances, in particular for visual acuity and absolute sensitivity, which are both greatly reduced in the first months of life. Also reduced are contrast sensitivity and binocular vision, i.e. depth perception.

The ability to adapt and to discriminate different colors is also reduced. Color discrimination, in particular, is not present before 2 months of age, but can be demonstrated for most 3 month olds, if large and highly saturated stimuli are tested against white (Teller et al. 1978; Allen et al. 1988; Packer et al. 1984). However, significant individual differences have been noted in the development of color vision: in the transitional age of 2 months, some infants can discriminate colors, while others do not (Clavadetcher et al. 1988; Peeples & Teller 1975).

Furthermore, the maturation of the blue-cone system seems to be delayed. A selective reduction of blue-cone sensitivity has been reported for young infants (Pulos et al. 1980), and this affects color discrimination as well as the detection of moving stimuli (Teller & Lindsey 1993). Thus, color discrimination appears to develop faster for longwavelength light, i.e. yellow and red stimuli, than for blue (Adams et al. 1986).

Another important performance of the color system, which develops within a similar time-frame as color discrimination is color constancy. The latter allows us to recognize objects under a wide range of different illuminations, e.g. from dawn to bright sun light, and from natural skylight to artificial tungsten light. This astounding ability of our color vision is completed between two and four months of age (Dannemiller & Hanko 1987). Studies on raising monkeys in different light environments showed that those monkeys which have been raised without changes of illumination later lacked the performance of color constancy (Sugita 2004). We can conclude from this that perceptual learning contributes to the development of our visual abilities and that a rich visual environment is therefore important for an optimal development of the visual system.

In the first months of life, performances improve very fast, and within 6 months of age, most visual functions have been successfully "installed". However, full adult performance is not reached before adolescence, while the visual system continues to mature and fine adjusts more slowly by learning and implementing visual experience. Knoblauch et al. (2001) carefully measured the development of chromatic contrast sensitivity in children aged 6 months and older by having them detect chromatic patterns on a monitor screen (e.g. patterns of red/green, or blue /yellow patches). They reported an approximately linear increase of sensitivity with increasing age (i.e. a doubling of sensitivity with each doubling of age) until adolescence (thereafter, a modest ageing begins, by roughly the same rate). Most importantly, Knoblauch and colleagues found a similar rate of improvement for all color contrasts, with blue/yellow contrast being only slightly delayed.

Taken together, it seems very likely that color perception in children older than 6 months does not differ *qualitatively* from that of adults. Rather, it differs *quantitatively*, in terms of contrast sensitivity and perceived saturation of colors. Thus, children's visual performance can be considered as a "scaled down version of adult colour vision" (Adams & Courage 1998).

2. Linguistic development: Color categories and color naming

Interestingly, adults divide the continuum of colors into few distinct categories, which are typically assigned basic color terms. Across many cultures, four basic color categories are common, namely "Red", "Green", "Yellow" and "Blue". These categories are distinct on a semantic level, i.e. assignment of color names, as well as a perceptual level in that colors across categorical borders are better discriminated than those within the same category.

It has been a long-standing controversy, whether perception or language take primacy in forming these categories. The universality of hue-categories (Berlin & Kay 1969) and the pre-linguistic acquisition of hue categories in infants (see below; Bornstein et al. 1976) favor a physiological explanation (the way in which color is encoded in the visual system). However, strong cultural and semantic influences on color perception have also been demonstrated: studying color categorization in the Berinmos, a tribe living in Papua-New Guinea, Davidoff and colleagues (1999) described five categories, which were significantly different from those used by Europeans. In particular, Berinmos combine the European categories "Blue" and "Green" in a common category ("Nol"), rather than discriminate between them. On the other hand, when testing color discrimination across categorical boundaries used by the Berinmos, like "Nol" (European "Blue" plus " Green" and "Wor" (European "Yellow" plus "Green"), Europeans performed worse. Thus, there seems to be a mutual interaction between color semantics and perception.

When and how do children learn these color categories and color names? Since color is a highly salient dimension of visual experience, more important than concepts of form or numbers, it can be expected that color names are learned early in development. Four month old babies have been shown to assign spectral wavelengths to four basic categories, which are already very similar to those of adults (blue, green, yellow and red; Bornstein 1975). By contrast and quite surprisingly, children learn color *names* relatively late in their development. One of the oldest reports on this developmental phenomenon comes from Darwin (1877) who described a "delayement" of the correct use of color names by his children, particularly by his boys and here especially for green and blue colors. Cook (1931) tested 2 and 6-year olds for naming and matching reds, yellows, greens and blues and found that the young children matched colors far more accurately than they named the same colors, whereas the older children were more successful in both tasks (see also Heider 1971; review by Bornstein 1985).

We know today that, in the beginning, color naming by young children is indeed unsystematic and unstable. At first, a single, random color term may be used for several targets, e. g. "red" for a ball, a car and a dog. Later, children may use several names, but again without proper and correct association to the right color. In fact, before the age of 4, it seems difficult to teach color names (Bornstein 1985). Only after 4 years of age do color names become more consistent and accurate. A significant increase in naming accuracy for basic color terms occurs around the age of 5 years and it has been argued this is prompted by school-training (Bornstein 1985; Anyan & Quilian 1971). Also, socio-economic and educational status appears to influence the development of color names (Kirk et al. 1975).

The order by which colors are learned and whether there is any learning order at all is controversial: whereas some researchers claimed that color names develop randomly (e.g. Bornstein), others found that children comprehend and name focal colors earlier and better than non-focal colors: Mervis and colleagues (1975) found that children learn the names of focal colors (blue, green, yellow, red) first, and colors of intermediate color regions (e.g. blue-green) later. By age 7, most children master color naming (e.g. Dale 1969; Mervis et al. 1975; Raskin et al. 1983). However, there are large individual differences, with acquisition among girls being generally faster than among boys (Bornstein 1985).

The late acquisition of color terms is puzzling because the sensory apparatus and perceptual organization are by that time already well established: children can discriminate and categorize colors, as well as have an awareness of color as a perceptual dimension. The latter is demonstrated by the fact that they answer questions like "what color is it?" correctly with a (random) color name. Yet they do not seem to be able to assign a correct name to a specific color. How can this discrepancy be explained? An interesting hypothesis put forward by Bornstein

(1985) considers the development of neurological maturation and integration. In brief this hypothesis assumes that the difficulties of young children to learn and use color names is related to the maturation of cortical functions connecting visual and verbal domains, as observed in specific forms of color agnosia in adults. In these patients, normal color discrimination and knowledge of color names coexists with an inability to correctly and consistently assign names to colors – similar to what is observed in young children.

In conclusion, it seems important to distinguish between the development of color *perception* and the acquisition of color *naming*: whereas color perception, including color categorization, is established for all spectral regions by 6 months of age the latest, color naming is acquired much later and needs several years to be consistent and correct. Therefore, even though infants and young children may not yet name colors correctly, they do perceive the "correct" colors and are able to form concepts based on color categories (provided there is no color vision deficiency). This is important for understanding the impact of the semantic use of color (terms) in the text as compared to the impact of the perceived colors in pictures. In other worlds, it highlights the significance of colored pictures in books.

Conclusions for the choice of colors in picturebooks

From what has been outlined above on the development of color perception and naming in young children, a number of questions arise concerning the choice of colors in picturebooks:

1. First of all, what does this mean for black & white drawings or gray scale photographs in books for very young infants: do they have any impact at all, or may the even be rejected by children?

Generally, people prefer colored pictures over black and white ones. Already infants older than 3 months show a spontaneous looking preference for certain colors. Whereas newborns prefer darker stimuli, 3 and 4 months old infants, respectively, seem to prefer colors from the spectral extremes (red and blue; Bornstein 1975; Zemach, Chang & Teller 2007), followed by yellow and blue-green (Adams 1987). No gender differences such as those known from adults (reddish hues by women and greenish hues by men; Hurlbert & Ling 2007) have been reported.

However, it can also be argued that black and white pictures allow imagining all colors desired, and thus encourage children's fantasy. But this requires an experience with colors typically assigned to objects which is just what needs to develop in young children.

Black and white line drawings deserve separate consideration: these may at first appear simple and clear, however, they are actually quite demanding. They require our visual system to group correctly lines belonging to the background and those belonging to the figures. For most (but not all) adults this is usually an easy task, based on our visual experience. However, Figure 3a demonstrates the actual challenge for an untrained observer. This picture consists of black and white dots exclusively; if you have never seen the picture before, it is difficult to see the featured figure. If, however you know the outlines of the figure (see Figure 3b on the following page), you will immediately recognize the dog in Figure 3a. Similarly, the interpretation of such black & white drawings may not be as straightforward for young, inexperienced children as it is for (experienced) adults.

Figure 3a. This black and white picture features a Dalmatian dog – do you see it?

2. There are concept picturebooks, especially designed to teach young children color names. In these books, color names such as "Red" or "Blue" are assigned to familiar objects. However, given the late acquisition of color terms, can concept books really fulfil their purpose?

Color-to-name associations can be trained in young children (see e.g. Bornstein 1985). It is quite plausible that children "trained" with such books do perform better then those without additional, specific experience on color names. However, the learning effect has, to my knowledge, never been tested specifically for concept books.

3. There are two main tendencies for choice of colors in picture nooks: there are those with primary colors only, without any shading by saturation or brightness; moreover, the colored areas are delineated by thick black lines. A typical example for this style of drawing is the *Miffy* Books by Dick Bruna (for example *Miffy's House* (2004)). The other tendency is to draw pictures realistically, using shadows, and a variety of different shades of hues, of brightness and/or of saturations. A typical example would be Hermann Spanner's *Meine ersten Sachen* (My First Things, 1998).

Which one of these very different styles we prefer is of course, first of all, a matter of taste.

Figure 3b. Here is the Dalmatian dog – you will now find it easily in Figure 3a

But considering the sensory development of color vision and their reduced color discrimination and contrast sensitivity, high purity (highly saturated) colors seem to be a good choice for the picturebooks for very young infants.

Whether or not some particular colors should be preferred in (e.g. yellow and red over green and blue) is a matter of debate: one may argue that these colors are better visible to young infants and some illustrators of picturebooks, therefore, prefer Yellow, Red, Black and White for their illustrations. The Danish picturebook artist Kamilla Wichmann refers to these preferences in the blurb of her leporello fold picturebook *Dyr på garden* (2007). While one side of the leporello is intended for children aged 3 to 7 months, reducing the color scheme to black and white contrasts, bright red and yellow, the other side appeals to children aged 8 to 18 months when they are usually able to distinguish almost every color under the condition that the hue is constant and that a prototypical color is chosen. However, as has been pointed out above, there is some controversy concerning the selectivity of the immaturity, and recent findings support the view of a more general immaturity of infant color vision. In that case, we cannot expect some colors to be more visible than others for infants. Also, it should be considered that a full palette of naturalistic colors provides the visual system with the necessary perceptual experience, and may support the acquirement of linguistic color knowledge.

Acknowledgments

I would like to thank Jürgen Heller and Bettina Kümmerling-Meibauer for their helpful and constructive comments on the manuscript.

Children's books cited

Bruna, D. 2004. *Miffy's House*. New York NY: Big Tent Entertainment (first published 1964).
Spanner, H. 1998. *Meine ersten Sachen*. Ravensburg: Ravensburger Buchverlag (first published 1977).
Wichmann, K. 2007. *Dyr på gården*. Copenhagen: Gorilla forlag.

References

Adams, R. J. 1987. An evaluation of color preferences in early infancy. *Infant behaviour and Development* 10: 143–150.
Adams, R. J. & Courage, M. L. 1998. Human newborn color vision: Measurement with chromatic stimuli varying in excitation purity. *Journal of Experimental Child Psychology* 68: 22–34.
Adams, R. J., Maurer, D. & Davis, M. 1986. Newborn's discrimination of chromatic from achromatic stimuli. *Journal of Experimental Child Psychology* 41: 267–281.
Allen, D., Banks, M., Norcia, A. M. & Shannonet, L. 1988. Chromatic discrimination in human infants. A re-examination. *Investigative Ophthalmology and Visual Science* (*Suppl.*) 29: 25.

Anyan, M. L.,Walter, R. Jr., & Warren W., II. 1971. The Naming of Primary Colors by Children. *Child Development* 42: 1629–1632.

Bang, M. 1991. *Picture This: How Pictures Work*. Boston MA: Little, Brown & Co.

Bieber, M. L., Knoblauch, K. & Werner, J. S. 1998. M- and L-cones in early infancy, II: Action spectra at 8 weeks of age. *Vision Research* 38: 1765–1773.

Berlin, B. & Kay, P. 1969. *Basic Color Terms: Their Universality and Evolution*. Berkeley CA: University of California Press.

Bornstein, M. H. 1975. Qualities of color vision in infancy. *Journal of Experimental Child Psychology* 19: 401–419.

Bornstein, M. H. 1985. Human infant color vision and color perception. *Infant Behavior and Development* 8: 109–113.

Bornstein, M. H., Kessen, W. & Weiskopf, S. 1976. The categories of hue in infancy. *Science* 191: 201–202.

Bornstein, M. H., Kessen, W. & Weiskopf, S. 1976. Color vision and hue categorization in young human infants. *Journal of Experimental Psychology: Human Perception and Performance* 2: 115–129.

Clavadetscher, J. E., Brown, A. M., Anchrum, C. & Teller, D. Y. 1988. Spectral sensitivity and chromatic discrimination in 3- and 7-week-old human infants. *Journal of the Optical Society of America* A 5: 2093–2105.

Cook, W. M. 1931. Ability of children in color discrimination. *Child Development* 2: 303–320.

Dale, P. S. 1969. Color naming, matching, and recognition by preschoolers. *Child Development* 40(4): 1135–1144.

Dannemiller, J. L. & Hanko, S. A. 1987. A test of color constancy in 4-month-old human infants. *Journal of Experimental Child Psychology* 44: 255–267.

Darwin, C. H. 1877. A biographical sketch of a young infant. *Kosmos* 1: 367–376.

Davidoff, J., Davies, I. & Roberson, D. 1999. Colour categories in a stone-age tribe. *Nature* 398: 203–204.

Fantz, R. L., Ordy, J. M. & Udelf, M. S. 1962. Maturation of pattern vision in infants during the first six months. *Journal of Child Physiological Psychology* 55: 907–917.

von Goethe, J. W. 1810. *Zur Farbenlehre*. Tübingen: Cotta.

Halliday, M. A. K. & Matthiessen, C. M. 2004. *Introduction to Functional Grammar*, 3rd revised edn. London: Arnold.

Heider, E. R. 1971. 'Focal' color areas and the development of color names. *Developmental Psychology* 4: 447–455.

von Helmholtz, H. 1866. *Handbuch der physiologischen Optik, I. bis II. Band, Die Lehre von den Gesichtswahrnehmungen*. Leipzig: L. Voss.

Hurlbert, A. C. & Ling, Y. 2007. Biological components of sex differences in color preference. *Current Biology* 17: R623–R625.

Kirk, G. E., Hunt, J. M. & Lieberman, C. 1975. Social class and preschool language skill, II: semantic mastery of color information. *Genetic Psychology Monographs, 91* (Second Half): 299–316.

Knoblauch, K., Vital-Durand, F. & Barbur, J. L. 2001. Variation of chromatic sensitivity across the life span. *Vision Research* 41: 23–36.

Kress, G. & van Leeuwen, T. 2002. Colour as a semiotic mode: Notes for a grammar of colour. *Visual Communication* 1: 343–368.

Kress, G. & van Leeuwen, T. 2006. *Reading Images: The Grammar of Visual Design*, 2nd edn. London: Routledge.

Lee, L. C. 1965. Concept utilization in preschool children. *Child Development* 36: 221–228.

Hansen, T., Olkkonen, M., Walter, S. & Gegenfurtner, K. R. 2006. Memory modulates color appearance. *Nature Neuroscience* 9: 1367–1368

Mervis, C. B., Catlin, J. & Rosch, E. 1975. Development of the structure of color categories. *Developmental Psychology* 11: 54–60.

Moebius, W. 1990. Introduction to picturebook codes. In *Childrens Literature: The Development of Criticism,* P. Hunt (ed.), 141–151. London: Routledge.

Nodelman, P. 1988. *Words about Pictures: The Narrative Art of Children's Picture Books.* Athens GA: University of Georgia Press.

Odom, R. D. & Guzman, R. D. 1972. Development of hierarchies of dimensional salience. *Developmental Psychology* 6: 271–287.

Packer, O., Hartmann, E. E. & Teller, D. Y. 1984. Infant color vision: The effect of test field size on Raleigh discrimination. *Vision Research* 24: 1247–1260.

Painter, C. 2007. Children's picturebooks: Reading sequences of images. In *Advances in Language and Education,* A. McCabe, M. O'Donnell & R. Whittaker (eds), 38–57. London: Continuum.

Painter, C. 2008. The role of colour in children's picturebooks: choices of ambience. In *New Literacies and the English Curriculum. Multimodal Perspectives,* L. Unsworth (ed.), 89–111. London: Continnum.

Peeples, D. R. & Teller, D. Y. 1975. Color vision and brightness discrimination in two-month-old human infants. *Science* 189: 1102–1103.

Pulos, E., Teller, D. Y. & Buck, S. L. 1980. Infant color vision: A search for short-wavelength-sensitive-mechanisms by means of chromatic adaptation. *Vision Research* 20: 485–493.

Schrauf, M., Lingelbach, B., Lingelbach, E. & Wist, E. R. 1995. The Hermann grid and the scintillation effect. *Perception* 24 (suppl.): 88–89.

Sugita, Y. 2004. Experience in early infancy is indispensable for color perception. *Current Biology* 14: 1267–1271.

Raskin, L. A., Maital, S. & Bornstein, M. H. 1983. Perceptual categorization of color: A life-span study. *Psychology Research* 45: 135–145.

Teller, D. Y. 1979. The forced-choice preferential looking procedure: A psychophysical technique for use with human infants. *Infant Behaviour and Development* 2: 135–153.

Teller, D. Y., Peeples, D. R. & Sekel, M. 1978. Discrimination of chromatic from white light by two-month-old human infants. *Vision Research* 18: 41–48.

Teller, D. Y. & Lindsey, D. T. 1993. Motion at isoluminance: motion dead zones in three-dimensional color space. *Journal of Optical Society of America* A, 10: 1324–1331.

Tomikawa, S. A. & Dodd, D. H. 1980. Early word meanings: Perceptually or functionally based? *Child Development* 51: 1103–1109.

Vernon, D. & Lloyed-Jones, T. J. 2003. The role of color in implicit and explicit memory performance. *The Quarterly Journal of Experimental Psychology* 56: 779–802.

Yuodelis, C. & Hendrickson, A. 1986. A qualitative and quantitative analysis of the human fovea during development. *Vision Research* 26: 847–855.

Zemach, I. K. & Teller, D. Y. 2007. Infant color vision: Infants'spontaneous color preferences are well behaved. *Vision Research* 47: 1362–1367.

CHAPTER 4

Parallel receptions of the fundamental

Basic designs in picturebooks and modern art

Martin Roman Deppner

Elementary shapes (in the tradition of Pestalozzi and later Fröbel) are of great importance in children's education and modern art. They appear, for example, in paintings such as "Die Hülsenbeckschen Kinder" (1805/06) by Philipp Otto Runge that exerted a great influence on modern art. The resulting reception enables an insight into children's perception. Minimal art, conceptual art, and other constructivist art forms have adopted this idea. However, the obvious impact of these movements and ideas on picturebooks for children has not been adequately investigated so far. The objective here is to reveal the aesthetically innovative dimension of elementary reductions, as well as to show how young children perceive basic shapes and objects that undoubtedly inspire the young child's imaginative powers. In this way, children's perception, the education of children, picturebooks for young children and modern art complement each other so that the underlying symbolic shifts relating to modernity become comprehensible (through the use of elementary shapes) and can be utilized productively.

Introduction

In spring 2009 the Museum Burg Wissem in Troisdorf held an exhibition, "Literature in the Playpen. Picturebooks for Young Children." It was advertised by a poster depicting colorful images of round objects that vividly illustrated two overlapping epistemological steps (see Figure 1).

To begin with, the objects depicted are all based on the circle. This basic form, extended to a sculptural sphere by illusionist shadowing and coloring, then diversifies into images of useful everyday objects. Five of these spheres are arranged as differently patterned balls juxtaposed to a square-based pattern, alternating with four images of an apple in various colors and shapes. One of these shows an apple cut in half, revealing pips and a halved sphere. Moreover, all the objects are surrounded by different colors that separate them from each other. Featuring first and second order primary colors, this object composition exhibits a further

Figure 1. Exhibition poster "Literature in the Playpen. Picturebooks for Young Children" (Picturebook Museum Burg Wissem, Troisdorf)
Design by Frank Georgy. Reprinted by permission of Frank Georgy

signal value: red is dominant, followed by green, white, blue and yellow. However, as this poster does not consist of two matching images like a Pelmanism game, but instead of similar images that can be differentiated according to function, the element of recognition becomes more difficult. The principle of similar appearance is established and simultaneously disrupted but not totally undermined; in the same way as the circle is not identical to a sphere yet still evokes it, various objects can be developed from the basic form.

In fact, the exhibition poster is not a picturebook but a compilation of illustrations from a variety of picturebooks from different periods. What the illustrations have in common is the representation of various objects as a circular shape. This is no coincidence because the circular shape in its many incarnations exerts a 'magical' attraction for pre-school children anyway – largely because it overlaps with the child's experience of not only being able to set an object in motion with a light push, but also being able to grasp it. Moreover, the sphere's regular form has inspired the imagination of educationalists since Johann Heinrich Pestalozzi and Friedrich Fröbel, for whom, as for many others, it symbolized a holistic experience of the world (Heiland & Neumann 2003).

The combination of elements in the poster refers to an important issue that offers insight for learning in general: how do abstract elementary shapes relate to the objects that emerge from them, and how can the signs accompanying these objects be related to each other to create meaning? It is the reenactment of phenomena that leads to a unifying principle behind the form, as a first exercise in abstract thinking.

In other words, the differentiation of comparable basic shapes, such as the circle and sphere, leads to additional meaning and understanding with regard to their object denotation. The realization of the symbol shift precisely to this basic form in relation to object denotation allows a sphere to mutate to a ball both as an image and in everyday life, and at the same time to assume the basic shape of an edible object, the apple.

Although this task is not easy, it can be found in many picturebooks for young children. In our life dominated by the media, it is a track that leads daily to even more abstract yet epistemological steps such as those that are important in works of modern art (Böhme 2004). The result, for example, if we were to pursue the implications of the poster, is that the same basic shape can describe different objects, which in turn can be assigned to different conceptual classes. If we included pears as well, we could have a variety of fruit; adding Christmas tree baubles to the series would extend the range of circular objects; adding pictures of other objects to the colors of the balls could show correspondences with the colors of these new objects. This principle could be continued with other artistic resources such as use of line, cross-hatching, or shade. This would overstep the boundaries of the educational age under consideration but is still worth mentioning here. This perception process, revealed and thought through by the post-structuralists, has been superimposed on the objects and is able to perceive meaning only in the resulting chain of symbols, no longer in the recognition of the object itself (Welsch 1990: 211ff.).

Fundamental forms in early childhood education

It has been established that in the kind of picturebooks now referred to as "early-concept books" – i.e., books that communicate not only "first images" but also "first concepts" to young children – "the two most common objects occurring both in early works and also in modern publications… [are] the ball and the apple" (Kümmerling-Meibauer & Meibauer (2005: 336). This applies to a period from around 1890 to the present day. Usually presented on a unicolored background, these and other objects appear isolated in a "negative space" without connection to the normal environment. At the same time, they are not mutually proportional, i.e. they are the same size independently of information from the external world. This presents an initial level of abstraction, since everyday objects are not usually shown in a negative space, nor are they the same size (Kümmerling-Meibauer 2009: 17ff.).

Let us begin with the basic shape highlighted in the poster and featured in various picturebooks for small children that focus on the representation of individual objects from the child's surroundings. As we have said, the fundamental nature of the sphere and other geometric bodies has influenced reflections on modern educational theory regarding the practice of epistemological steps since the 18th century, as part of the quest for patterns that might explain the structure of the world. Pestalozzi, and above all, Fröbel, left no stone unturned in their attempts to describe and test the developing intelligence of a child in its play with basic shapes as a path from the simple to the complex, as a path from basic natural shapes to cultural constructions (Pestalozzi 2006).

Let us compare our poster with a visual testimony from the era of the elementary education movement: the draft for a color sphere designed by Philipp Otto Runge in 1810. This is a design that exhibits the contrasting polarization of the three-dimensional color sphere and the vertical and horizontal sections. It is striking that Runge's color sphere occurs in a context that provides more than a superficial comparison with the conference poster. Runge's conception of art shows a constructive understanding of the world that already departs from assigning symbols to objects. Runge understood both color and geometry as elements that can be used to reconstruct what Werner Hofmann (1977) called the "lost paradise" (31f.), a metaphor alluding to the Romantic idea of childhood representing the lost "Golden Age of Mankind." Runge reveals himself as a Romantic who had a sense of the harmony of colors, but at the same time as a reflective person, i.e. he subscribed to the contemporary idea that the world had to be designed in people's heads. In paradigmatic terms he applied this standpoint demonstratively in one of his most significant paintings – a standpoint that also had the basic aim of adopting a child's perspective, thus bringing it into the realm of pre-school education (see Figure 2).

The painting, "Die Hülsenbeckschen Kinder" (The Hülsenbeck Children), dates from 1805/6. Along with other works by Runge and similar Romantic artists, it was used as a reference by Maurice Sendak for his picturebooks *Outside Over There* (1981) and *Dear Mili* (with a text by Wilhelm Grimm, 1988). Sendak also cited Runge's "Morning" of 1810, adopting elements from it such as the climbing plants with cherubs. In this context Sendak was interested in the emotional quality of the Romantic period, orienting himself on the painterly qualities of transitions that illustrate different moods and feelings. Moreover, he was intrigued by the characteristics that convey Romantic sensibility not only as a longing for harmony and security but also as a path through a dark, mysterious world (Deppner & Thiele 1994: 52).

Figure 2. "Die Hülsenbeckschen Kinder" (1805/06), painting by Philipp Otto Runge

Runge's "The Hülsenbeck Children" shows the symbolic path in a constructive worldview that was important for the educational theory of that time. It is paradigmatic, for example, that the girl pulling the handcart with the infant is turning back her head, arm and hand and making a grasping movement – towards the infant, in fact. The implied diagonal intersects with a sphere fastened to the garden fence that resembles an object to be grasped. If we envisage the diagonal as a connecting line between the children, then all three heads are located on this line and brought into a structural relationship with the sphere. The heads are spherical, indicating the special status assigned to this basic shape (Brodersen et al. 1978: 23).

The sphere embodies, so to speak, the symbolic centre of action in a picture that changes the children's proportions to their environment – the children seem like adults in their gestures and in relation to the fence and house. The basic shape of the sphere also relates to the circular movement embodied by the sunflowers with their changing alignments following the sun's circuit. Sphere and circle form a unit in the unity of nature and culture, connecting with other Romantic ideas about the unity of humans with nature and – deriving from this – the natural equality of nature as a model for the human being, visible, for instance, in the equivalence of the subject-related elements of landscape and children in the picture (Träger 1987: 51).

Runge correspondingly transferred the structures of the fundamental shapes to nature or, one might say, attempted to reveal one form in the other. One example here is Runge's depiction of the structure of a cornflower. Here, as in his "Hülsenbeck Children", we can discern a reference to microcosm and macrocosm, embodied as sun and flower (Hofmann 1977: 136–147).[1]

In addition to circular and spherical shapes, other nature-related structures used by Runge correspond to the fundamental forms that Pestalozzi used as examples in elementary teaching – just as the bodies of the Hülsenbeck Children are based on stereometric forms.

Pestalozzi's tripartite division of "head, heart and hand," standing for intellect, moral values and practical ability, as well as the fundamental subjects of speech, song, writing, drawing and arithmetic and, ultimately, the ability to form abstract judgments, can also be understood as a building set in Runge's sense, a construction kit for ideal communication of the structural principle as demonstrated by nature (Kuhlemann & Brühlmeier 2002).

The children's heads in Runge's painting appear as differentiated physiognomies emerging from the pure spherical form. Runge himself wrote about

1. This idea was also reflected – consciously or unconsciously – in the illustrations in Hilde Heyduck's picturebook for small children *Wenn die Sonne scheint* (When the Sun Shines, 1961).

one of his sons, "The young child is very fat and getting ever closer to perfection, namely the spherical form" (Runge 1940: 343). At that time the spherical form was also viewed as an educational model. For example, Johann Friedrich Herbart wrote in his *Allgemeine Pädagogik* (General Pedagogy, 1806): "Once the work (of education) has been begun with the individual, the contours of this individual increasingly change, as if a sphere were gradually to grow from a certain central point on an irregular angular body, although the sphere can never fully encompass the outermost projections. These projections – the strengths of individuality – may remain as long as they do not corrupt the character" (Herbart 1976: 66f.).

It was Friedrich Fröbel, the founder of the first German "Kindergarten" in 1840, who eventually developed play and learning materials that were intended to introduce young children to the adult realm of experience by means of basic educational forms, understood as the three-dimensional forms of the sphere, the cylinder and the cube. The monument dedicated to Fröbel is consequently constructed like a model created from his favorite basic shapes, as a metaphor for the human being itself (Fröbel 1998).

This concludes our digression on these basic forms of elementary education, which have lost nothing of their relevance to this day, even if they no longer serve as models for explaining the world but instead for understanding the constructability of the world and for practicing the corresponding methods. We can mention other parameters as well. Around 1800 the basic forms came to be viewed as a symbol of the ability to see the world constructively – as shown by William Blake's "Ancient of Days" (1794), which he also saw as a prophecy for the future – while today, the basic forms tend to be assigned the role of learning to deal with mutable processes. This represents a paradigm change in the understanding of structure that also took place in art.[2]

Friedrich Fröbel and abstract concepts in picturebooks for small children

If we compare a Fröbel building set with a formally related floor sculpture by Carl Andre from the 1970s, and ignore the differences of size, we can recognize a similar structural principle in the arrangement of the same elements (see Figure 3).

A closer look reveals that Andre dispenses with a border. The play of shadows also indicates a possible extension – signals directed outward. If we now compare an Andre sculpture consisting of rectangular wooden blocks to a drawing

2. Cf. Deppner on Moholy-Nagy (1997); on the 100th birthday of this artist and Bauhaus teacher, see pp. 163–180.

Figure 3. Building set by Friedrich Fröbel (left side), and floor sculpture by Carl Andre (right side)

by Fröbel that also depicts the structure of open forms, we see once again a close relationship between children's toys and minimal art. Moreover, both are realized on the floor, which in the case of art means that art itself is removed from its pedestal – with what might almost be called a childish gesture (Friese 1998).

But there is a difference as well: the purpose of Fröbel's building set was, and is, to foster the perception that a whole can be divided into many identical parts and that these in turn can form a whole. The minimal art of Andre and other artists has a very different goal. In minimal art the juxtaposition of the basic forms – as we can see, for example, in the development of a Pythagorean formation – aims at reduction for two reasons: first, so as not to establish any additional references, and second, to shift the point of reference outwards, aiming at and transferring to the recipient, who then continues constructing the world in his head, and so on (Held 1995: 447f.).[3] While Fröbel was concerned with the unity of the parts, in minimal art the focus is on the whole as a starting point, expanding into the space and beyond. This is how the works of Sol LeWitt and Donald Judd can be understood: an intention that also corresponds to the

3. Cf. Westheider (1997: 30f.) on conceptual art.

open object forms, to the expansion in space towards an imagined eternity, and to the materials that are directed outwards from the work of art, for instance as mirroring surfaces.[4]

Early on, in the 1920s, El Lissitzky designed a picturebook for children with a story developing from two squares and illustrated with abstract relationships between forms, numbers and letters. But here, too, one still finds the idea of a unifying construction with mobile elements as part of a holistic concept and the search for meaning. In this case the Russian revolution was the guiding principle of the picturebook's story. This also corresponded to Lissitzky's concept of art, epitomized by Kazimir Malevich's Suprematist painting, "Black Square" (1920). The demonstration of an abstraction that aimed to encompass everything, it could still only function as sensation or feeling (Schneede 1998). The reference to sensation derives from Malevich himself and indicates how the carefully calculated arrangement of geometrical forms leads to an impression that would prove important to post-war modern art and has also made its mark on picturebooks dealing with abstract geometrical forms. In this way the structures of minimal art and color-field paintings, variations of the basic forms, are released, as it were, from a purely geometrical idea of wholeness by becoming

---

4. For a long period, the exemplary role of Fröbel's elementary pedagogy, especially for the abstractions of the European avant-garde, was not generally recognized, although individual scholars and artists acknowledged its influence earlier. According to Brigitte Werneburg, Fröbel's square pattern influenced the architect Frank Lloyd Wright (1867–1959), the art historian and founding director of MOMA, Alfred H. Barr (1902–1981), and the cultural theorist Buckminster Fuller (1895–1983) while they were still children: "On this square pattern she had arranged the simple, unembellished wooden blocks of her building set and had built houses, temples and villas using its cubes, triangular forms and cuboids. With the help of colourful, geometric cardboard tiles it was possible to create floral patterns on this grid, to install a windmill or also abstract patterns of purely symmetrical beauty. [...] For *Fröbel*, the child and its play formed an almost religious unity [...] However, his programme centred on the twenty 'toy gifts': strictly geometric play elements of wood, paper and other materials, with the help of which the children could develop structures divided into three basic categories: shapes of nature and life, shapes of science and mathematics, and shapes of beauty and art. In this context, an armchair built from eight cubes could simply signify the number eight, or could also become a tower, and so on. However, what could never be created with these 'toy gifts' were the artistic and architectural forms of the 19th century. The play elements were too puristic, too abstract and too minimalistic for this purpose. They did not reproduce the aesthetic forms of the age, but instead the scientific forms, particularly those of mathematical crystallography. In the mental and concrete interaction of their shapes, they were thus intended to symbolise all conceivable forms and things." As examples of a later aesthetic application of Fröbel's fundamental 'toy gifts' we can also cite Georges Braque (1882–1963), Piet Mondrian (1872–1944) and Wassily Kandinsky (1866–1944), and the Bauhaus movement as a whole (Werneburg 1997).

mobile in terms of "technical perception", through twisting and distortion – as with the work of Elsworth Kelly – or through a structure of strokes spreading across image field – as in Sol LeWitt's work. This is another approach that stimulates the feelings in the sense that we perceive a change occurring within fixed dimensions (Honnef 1971).

I would argue that abstract art, minimal art and conceptual art have much in common with picturebooks for small children that focus mainly on the representation of everyday objects in a more or less abstract manner. Abstraction and contrasts between forms and colors also occur in picturebooks designed for infants and toddlers, as can be seen in Chez Picthall's *Baby Sees. Spots and Dots* (2005). The underlying concept is stressed in the blurb on the back cover: "Babies find high-contrast images stimulating and focusing on them helps the brain and eyesight to develop." The contrasts featured in this picturebook correspond, not only in terms of form, to the kind of painterly solutions proposed by Kenneth Noland and Jasper Johns in the 1960s and '70s.

Figure 4. Book Cover and Image from *Baby Sees. Spots and Dots* by Chez Picthall. Bromley: Picthall & Gunzi 2005

The different media are all concerned with perceptual events that occur when colors are combined to create contrasts and assigned to forms that, for example, lead the gaze backwards or forwards and make the eye move between focus and field of vision, between light and dark. In addition to the realization that fixed forms can become mobile through visual symbols, there is the experience that colors and forms do not exist in a fixed relation to each other. This idea can also be applied to assigning colors to objects. This involves the symbol shift we mentioned at the start in relation to a basic shape such as the sphere, and to the symbol shift in relation to object denotations: a sphere can actually mutate to a ball in both image and everyday life and simultaneously refer to the basic shape of an edible object, the apple, and so on. Basic designs and abstract forms therefore play a significant role in modern art, and in picturebooks as well. When renowned artists such as Andy Warhol and Keith Haring created picturebooks directly referring to artistic concepts derived from pop art, minimal art or conceptual art, they made the link between modern art movements and picturebook illustration.

Basic designs in modern art

The symbol shift that can lead to an object or person being totally transformed and given a different image, particularly in a media-dominated reality, was taken up and pursued by pop art in a variety of ways. Andy Warhol's countless variations on Marilyn Monroe demonstrate enduringly how, a person's facial characteristics can be transformed through color changes, emphasizing his or her existence as an artificial figure. In his day, Runge already sought to construct a world of color. He discovered colored light as a property of color independent of the object that could be used to construct objects and persons and shift them into different moods (Träger 1987). He initiated a process that Cézanne further developed into a system and that already takes us toward to the principle of the computer. From the elements of sphere, cone and cylinder he developed what we would now call a computation system, which completely corresponded to the binary code and was intended to do everything, as Cézanne himself said (Bernard 1982: 85).

This not only reveals a structure parallel to nature; Cézanne's work reflects the process of separation of the symbol which makes the external aspect of an object into a constructible, autonomous symbol and reference area. Cézanne's color passages released from the motif are, strictly speaking, no longer reliant on a motif – for instance a mountain – as semaphore, even if their origin can still be reconstructed – as in his famous painting of "Mont Sainte Victoire." It is now just a small step to the autonomy of the visual means and to that of playing with definition that can be used to transpose the symbols to an infinite number of semaphores. This reveals a paradigm that recognizes a materiality in the repertoire of symbols of pre-existing symbol networks that can be used for construction and deconstruction of objects and persons – networks that are interactively structurable, and both manipulative and consciousness-raising.

Artists such as Picasso, and later, Warhol, extended the process of combining splintered-off symbols derived from existing representations and visual relationships. Picasso cited various positions from art history (e.g. in the monumental work "Guernica" from 1937) and operated with individual components from the symbolic repertoire, constructing a new picture from individual elements. Warhol "borrowed" from fields such as product aesthetics and its packaging codes, and transformed these by dimensional changes and the abstract use of color. In this way, iconic symbols are recombined like linguistic signs and transposed into a new syntax, precisely as if one were to apply Ferdinand de Saussure's *Cours de linguistique générale*, written before the start of the 20th century and equally path-breaking for similar processes in linguistics. Saussure's differentiation of "signifiant" and "signifié", of sound and meaning – that became a differentiation in semiotics between the description and the thing described, between the external casing of a symbol (or signifier) and its core (or significatum), embracing both the outside and the inside of a mediatized object – relates to the realization that a communicating person is able to transfer the external shell of one thing to another (de Saussure 2006). This is similar to the way that Ludwig Wittgenstein interpreted the handling of color: "It is," he wrote in his *Philosophical Investigations* (1990), "almost as if we peel off the color impression like a membrane from the viewed object" (227). In this sense, modern artists such as Picasso und Warhol extracted elements from other pictures, recombined them and transposed the cited elements and semantic structures to other contexts – to the point where they sometimes lost their original meaning and were assigned new ones.

The distinction between "signifier" and "signified" , along with the slogan "images as text," has become a characteristic of the 'linguistic turn' in art history. It is used to explain what happens with the adoption of and the construction with signifiers in art and the media communication that defines our society. In my opinion, pop art can be seen as the type of art that has actively and consistently adopted the basic principles and insights of this process, especially in reflecting the daily media routine in which symbols are increasingly mutually referential and the medium itself becomes the message (McLuhan 1964). Whether we are talking about Andy Warhol's paintings of Marilyn Monroe or the Campbell's soup cans, understood as a symbol separated from its carrier, the image of the actress and the logo of the product are mutually referential in their aligned aesthetics. They are perceived as being of equal beauty, which prompted Andy Warhol to the inspired remark, "All is pretty."

In philosophical terms, a self-referential system becomes effective because the reflection of the reflecting person converts the act of observation into a mental principle. This is the starting point for all mental operations that lead to a constructivist attitude to reality. "This experiment is not based on any question directed to nature," wrote Walter Benjamin, referring to the artists of the Romantic era. "Instead, observation fixes in its view only the self-knowledge nascent in the object; or rather it, the observation, is the nascent consciousness of the object itself" (Bullock & Jennings 2008: 148). This completes a Copernican reversal in philosophy that principally shifts the act of recognition to the person who is experiencing, to the subject's possibility of experience and perceiving. (It is not the subject that orientates itself to the object, but the object to the subject.)[5] In this view, the ability to continually reconstruct an object through action, as the educationalist Jean Piaget later formulated it (see below), prevents the self-referentiality of individual reality construction from being fulfilled outside a social context.

Representation of basic designs in picturebooks

Since basic designs are important in picturebooks for young children, its is obvious that there is a close link between the basic design presented in modern art on the one hand, and the educational issues raised by Fröbel and Piaget on the other. According to Jean Piaget, author of *The Construction of Reality in the Child*, this construction arises precisely from dismantling and subsequent reconstruction (equilibration), not from a repetition of reality (Piaget 1959). In this sense, a child does not simply reflect or 'report on' a given situation, but dissects it into separate components to create something new. This is illustrated perfectly by the dismantling and reorganization of individual elements in the playroom, and constitutes adaptation between the organism and its environment. The behavior of young children presents the ultimate model for describing the human ability to construct in the first place. This includes understanding the isolation of the object as a construction element – which is apparently easier for a young child. An isolated object can develop a life of its own in an image, independently of its intended use. One example from the world of art would be Andy Warhol's early drawings of isolated shoes as the object of an aesthetic form of observation. Children's books were quick to prestructure this kind of isolation of the object and to highlight it in accordance with a child's perception.

5. This achievement can be ascribed to Immanuel Kant, and completely negates the basis for viewing the act of understanding as a mere act of imitation or depiction. For Kant, nature was the epitome of all objects of experience, and space and time were consequently pure forms of perception of what is experienced. Everything we perceive necessarily refers to experience, which forms the precondition for interpreting, organizing, and constructing the world we live in. (Kant 1979: 359ff.).

Artists such as Keith Haring further developed the principle of separation of the symbol and of the isolation of objects. These artists recognized that their logograms could certainly stimulate childish imagination, so that, with the aid of this abstraction of objects, children can arrive at principles of ordering such as numbers and words. Haring's book *Ten* (1998) completely eliminated the distinction between art and picturebook.

Kurt Schwitters already recognized the value of picturebook illustrations that anticipated the modern way of seeing objects. He incorporated the familiar illustration of a picturebook cherry – see, for instance, Kurt Wick's *Babys Bilderbuch* (Baby's Picturebook, 1948) – into his montage of 1921, and titled the whole picture after this image. In Schwitters' work the interpolated "cherry picture" is the island in a cosmos of incoherence, an oasis of easily understandable childhood days standing against the decay of symbols.

In the 1960s, Joseph Kossuth united three states of perception of an object in the form of a real object (e.g. a chair), an illustration (photo of a chair) and an idea (the dictionary definition of "chair") – to form a three-part work of art. An easily identifiable object becomes part of a constructing philosophy when the recipient relates different signs to the same object. The perception of the differences between signified and signifier recreates the work, making this an experience that reaches beyond the work itself.

This is similar to picturebooks for young children, particularly when they function as a conceptual book in such a way that even linguistic aspects in them have an effect. Taking image acquisition as the point of departure, we can say the following: first, a distinction can be made between figure and background. Secondly, it is understood that lines, points, colors etc. delineate the depicted object, although these delineating elements are not present in the real objects. Thirdly, the books train the skill of projecting a three-dimensional object onto a two-dimensional surface. Finally, we note that the observation of the image reveals distinctions, even between images and referents. Comprehension of representations leads to the realization that the discoverable similarities between the real object and the various representations can indicate shared characteristics, which in turn enable the distinction between essential and inessential properties in the transposition process (Kümmerling-Meibauer 2009: 31). These four aspects pave the way to discovering visual codes in the images. This ability is known as visual literacy and is seen nowadays as a type of image acquisition that can almost be said to 'provoke' verbalization. By the same token, we can concur with the conclusion that "early-concept books play an important role in language acquisition" (Kümmerling-Meibauer & Meibauer 2005).

This is also a reason why fundamental objects and forms are repeatedly represented in picturebooks, and rightly so. Margret Rettich's *Dies und Das* (*This and That*, 1970) makes the visual perception of objects shift into a perception of colors and forms. The issue here is not the precision of the object, but that the shift which is so integral to pop art and conceptual art occurs before one's own eyes. An object such as a pear can be depicted as a green surface against a red background, so that the juxtaposition of these colors can create a simultaneous contrast that triggers neural activity and evokes impressions that exist only in the perception itself.

In my view, Vladimir Radunsky has provided a variegated summary of the most important stages of the perceptual constellations described here. *Square triangle round skinny* (2002), which consists of four books in a box set, guides young readers through a haptic book experience that offers an interplay of the senses (see Figure 5). The flexible use of the four picturebooks in the slipcase offers an opportunity to make changes visible entirely through usage, and this approach is pursued in the assigning of forms and colors to the illustrated objects. The books' bindings correspond to the forms in question, which are linked in turn to image reductions of various objects. Because a pair of spectacles is "round," this illustration is inserted into the book *Round*, whose shape is almost circular. The selection of the terms refers to corresponding yet differing forms and descriptions of condition. While "square" and "triangle" describe geometric and abstract forms, the adjectives "round" and "skinny" emphasize qualities that cannot be associated with the forms alone, but give them attributes with emotional connotations.

Figure 5. Book Case and Image from *Square triangle round skinny* by Vladimir Radunsky. Cambridge, MA: Candlewick Press, 2002

Understanding symbols in media-dominated realities

In English-language aesthetics this combination of different perceptual impressions linked to the symbol shifts is traditionally described as "dissociation of sensibility."[6] This is an attempt to describe how the visual symbol transmits feelings that, however, can scarcely form a whole in the process of fragmentation and overlapping. The assumed whole or integral qualities of an object actually contain the seeds of dissociation. The forms that overlap each other as the books are used become heterogeneous fragments that create different effects such as round and skinny, effects that have an impact on the recipient as (aggregate) totals. The emphasis on individual senses is achieved with the symbols and thus allows the emergence of a new construction in one's consciousness (Iser 1966). A Radunsky dachshund is thus not only skinny: the shape of the book in which it is depicted makes it into an elongated rectangle; in turn, the form can correspond to books in other shapes such as square or round objects known as spectacles, ball, or sun.

The media theories of Marshall McLuhan made early reference to this creation of percepts, of art products relating to perception. It was during his time at Cambridge that McLuhan first had the insights that would later lead to his pathbreaking proposition that in the age of mass media the medium was the message. Prior to this he must have become aware how, and with what effect, sensory effects could be separated from their traditional positions, or in other words, the dissociation of the medium from reality is based on the realization of the dissociation of the senses in the media age (Hagen 2008). Picturebooks such as *Square triangle round skinny* can help to utilize this dissociation to create new compilations as a way to record further combinations in a world apparently cluttered up with signs and symbols. The same purpose is fulfilled by transition to alphabetic letters through shapes that may look similar but describe something different, such as the triangular pizza slice and the triangular letter A.

One way of understanding these combinations for discovering the world and the reality dependent on one's own perceptions and actions is provided by an understanding of the symbol that comprehends the world as codified and thus decodable and modifiable. This is also noticeable in education for young children influenced by Jewish tradition. Letter cases and other devices for playing with alphabet letters stimulate early practice in the letter-based creative process. A word

6. The term "dissociation of sensibility" was first used by T. S. Eliot in his essay, "The Metaphysical Poets", *Times Literary Supplement*, 20 October 1922. It was understood as an adaptation of Remy de Gourment's concept from "La dissociation des idées" (1899). Regarding the significance of this "dissociation of sensibility" for the "disordering of all senses" in the modern age, see Edgar Wind (1963: 130f.).

abacus (customary in Jewish nursery schools) containing the square Hebrew print characters allows infinite combinations. By turning the letter cubes, children can create a huge variety of different Hebrew words, helping them to recognize that a single letter is capable of many meanings and nuances (Kilcher 1998, 2004). This is not possible with the Latin alphabet.

In a metaphorical sense this also paves the way generally to art and the picturebook. The spatial sculpture of Sol LeWitt, for instance, combines squares into a pyramidal form, showing that a square can also be an empty space and a shape can also enable perspectives, while a form can embody different impressions and meanings simultaneously, and can therefore differ within itself.[7]

These combinatory methods, which also have many facets in terms of perception, bring us back to the first picture we examined, to the combinations of a single form assigned to diverse objects derived from numerous picturebooks for young children. As I have attempted to show, modern art and the aesthetics presented in picturebooks for young children share related and fundamental perceptual constellations. In addition to the reduction to basic geometric shapes that have served as components for an exemplary construction of reality in art and education since the 18th century, it is the symbol shifts in the art of the 20th century and above all in the art after 1945 – resulting especially from the dissolution of the contract between symbol and object – that influenced art and imbued the picturebook with fresh perspectives. Conversely, art has responded to the isolation and highlighting of individual objects in the picturebook.[8] What they share is the recognition of the need to accept perception as the basis for changing action, i.e., an action capable of imposing a design on the emerging subject world. The earlier this attitude can be communicated – through shapes, colors, elementary objects and their corresponding pictures – the better. This can be a foundation for further development of the differences and common features of a world bound together by its inherent contrasts.

Conclusion

Basic shapes, such as the wide variety of ball forms that exist in the child's world, are helpful in playfully applying the basic elements of abstract principles as well as drawing attention to the constructible nature of the world. These insights have been influential in educational science and in art. The use of these basic shapes in

7. For the influence of Jewish tradition on modern art, see Deppner (2008).

8. Cf. Deppner (2007), Oetken (2007) and Thiele (2000).

picturebooks for small children clearly shows that a supposedly naive relationship with the world can open up a complex approach. The process becomes complex when the basic shapes become signs or symbols that refer to something and simultaneously develop a life of their own. Signs can, for instance, communicate sensations and both confuse and stimulate the senses through altered combinations of meaning. This has been highlighted not only by modern art, especially pop art, but also by picturebooks, and has allowed even young children to practice dealing with a world that can altered by signs, and can also be coded or decoded. We have discussed some of these works here. It would seem that the interrelationship between modern art and picturebooks that feature basic shapes provides a productive foundation for learning abstract principles, even in early childhood. By fostering experience of visual signs and symbols, these principles can make an essential contribution to the understanding of writing and other codification.

Children's books cited

Ehmcke, S. 1953. *Bunter Kram*. Ravensburg: Otto Maier Verlag.
Grimm, W. & Sendak, M. 1988. *Dear Mili*. New York NY: Farrar, Straus & Giroux.
Haring, K. 1998. *Ten*. New York NY: Hyperions Books.
Picthall, C. 2005. *Baby Sees. Spots and Dots*. Bromley: Picthall & Gunzi.
Radunsky, V. 2002. *Square, Triangle, Round, Skinny*. Cambridge MA: Candlewick Press.
Rettich, M. 1970. *Dies und Das*. Hamburg: Oetinger.
Sendak, M. 1981. *Outside Over There*. New York NY: Harper & Row.
Wick, K. 1948. *Babys Bilderbuch*. Düsseldorf: H. D. Schaack Verlag.

References

Bernard, E. 1982. Erinnerungen an Paul Cézanne 1904–1906. In *Gespräche mit Cézanne*, M. Doran (ed.), 68–100. Zurich: Verlag der Arche.
Böhme, G. 2004. *Theorie des Bildes*. Munich: Fink.
Brodersen, W., Deppner, M., Gross, F., Haubner, K., Huhn, R., Jarchow, M., Mewes, C., Rautmann, P., Schulze-Altcappenberg, H.-T. & Voigt, D. 1978. *Philipp Otto Runge. Historisch-kritische Analysen zu seinem Werk*. Gießen: Anabas-Verlag.
Bullock, M. P. & Jennings M. W. (eds). 2008. *Walter Benjamin 1913–1926*. Cambridge MA: Harvard University Press.
Deppner, M. R. 1997. Konstruktion und Dekonstruktion im kunstwissenschaftlichen Diskurs. In *Über Moholy-Nagy, Ergebnisse aus dem Internationalen László Moholy-Nagy Symposium*, G. Jäger & G. Wessing (eds), 163–180. Bielefeld: Kerber.
Deppner, M. R. 2007. Kunst als Simulation kindlicher Identitätsformung. In *Neue Impulse der Bilderbuchforschung*, J. Thiele (ed.), 70–88. Baltmannsweiler: Schneider Hohengehren.

Deppner, M. R. (ed.). 2008. *Die verborgene Spur. Jüdische Wege durch die Moderne.* Exhibition catalogue. Felix Nussbaum-Haus Osnabrück. Heidelberg: Vernissage-Verlag.

Deppner, M. R. & Thiele, J. 1994. Das Bild hinter dem Bild. Bildspiegelungen in David Lynch Blue Velvet. In *Film, Fernsehen, Video und die Künste. Strategien der Intermedialität*, J. Paech (ed.), 50–61. Stuttgart: Metzler.

Friese, P. (ed.). 1998. *Minimal Maximal. Die Minimal Art und ihr Einfluss auf die Kunst der 90er Jahre.* Exhibition Catalogue Neues Museum Weserburg Bremen. Heidelberg: Umschau/Braus.

Fröbel, F. 1998. *Ausgewählte Schriften.* Vol. 3: *Vorschulerziehung und Spieltheorie*, 3rd edn, H. Heiland (ed.). Stuttgart: Klett-Cotta.

Hagen, W. 2008. Die 'Closure' der Medien: Wyndham Lewis und Marshall McLuhan. In *MacLuhan neu lesen. Kritische Analysen zu Medien und Kultur im 21. Jahrhundert*, D. de Kerckhove, M. Leeker & K. Schmidt (eds), 51–60. Bielefeld: Transcript.

Held, J. 1995. Minimal Art – eine amerikanische Ideologie. In *Minimal Art. Eine kritische Retrospektive*, G. Stemmrich (ed.), 444–470. Basel: Verlag der Kunst G+B Fine Arts.

Heiland, H. & Neumann, K. 2003. *Fröbels Pädagogik verstehen, interpretieren, weiterführen: internationale Ergebnisse zur neuen Fröbelforschung.* Würzburg: Königshausen & Neumann.

Herbart, J. F. 1976. *Allgemeine Pädagogik*, H. Holstein (ed.). Bochum: Kamp (Originally published in 1806).

Hofmann, W. 1977. *Runge in seiner Zeit.* Exhibition catalogue of the Hamburger Kunsthalle. Munich: Prestel.

Honnef, K. 1971. *Concept Art.* Cologne: Phaidon.

Iser, W. 1966. Image und Montage. Zur Bildkonzeption in der imaginistischen Lyrik und T. S. Eliots Waste Land. In *Immanente Ästhetik, Ästhetische Reflexion. Lyrik als Paradigma der Moderne*, W. Iser (ed.), 361–393. Munich: Fink.

Kant, I. 1979. *Kritik der Urteilskraft.* In *Collected Works.* Vol. 10, 4th edn, W. Weischedel (ed.). Frankfurt: Suhrkamp.

Kilcher, A. 1998. *Die Sprachtheorie der Kabbala als ästhetisches Paradigma. Die Konstruktion einer ästhetischen Kabbalah seit der frühen Neuzeit* Stuttgart: Metzler.

Kilcher, A. 2004. Die Sefirot. In *10+5=Gott. Die Macht der Zeichen*, D. Tyrandellis & M. S. Friedländer (eds), 83–90. Cologne: Dumont.

Kümmerling-Meibauer, B. 2009. Erste Bilder, erste Begriffe: Weltwissen für Kleinkinder. In *Literatur im Laufstall. Bilderbücher für die ganz Kleinen*, Exhibition catalogue of the Bilderbuchmuseum Burg Wissem Troisdorf, B. Kümmerling-Meibauer & M. Linsmann (eds), 14–33. Troisdorf: Burg Wissem.

Kümmerling-Meibauer, B. & Meibauer, J. 2005. First pictures, early concepts: Early concept books. *The Lion and the Unicorn* 29: 324–347.

Kuhlemann, G. & Brühlmeier, A. 2002. *Johann Heinrich Pestalozzi* [Basiswissen Pädagogik. Historische Pädagogik 2], C. Lost & C. Rizzi (eds). Baltmannsweiler: Schneider Hohengehren.

McLuhan, M. 1964. *Understanding Media.* Maidenhead: McGrawHill.

Oetken, M. 2007. Bilderbücher der 1990er Jahre. Kontinuität und Diskontinuität in Produktion und Rezeption. Ph D dissertation, University of Oldenburg.

Piaget, J. 1959. *The Construction of Reality in the Child.* New York NY: Basic Books (Original French edition first published in 1950).

Pestalozzi, J. H. 2006. *Wie Gertrud ihre Kinder lehrt.* Bad Schwartau: Wfb Verlagsgruppe (Originally published in 1801).

Runge, P. O. 1940. *Briefe in der Urfassung*, K. F. Degener (ed). Berlin: Nicolai.

de Saussure, F. 2006. *Course in General Linguistics*. Oxford: OUP (Original French edition first published in 1916).

Schneede, U. M. (ed.). 1998. *Chagall, Kandinsky, Malewitsch und die russische Avantgarde*. Exhibition catalogue Hamburger Kunsthalle and Kunsthalle Zürich. Ostfildern-Ruit: Hatje.

Thiele, J. 2000. *Das Bilderbuch. Ästhetik. Theorie. Analyse. Didaktik. Rezeption*. Oldenburg: Isensee.

Träger, J. 1987. *Philipp Otto Runge, Die Hülsenbeckschen Kinder. Von der Reflexion des Naiven im Kunstwerk der Romantik*, K. Herding (ed.). Frankfurt am Main: Fischer.

Welsch, W. 1990. *Ästhetisches Denken*. Stuttgart: Reclam.

Werneburg, B. 1997. Der Kindergarten der Abstraktion. Neues aus den Anfangsgründen der modernen Kunst. *Frankfurter Rundschau* 5 July.

Westheider, O. 1997. *Konzeptkunst in der Hamburger Kunsthalle*. Exhibition catalogue. Hamburg: Hamburger Kunsthalle.

Wind, E. 1963. *Art and Anarchy*. London: Faber & Faber.

Wittgenstein, L. 1990. Philosophische Untersuchungen, Absatz 276. In *Tractatus-logico-philosophicus/Philosophische Untersuchungen* by L. Wittgenstein. Leipzig: Reclam.

PART II

Picturebooks for children under three

CHAPTER 5

Picturebooks

Where literature appreciation begins

Kathleen Ahrens

When selecting books for children age zero to two a natural tendency is to choose naming and/or categorizing books. Other default selections for the very young include nursery rhymes, books based on songs, or counting, color, and alphabet books, as it is easy to evaluate the suitability of such texts for very young children. It can be more difficult, however, for caregivers to evaluate which narrative texts are most suitable for the youngest children, given the range of offerings available in picturebook format. In order to aid caregivers and early childhood teachers in the selection of stories for the very young, this paper will propose three easily implementable criteria for picturebook selection and then analyze eight picturebook classics in order to evaluate to what degree they match these criteria. Given the range of evidence that reading aloud to infants is a precursor toward literacy success, the guidelines provided will allow caregivers to confidently select narrative texts to enjoy with babies and toddlers.

1. Benefits of reading aloud to infants and toddlers

It is all too easy to worry about the future of literature – not because of time children spend reading blogs on the computer or interacting with the latest gadgets – but because parents often do not read to their children from a very young age. Even relatively well-off, educated, and well-meaning parents will look blankly at me when I ask what they have been reading to their 0–24 month-old child. "Nothing," they say in reply to my question. "Isn't it too early to teach them to read?"

"Of course, it's to early to teach them to read," I respond. "But it's never too early to read to them."

In fact, gains in language and literacy in relation to early exposure to texts have been well documented for quite some time. Ninio (1983), for example, studied the ways in which mothers reading picturebooks helped infants acquire new vocabulary, while Snow and Godfield (1983) documented how a one-year ten-month child learned vocabulary through scaffolding based on picturebooks his mother read to him. Moore and Wade (2003) in a paper discussing the success of their Bookstart project, detailed the qualitative evidence for giving books to families of infants to facilitate language learning and literacy.

In addition, in just the past decade, there have been a range of studies showing that reading early and often is the greatest predictor for later achievement. Karras and Braungart-Rieker (2005) looked at 87 infants at four month intervals between four and sixteen months, and found that shared book reading at four months was related to shared book reading at eight months, which was, in turn, linked to the infant's ability to express him- or herself at twelve and sixteen months. Simcock and DeLoache (2008) showed that 18- and 24-month olds improved in their imitation scores when they were exposed to a picturebook four times in succession as compared with two times. Westerlund and Lagerberg (2008) found that 18-month-old children whose parents read to them six times a week had a larger amount of expressive vocabulary, regardless of the child's gender. Rodriguez et al. (2009) found evidence that the overall literary experiences of toddlers at 14, 24 and 36 months explained the differences in the children's respective language skills at the age of three. And in an interesting study that also looked at video watching, it was found that children between 12 and 15 months who watched eductional DVDs had no increase in vocabulary comprehension or production, but that an increase in both areas could be seen in relation to the amount of time spent reading aloud (Robb et al. 2009).

With study after study showing that reading often and early to young children gives them a leg up on expressive language abilities and literacy learning, it seems obvious that reading to one's child is a key precursor to later literacy achievements during the school years. And often, after a bit of discussion concerning the above findings, the parent in question will then ask: "Fine. I see your point. But what should I be reading to them?"

This is a legitimate but loaded question – one that academics, educators, and librarians, are faced with on a regular basis. Our own personal answer may vary considerably depending on our cultural, educational and familial background. Books are one of the many ways in which humans transmit knowledge over distance and time, and the choice of what we read ourselves or what we read to our children is a reflection of our own identity as well as the identity we want to forge for our child. But as educators, we are also aware that the answer that is suitable for our family circumstances may not be suitable for another's. How then can we go about answering the question so that parents can take ownership and feel confident about the choices they make for their child? Given that transmitting one's cultural identity is one implicit goal in raising a child, one reasonable answer therefore is: read to your infant whatever you yourself find interesting to read aloud. A person interested in design could share a beautiful book on chairs with a child, and a financial analyst could read the stock report. Most infants would be quite happy to sit on a caregiver's lap and feel the rumble of his or her voice as they pat (or drool on) any page in front of them. In fact, whatever one finds relaxing to read to their children when they are newborns (or even in utero) is fine. They will respond to the fact that their caregiver is relaxed and happy, and enjoy the cadence of his or her voice. But once they can wriggle around and/or take interest in the object being held, the question takes on more urgency and is not as easily answered, as at this point the caregiver will most likely want to put his or her hands on something that is more suitable to the child's cognitive level. And in order for the caregiver to continue to enjoy the reading time, it is also an important (but often overlooked) point that the material also be engaging at some level for him or her.

The most likely candidates once infants start reaching and teething are sturdy board books, which may be picturebooks resized (and perhaps edited) for the shorter, chunkier format, or board books specifically designed for the very youngest readers. Books having to do with naming objects or events are popular choices, as are counting, color and alphabet books, and nursery rhymes and song books. Kümmerling-Meibauer and Meibauer (2005), for example, point out that early-concept books often present information thematically, through similarity, or contrast, or through the grouping of related objects, and that these books are in fact important precursors for the acquisition of language and literacy.

However, narrative texts have always held a special place in the hearts and minds of children and the adults who read to them. The satisfying thump of a book closing at the end of a well-loved narrative is entirely a different sensation from reaching the end of a straightforward naming or counting book. Moreover, narratives that resonate in the hearts of reader and child alike are the ones that are read repeatedly, which benefits the child's language acquisition.

Given the above suggestions, the question the caregiver is asking can then be rephrased from "What should I be reading to them?" to "So you're asking what books, in addition to concept books and nursery rhyme books, will provide you and your child with a sense of emotional satisfaction when you reach the end of the story?" This places their request in a context that acknowledges that they can and should provide the staples for infant reading, at the same time that it opens a window to the possibility of the additional pleasure to be gained from reading narrative texts. But how then should caregiver determine which books provide emotional satisfaction?

Of course, the simple response is to suggest a book list from a reputable source. There are many out there, including Trelease (2006) and Fox (2001) for all age ranges, and Dell'Antonia & Straub (2006), who focus on the ages of zero to two years. In their book, Dell'Antonia & Straub not only provide a range of suggested titles, but they talk about how to read to a child who is crawling away or gnawing on a book, and they also discuss choosing books for this age group. However, while they discuss how to choose among the different types of books that can (and should) be read to young children (i.e. nursery rhymes, counting books, categorizing books, and naming books, among others), in this paper, I will focus exclusively on what questions we as researchers can suggest that parents ask themselves when they select narratives for their newborn-to-two-year-old child. In this way, caregivers can more easily discern the wheat from the chaff when they enter a library (and face a basket of gnawed-on board books) or a bookstore (where they face tables of the hottest movie tie-ins before getting to the shelves filled with thin book spines). In addition, it allows caregivers to move away from static book lists that can become out-dated (i.e. McMahon's 1996 book list for infants only contains a few books still in print), or that, even when updated, lists books that for one reason or another may be difficult to locate. Indeed, what this paper will propose is that it is possible to identify a certain set of questions that can be asked when a caregiver flips through any picture-or board book, and that these questions can help them select relevant narratives for the children in their care. In this way, a commonality of shared experience will grow between the caregiver and the child, setting the child on the path to appreciating literature not only for its aesthetic value but also for the emotional resonance that it creates when it is read and shared with others.

2. The secrets of emotionally satisfying picturebook narratives

While an examination of the literature shows that an analysis of how complex picturebook narratives relate to their readers has been done for older readers (Goodwin 2009), there is no such analysis to examine how picturebooks for the very young (0–24 months of age) do the same. For example, although Lowe (2007) presents children's experiences with, and reactions to, narratives from a very early age, the work does not examine the narratives of the texts themselves. The goal of this paper, thus, is to examine and explain how in two hundred words or less, seemingly 'simple' narratives provide a sense of closure and emotional satisfaction. As with fiction that has evolved from the Aristotelian tradition for older readers, the starting point is to examine what tension exists in the story and how it is resolved. This resolution of tension brings about a change in the main character or the state of events between the beginning and ending of the book. Thus, the first key point is to check whether a change of state – this may be either a physical, physiological, or emotional change has occurred between the beginning and the end of the book. Books that simply list the animals found on a farm in declarative sentences do not qualify under this condition. They are still valuable for the purposes of classification and naming and learning more about the world around the child, but they are not literary narratives. Manipulative concept books, such as Cheerio books (in which a circular type of breakfast cereal is placed in a hole in the book) also do not qualify under this criteria. Again, these books have their value, but they are not a pre-cursor to literature appreciation in that they do not expose the child to a narrative story arc.

In addition to evaluating whether there is a change of state, looking at whether the text deals with a relevant developmental stage for the child should also be a consideration in choosing a narrative text. For example, going to bed and falling asleep, learning about cause and effect (objects moving in space) are developmental issues for children zero to two, but are no longer usually issues for children who are older. Moreover, as Lukens (2003) points out, literature serves many functions (i.e. brings pleasure, brings about understanding, and shows human motives, among others), but I would like to propose that one function she mentions is particularly important for the youngest readers; that is, it serves to provide form for experience (i.e. makes order of randomness). For example, the seven-month-old child who cannot push the car in the direction he or she wants it to go, will find a similar problem in *Sheep in the Jeep* (and in addition, a wonderful rhyme scheme). Or the 18-month old who is being told he or she cannot do something will find it fascinating that a pigeon has the same problem in Mo Willems's *Don't Let the Pigeon Drive the Bus*. As a child's range and depth of experience is limited at this age, finding problems similar to one's own between the pages of a book is a meaningful discovery.

The last point, or secret, to selecting an emotionally satisfying book to read with an infant or toddler, in addition to the above two points of ensuring that there is change, and that it is developmentally appropriate for the child in question, is that it be short and easily read aloud. This is not only because the attention span of a young child may be limited, but because young children love to hear stories again and again and it is much easier to gear up for another reading as a caregiver when it will take only a minute or two to complete the task, and if it will be a linguistically pleasurable event to read it through for the thousandth time. The smoothness of the language is something that can be evaluated independently by reading it aloud prior to bringing it home. If a caregiver stumbles over words because they cannot find the flow of language, then reading it aloud will not be enjoyable for them or the child they are reading aloud to. Many children's movies or TV shows that are later put into book format suffer from verbosity – they contain too many non-informative words and often use syntax that sounds stilted or unnatural when read aloud.

Thus, three guidelines have been proposed: (1) there is physical, physiological or emotional change, (2) it is developmentally appropriate such that it provides form for experience, and (3) it is quick and pleasurable to read. These guidelines have been selected for their ease in application when making a picturebook selection for a very young child with the express purpose of developing their appreciation of a story and all that it entails in becoming fully engaged with the human condition. In order to evaluate the usefulness of these guidelines, in what follows below I will look at the picturebooks that are identified as being for the youngest child in Knopf's *The 20th Century Children's Book Treasury* (1998).

3. Analyzing picturebook classics

In *The 20th Century Children's Book Treasury,* forty-four picturebooks from a variety of publishers are included in one volume by reformatting the original picturebook text. Eight books of the forty-four are identified as being for the youngest readers. However, as the editor Janet Schulman notes in her introduction: "there is no pre-tested way to know precisely which stories a child will most enjoy at a particular age" (1998: ix). While I certainly agree with this statement, I would like to propose that a parent or educator or caregiver can make a good guess based on the criteria proposed above (along with their own knowledge of their child's development, likes, and interests).

In addition, it is noteworthy that of the eight stories proposed as being for the youngest child in this volume, seven of the eight are narratives, with only one being a concept book: Helen Oxenbury's *I Hear, I See, I Touch.* As this book has no change of state from beginning to end, it does not count as a narrative text. Of course, it is still a wonderful text for children, and if the caregiver wanted to select a categorizing book, this would be an excellent choice.

Goodnight Moon, the first book identified in the Knopf's *Treasury* as being for the youngest child, is also a selection in the *HarperCollins Treasury of Picture Book Classics* (and it is the only text that is included in both collections). Written and illustrated by Margaret Wise Brown, it was published by Harper (now HarperCollins) in 1947. The classic goodnight book, it tells the story of a bunny who looks around and says, "Goodnight!" to everything in his or her room before finally falling asleep. It has a clear change of physiological state portrayed in the story: at the beginning the rabbit is awake, and by the end of the story he or she is asleep. It deals with a developmentally appropriate issue, as young children find it difficult to settle down when they are tired: just when they find life at home is at its most stimulating, they get sent off to sleep. The word count is low (approximately 130 words), which means the story can stand repeated consecutive readings. And the language is lyrical and soothing. As noted in the HarperCollins's Afterword to the story, "When *Goodnight Moon* is read aloud, it takes on the quality of a classic lullaby, as though it had been around for centuries. And because the lullaby works, parents never tire of reading *Goodnight Moon* over and over again" (p. 48). All in all, it is an excellent choice for children between the ages of 0 and 2.

The second is *Freight Train*, a deceptively simple story that captures the heart of children aged 24 months and below. The first page starts out with a train track at the bottom of a white page, with the words "A train runs across this track" at the top. Then in rhythmic and concise language (with 55 words in total), the trains cars and train engine are introduced, after which they move across the page until they are "Going, going, gone." The last page has the last word at the top left, and a faint stream of smoke running back from the right above the same train tracks as the beginning. The change of state in this case has to do with physical objects appearing and disappearing again. The behavioural development issue is one the young child is dealing with as he or she watches toy cars and trucks being pushed or learns to push them him or herelf. On all three counts of language, change, and relevance to the young child, this book hits the mark.

In *Titch*, by Pat Hutchins, the problem is quite simple: Titch is smaller than his siblings and his toys are smaller than his siblings' toys. But Titch has a seed and the seed grows taller than his siblings, thus resolving the problem. In about 120 words, the author has skillfully laid out a problem that is a developmental issue for all children – the fact that they are smaller than everyone else around them, and solved it in a realistic manner. The language is simple, with a grammatical structure of subject-verb-object as the primary sentential structure throughout the book. This, in addition to the use of 'and' to start sentences having to do with Titch, make for a very structured cadence throughout the book, as if a drummer is drumming repeated lines. To emphasize that Titch (and his toys) were smaller than everyone else and their toys, 'and' is used at the beginning of the contrastive sentences, as in "Peter had a big drum. Mary had a trumpet. And Titch had a little wooden whistle." However, in the final sentence, "and" conjoins not only the sentence about Titch, but also conjoins verbs describing the growth of his seed: "And Titch's seed grew [page turn] and grew [page turn] and grew." This skillful use of language contributes to the sense of closure at the end of the story.

Peggy Rathmann's *Goodnight Gorilla*, tells a classic goodnight wish of every child. Like the animals in a traditional zoo, a majority of young children in America sleep behind bars at night, in a crib. From the adult point of view, this is to keep the child safe while the parents rest and cannot watch over him or her. But in this story, a child's wish to be let out of his or her crib and sleep with his or her parents is fulfilled as the gorilla takes the keys from the zookeeper and lets the animals into the zookeeper's house. Then, even after the zookeeper's wife sends all the animals back to the zoo, the gorilla (with a mouse) still manages to sneak into their big bed and sleep with them. The developmental issue (wanting to not sleep in a crib, but be out and about, or at least, sleeping with the parents) is skillfully dealt with implicitly. But explicitly there is the problem, endemic to all children and their tired parents, that children want the reassurance that their parents are there and will be there when they wake up. Thus, the multitude of "Goodnights" that echoes throughout this text also echoes in the hallways outside bedrooms night after night. Those "Goodnights", along with the animal names, take up around fifty words of text. Again, this text succeeds in the three proposed criteria, as the text is short and easily read, there is a clear change of state at the end (i.e. the gorilla is no longer in his cage; instead he is in the bed of the zoo-keeper and his wife), and the story focuses on the classic developmental issue of going to sleep, with the added twist of providing form for an experience the child would like to have!

Molly Bang's classic goodnight book, *Ten, Nine, Eight* is a short, simple, rhyming text that takes the main character from checking out all her toys (from 10 down to 6) and then preparing herself to go to bed (from 5 to 1). Told in less than 70 words, in short, simple adjective-noun-prepositional-phrase phrases fragments, the main character moves from being outside her crib to being tucked happily in her crib, and is another example of a classic bedtime story.

Simple sentence structure is also found in *I Am a Bunny* written by Ole Risom and illustrated by Richard Scarry. The story shows Nicolas Bunny and recounts what he likes to do in the spring, summer, fall, and winter in the simple present tense, which implies he does this year after year. The story, told in less than 150 words, shows the physiological change that the bunny goes through (again, from awake to asleep, but in this case, the time period is over the course of a year, and the sleep is the longer winter sleep). In addition, the story gives form for experience as the seasons are named. Moreover, the ending provides a circular closure, as the bunny dreams about spring. Thus, the listener realizes that the bunny will wake up and do all the same activities again next year. This story thus provides linguistic and cognitive structure for the experience of seasonal change.

Whose Mouse Are You?, written by Robert Kraus and illustratred by Jose Aruego, is an interesting contrast to the previous stories for the very young, as it deals with issues of identity and loss. It is the story of a mouse whose parents and sister are all individually lost or trapped, and how he goes and saves them all. There is clearly a change from start to finish as first he is alone, and by the end he is with his whole family, including a new brother. In addition, the language of the story is wonderful with a question-answer pattern that moves along quickly in a lovely near-rhyme pattern. This 100-word manuscript is the quickest read of all the ones mentioned above precisely because of the short question-answer format and the judicious use of rhyme. However, this picturebook cannot be argued to provide form for experience for most children in the first two years of life, as they are not questioning their identity, or their role in the family, or saving their parents from imminent death. So this text alone, of all the texts examined above, does not meet the suggested criteria for being developmentally relevant. However, the delightful rhyming text and bright illustrations in this case override the criteria of developmental appropriateness.

Thus, after examining eight books in *The 20th Century Children's Book Treasury* according to the criteria suggested above, one is found to be a concept book, and not a narrative (i.e. Helen Oxenbury's *I See; I Hear; I Touch*), and one (*Whose Mouse Are You?*) is considered to be a narrative with strong use of language, but not developmentally relevant for the age group discussed in this paper, namely newborn to two years of age. This is not to say that they should not have been included in the treasury; what I am suggesting is that if a parent were to use these three questions to evaluate the eight books contained in the treasury, they might exclude these two books from consideration, while they might include as suitable narratives for their infant or toddler the other six selections. Moreover, of the seven narrative texts included in this treasury, six clearly fit all three guidelines suggested herein, indicating their usefulness.

Of course, there are a variety of other criteria that can be used for picturebook selection. In 2002, HarperCollins published the *HarperCollins Treasury of Picture Book Classics: A Child's First Collection*. It included 12 reproductions of HarperCollins' picturebooks from 1947 to 1998. In the Acknowledgements and a Little History, HarperCollins editor Katherine Brown Tegen noted that all the books "share some universal qualities: they tap into children's emotions, the stories are told with language that endures repeated readings because of its poetry and simplicity; the artwork extends the text so that the whole of the book is always more than the sum of its parts" (p. 442). There are differences in the criteria with what I have suggested above, but the issue of language is considered crucial in both instances. In the latter set of criteria, however, it is noted that the artwork is evaluated as to whether it extends the text, and while it is certainly an important consideration from an editorial point of view, it is more difficult for a caregiver to make that evaluation immediately. This is not to say that illustrations are not important, only that it may be difficult to determine if it is extending a text. Parents and readers of all ages respond viscerally to images, and as such it is obviously a crucial consideration, and one that bears further analysis on the relation of pictures to a child's emergent visual literacy. My point is that this particular criteria of how the pictures extend a text does not lend itself well to analysis while a parent is standing in a bookstore or a library. A 'naive' reader will either be drawn to the visual images or not, and this response will result in either the reader moving his or her eyes to the words to ascertain the suitability of the text or closing the book and returning it to the shelf.

Similarly with the issue of tapping into the emotions of the child: it is important, but difficult to evaluate when stated in that way. While this is obviously a critical criteria for an editorial team, for a parent or caregiver who wants to select a book that will engage their 0-to-24-month-old child and provide a sense of completion and satisfaction at the end of each reading, assessing the criteria of change and behavorial development portrayed in the book are argued here to be more easily graspable and implementable when trying to make a quick decision.

In sum, if caregivers want to begin leading the child into the world of literature appreciation, the three guidelines proposed should help them get there: select books that (1) show a change of state (in the object or character) from beginning to end, (2) are developmentally relevant to that particular child (i.e. deal with emotional, behavioral, physiological or social issues that that child is currently experiencing, or has recently experienced and can identify with) and (3) are very short and are well-written in that they invite repeated readings with the child.

4. Conclusion

In this paper, I have discussed the rationale for reading picture narratives to babies and toddlers: to create a commonality of experiences between the caregiver and child. In addition, I reviewed the recent psycholinguistic literature that clearly points to the benefits of reading, especially repeated reading, to the very young. Lastly, I have proposed three criteria that educators, academics, and librarians can suggest to parents to help them quickly identify an emotionally satisfying picturebook narrative, and then I tested those criteria on picturebooks that are considered to be classics in the American picturebook tradition of the past fifty-some years. The findings suggest that caregivers can use these three questions in the bookstore or in the library to judge whether or not the text will provide a satisfying experience for both reader and child, which will, in turn, pave the way for language and literacy development, as well as extend the emotional and cognitive landscape of the child by providing a range of situations and experiences through the pictures and text.

However, what if there is a conflict between the three questions? That is, what if the picturebook has concise and lovely language and a change of state, but is not developmentally appropriate? Or what if there is no change of state, but it is developmentally appropriate and has a wonderful sense of rhythm? Does that mean a book should not be selected? Certainly not. The questions, first off, are simply guidelines. Second, they are provided to stimulate the caregiver's own evaluation process. If, for example, the caregiver was planning to select a narrative, but instead found a wonderful counting book in rhyme, these questions then allow him or her to realize she was hoping for one kind of book, and came away with another. If a book is not developmentally appropriate, but has a wonderful sense of rhythm (as in *Whose Mouse Are You?)* it would still be worth selecting that picturebook if the caregiver found it so enjoyable to read that it encouraged repeated readings (*Whose Mouse Are You?* is, in fact, very enjoyable to read, as are *Madeline* and *Where the Wild Things Are* even though they are also not developmentally relevant for a newborn-to-two-year-old child.)

In fact, as the psycholinguistic literature clearly shows that repeated readings increase a toddler's vocabulary and pave the way for acquiring language and literacy skills, what is critical is that parents enjoy the reading-aloud process. This paper suggests that providing guidelines to caregivers to seek out short, well-written narrative texts which involve change and are developmentally appropriate will aid caregivers in their selection of picturebooks and, in turn, add to their enjoyment of the reading-aloud time for both themselves and their child.

In conclusion, narrative picturebooks may be considered beneficial for the youngest readers, not only for purposes of language and literacy acquisition, but also so that infants and toddlers may begin to join in one of the benefits of being part of the human race: to appreciate another's point of view as one's own and to enter into the greater humanity of a shared knowledgebase that embraces individual and cultural differences at the same time that it transcends them.

Acknowledgements

The author would like to acknowledge the support of Hong Kong Baptist University for providing a partial travel grant to attend the conference "Children's Books from 0 to 3: Where Literacy Begins," as well as the organizer of the conference itself, Dr. Bettina Kümmerling-Meibauer at the University of Tübingen. Thanks also go to Ivy Chan, for her help in preparing the PowerPoint slides, and to all the participants of the conference, with special thanks to Dr. Janet Evans and Dr. Virginia Lowe for commenting on the talk presented at that conference, and to Dr. Kümmerling-Meibauer and two reviewers for their comments on an earlier draft of this paper. Any errors are my sole responsibility.

Children's books cited

Bemelmans, L. 1939. *Madeline*. New York NY: Penguin Putnam.

Bang, M. 1983. *Ten, Nine, Eight*. New York NY: Greenwillow Books.

Brown, M. W. & Hurd, C. 1947. *Goodnight Moon*. New York NY: Haper Publishers (now HarperCollins).

Crews, D. 1978. *Freight Train*. New York NY: Greenwillow Books.

Hutchins, P. 1971. *Titch*. New York NY: Simon & Schuster.

Kraus, R. 1970. *Whose Mouse Are You?* New York NY: Simon & Schuster.

Oxenbury, H. 1985. *I See; I Hear; I Touch*. Cambridge MA: Candlewick Press.

Rathmann, P. 1994. *Goodnight Gorilla*. New York NY: Penguin Putnam.

Risom, O. 1963. *I Am a Bunny*. New York NY: Golden Books.

Sendak, M. 1963. *Where the Wild Things Are*. New York NY: HarperCollins.

Shaw, N. & Apple, M. 1988. *Sheep in a Jeep*. New York NY: Houghton Mifflin Harcourt.

Willems, M. 2003. *Don't Let the Pigeon Drive the Bus!* New York NY: Hyperion Books for Children.

References

Dell'Antonia, K. J. & Straub, S. 2006. *Reading with Babies and Toddlers and Twos*. Naperville IL: Sourcebooks.

Fox, M. 2001. *Reading Magic: Why Reading Aloud to Our Children Will Change Their Lives Forever.* San Diego CA: Harcourt.

Goodwin, P. 2009. Developing understanding of narrative, empathy and inference through picturebooks. In *Talking Beyond the Page: Reading and Responding to Picturebooks*, J. Evans (ed.), 152–167. London: Routledge.

Karras, J. & Braungart-Rieker, J. 2005. Effects of shared parent-infant book reading on early language acquisition. *Journal of Applied Developmental Psychology* 26(2): 133–148.

Kümmerling-Meibauer, B. & Meibauer, J. 2005. First pictures, early concepts: Early concept books. *The Lion and the Unicorn* 29(3): 324–347.

Lowe, V. 2007. *Stories, Pictures and Reality: Two Children Tell.* London: Routledge.

Lukens, R. 2003. *A Critical Handbook of Children's Literature*, 7th ed. Boston MA: Pearson Education.

McMahon, R. 1996. Introducing infants to the joy of reading. *Dimensions of Early Childhood* 24: 236–239.

Moore, M. & Wade, B. 2003. Bookstart: A qualitative evaluation. *Educational Review* 55(1): 3–13.

Ninio, A. 1983. Joint book reading as a multiple vocabulary acquisition device. *Child Development* 54: 445–451.

Robb, M. B., Richert, R. A. & Wartella, E. A. 2009. Just a talking book? Word learning from watching baby videos. *British Journal of Developmental Psychology* 27(1): 27–45.

Rodriguez, E. T., Tamis-LeMonda, C. S., Spellmann, M. E., Pan, B. A., Raikes, H., Lugo-Gil, J. & Luze, G. 2009. The Formative role of home literacy experiences across the first three years of life in children from low-income families. *Journal of Applied Developmental Psychology* 30(6): 677–694.

Schulman, J (ed.). 1998. *The 20th Century Children's Book Treasury.* New York NY: Alfred A. Knopf.

Simcock, G. & DeLoache, J. 2008. The effect of repetition on infants' imitation from picturebooks varying in iconicity. *Infancy* 13(6): 687–697.

Snow, C. E. & Godfield, B. A. 1983. Turn the page please: Situation specific language acquisition. *Journal of Child Language* 10: 551–569.

Tegen, K. (ed.). 2002. *HarperCollins Treasury of Picture Book Classics.* New York NY: HarperCollins.

Trelease, J. 2006. *The Read Aloud Handbook,* 6th edn. New York NY: Putnam Books.

Westerlund, M. & Lagerberg, D. 2008. Expressive vocabulary in 18-month-old children in relation to demographic factors, mother and child characteristics, communication style and shared reading. *Child: Care, Health and Development* 34(2): 257–266.

CHAPTER 6

Early-concept books

Acquiring nominal and verbal concepts

Bettina Kümmerling-Meibauer and Jörg Meibauer

This article focuses on picturebooks for young children aged 12 to 24 months. This type of picturebook has been largely neglected in picturebook research, albeit it provides fascinating insights into the literary and cognitive development of young children. Two types of picturebooks will be analyzed: First, those that show single objects from the child's surroundings which are denoted by nouns, second those that show actions that are usually denoted by verbs. Both book types serve to support the child's acquisition of early concepts, i.e. mental devices the child needs when referring to objects (*ball, apple*), persons (*mummy, baby*), or actions (*to hit the ball*). These early-concept books, as we call them (see Kümmerling-Meibauer & Meibauer 2005), have important properties from the point of view of cognitive and literary development. Not only do they reflect the child's order of lexical acquisition, they also serve as an introduction in elementary picture-text relations and text structures. Hence this article is a plea for a developmental approach to picturebooks. Such an approach should integrate insights from a number of disciplines, such as psycholinguistics and developmental psychology, picture theory, and narratology.

Introduction

Picturebooks for children aged 12 to 18 months typically show pictures of everyday objects such as apples, balls, teddy bears, dolls, chairs, or shoes. These books are made from cardboard, cloth, wood, or plastic and they have a handy format. Their titles often refer to implied users (*For Our Child, Baby's First Book*), depicted objects (*First Things, What is that?*), or the book's pictures (*First Pictures, Pictures for the Little Ones*). Sometimes the title stresses the act of seeing (*Come and See! Look!*), or the child's ownership (*My First Picturebook, That Is Mine)*. Most of these picturebooks have less than ten pictures. These picturebooks do not contain text; sometimes one may find a single word denoting the depicted object. The pictures are either color drawings, or photographs in color or black and white.

The most common term for this book type is "baby book" (Nodelman 1988). But this term is far too general, since it refers to most books for young children, ranging from simple board books to complex I-Spy books. More adequate terms would be "object book" (cf. Japanese "mono ehon" (object book)), Swedish "sakbok" (thing book) and "pekbok" (pointing book), or the Dutch notion "anwijsboek" (instruction book)), because they all focus on a characteristic property of this book type.

In our article published in 2005, we proposed the more specific label "early-concept book", because the basic function of these books has to do with early concepts (Kümmerling-Meibauer & Meibauer 2005). A concept comprises the verbal knowledge that the child needs to be able to refer to a given entity. For instance, the concept BALL enables the child to refer to balls, and the picture of a ball is intended to support the child's acquisition of early concepts. Early concepts belong to the young child's early lexicon and are acquired between 12 and 18 months of age. These early concepts are not only related to nouns, but also to verbs, such as *to have*, *to make*, or *to hit*, and adjectives, such as *hot* or *big* (cf. Clark 1993; Barrett 1995; Meibauer 1995).

To possess just one word is a major step in lexical acquisition. For example, if the child is able to refer to her mother using the word *mama* while her mother is not co-present, she might be said to have acquired the word *mama*. But the ultimate goal is to realize speech acts and texts, and these units are typically composed out of sentences. So picturebooks should exist that path the child's way towards this goal. And indeed, there are picturebooks which focus on actions which are usually denoted by verbs, thus supporting the acquisition of verbal concepts. Nouns and verbs typically make up the semantic core of a sentence, its proposition. Moreover, they are related by argument structure, that is, the linguistic fact that a verb takes subjects and objects as its complements. Although verbal concepts are acquired at a very young age, it appears that they usually follow the nominal concepts. The respective book type may be more marginal than the nominal one, but nevertheless it exists, and moreover, is of great interest for a more systematic approach to the relationship between picturebooks and the cognitive development of the child.

Considering the assumption that most children in Western countries, but even in other continents as well, are familiar with one or more books of this type when they are about twelve to eighteen months old, one wonders why so little research has been devoted to the topic (see Tucker 1990).

The outline of our article is as follows: First, the essential features of early-concept books focussing on nominal concepts will be pointed out. Second, a thorough analysis of early-concept books concentrating on the acquisition of verbal concepts will show to what extent this book type is connected to the first book type, and in which regard it might be considered a further step in the acquisition of early concepts. Finally, it will be shown how these picturebooks are related to similar book types that display conceptual classes. Thus, we will attempt to develop a typology of picturebooks targeted at young children that is closely related to recent findings in children's cognitive and linguistic development.

Early-concept books: Nominal concepts

This section shortly summarizes the main findings of our previous research into early-concept books focusing on nominal concepts (Kümmerling-Meibauer & Meibauer 2005). The early-concept book has prominent precursors, such as Johann Amos Comenius's *Orbis Sensualium Pictus* (1658) and Friedrich Johann Bertuch's *Bilderbuch für Kinder* (Picturebook for Children, 1792–1830), since they also display pictures of everyday objects (Fassbind-Eigenheer & Fassbind-Eigenheer 2002). However, those books were meant for school children and conveyed an encyclopedic knowledge of the world. In contrast, early-concept books that focus on young children originated in the last two decades of the nineteenth century. Typical examples are the Swiss Picturebook *Mim Chindli. E neus Bilderbuech für die ganz Chline* (To My Child: A New Picturebook for the Little Ones, c. 1910) by an unknown illustrator, Edward Steichen's and Mary Steichen Calderone's photobook *The First Picture Book* (1930), and the widespread cloth books from the British publishing house Dean's Rag Book since the beginning of the twentieth century, such as *Baby's Object Book* (1905) and *What Is It?* (c. 1910).

When looking at a modern picturebook of this type, for example the seminal picturebooks about *Miffy* (1964) by Dick Bruna, some visual features are striking. One object is usually shown on each page, but sometimes two to five objects constitute a scene. The objects are depicted as a whole object, never in their parts. A black line usually frames the object, so that it stands out distinctly from the background and is shown either from the front or from one angle. In general, the viewer is at eye level with the object. The objects are characterized by bright and rich colors with a dominance of primary colors (cf. Bornstein 1975; Bornstein, Kessen & Weitkopf 1976; Koerber 2007; Werner, this volume). The hue is consistent and modulations of colors are lacking. The depicted objects are usually presented as clean and intact, as if they were brand-new.

Surrounded by empty uncolored or single-colored backgrounds, the objects seem to float in a negative space. Movement is not shown, so that the objects are always static. Moreover, they are often depicted without shadows or a source of light, so that the objects' three-dimensionality is reduced. The proportions are striking: objects seem to be of the same size, even though they may have different actual sizes. A concise description reveals that the objects in these books are not shown naturally. Actual objects apparently are not outlined in black, nor are they presented in bright colors without modulations. Because of this stylized representation, most of these picturebooks can be characterized as showing a certain degree of abstraction.

Hence, the supposed simplicity of the illustrations in these picturebooks turns out to be problematic since they demonstrate, on closer inspection, a remarkable complexity. Young children certainly have to acquire some basic skills of perception in order to understand these images. These skills concern (i) the differentiation between figure and background, (ii) the recognition of lines, points, and colors as inseparable parts of the depicted object, (iii) the insight that two-dimensional pictures stand for three-dimensional objects, and finally, (iv) the knowledge of learned visual schemata (DeLoache, Strauss & Meynard 1979: 77–89; Nodelman 1988: 35; Kümmerling-Meibauer & Meibauer 2005: 332–333; for examples, see Kümmerling-Meibauer & Linsmann 2009).

These four essential skills show that images comprise visual codes which must be learned (Kress & Van Leeuwen 1996: 22–23). Therefore, children must acquire these visual codes in order to make sense of pictures. By joint looking at these picturebooks, children are stimulated to acquire these conventions that constitute a sort of "visual grammar" (cf. Kress & Van Leeuwen 1996: 18). The authors claim that "language and visual communication both realize the same more fundamental and far-reaching systems of meaning that constitute our cultures, but that each does so by means of its specific forms" (17). Moreover, psychological research in picture perception emphasizes that at an early age, children develop a surprising ability to acknowledge elements of visual grammar which is described as visual literacy, i.e. the competence to understand visual signs and codes (Goldsmith 1984: 111). Visual literacy is not innate, but is acquired by a long-lasting and permanent process of learning.

Now, we argue that the presentation of pictures is not only important for the acquisition of visual literacy, but also for lexical acquisition. Obviously, in the process of language acquisition, the acquisition of words plays a significant role. A child's first words are learned when she is about one year old. By eighteen months, most children have a repertoire of fifty words which constitutes the "early lexicon". From about age two, the lexicon seems to explode; children acquire new words on a daily basis. Some researchers estimate that by age six, children possess a vocabulary of about 14.000 words (Bloom 2000: 26–35).

It is not a mere coincidence that the objects depicted in early-concept books are labelled through nouns, because it is the linguistic function of nouns to denote objects. Nouns play an important role in the early lexicon; approximately 44 % of the first 50 words learned by children are nouns (Bloom 2000). According to research by Kauschke & Hofmeister (2002) on early lexicons in German, there is a continuous increase of nouns during early lexical acquisition (see Meibauer & Rothweiler 1999).

The acquisition of the meaning of words is not quite as simple and automatic as it seems to be at first glance. Of the numerous and sophisticated theories that are on the market (see Bloom 2000; Bowerman & Levinson 2001; Murphy 2002; Rakison & Oakes 2003), prototype theory is of particular interest with respect to early-concept books. Children have to learn the prototypical features that constitute a category or concept on the one hand, and to avoid overextension and underextension on the other hand. Research in prototype semantics has shown that prototypes, the best examples of a category, are crucial for categorization (Gelman 2006; Markman 1989). A chair appears to belong to the category furniture rather than a bench, and robins are in the category birds rather than penguins (Taylor 1995: 38–55). In language acquisition, prototypes seem relevant for conceptual development and lexical acquisition. It is tempting to argue that the illustrators make proposals as to what should constitute a prototype for the child. An apple may be a prototypical fruit even for an adult, but a crib is certainly prototypical furniture only for a child. Hence, there is some evidence that adults try to give conceptual information that is interesting from a child's point of view (Snow & Goldfield 1983). Of primary interest are therefore things in the child's immediate surroundings: food, toys, and animals, among others.

In the course of language acquisition, children also have problems with context-bound references, overextension, and underextension. Children overextend a word's meaning, if, for instance, they use the word *cat* to refer not only to cats, but also to dogs, rabbits, and guinea pigs. They underextend a word's meaning, when, for example, they use the word *doll* to refer just to a specific doll (Barrett 1995: 372).

Children typically learn words by listening to people's talk. This learning process is not guided, because there is no systematic and explicit instruction through parents or peers. However, when an adult looks at a picturebook together with a child, the learning situation is different. Since these picturebooks usually do not contain any text or story, the situation is dominated by a pointing and naming game, as is demonstrated in the following dialogue between a father and his daughter Katrin who is seventeen months old:

> Daddy: "Oh, what kind of animal is that?"
> Katrin: "Kind of animal"
> Daddy [points to the picture]: "What is that?"
> Katrin: "Crocodile."
> Daddy: "A crocodile."
>
> (Wagner & Wiese 1996: 14; translated from German)

This example demonstrates that joint reading of an early-concept book usually consists of a pointing and naming game. The adult points to the respective image and simultaneously asks the child what the picture shows; the child has to answer correctly. If the child gives the wrong answer, the adult might correct her. Thus, joint looking at these picturebooks supports the young child's vocabulary acquisition. This is in line with case studies on language learning and emergent literacy suggested by scholars such as Moerk (1985), Ninio (1983), Snow & Goldfield (1983), Jones (1996), and others.

In the above discourse, Katrin knows that the depicted object is called a crocodile. What is unclear is whether she is already able to learn from this particular picture and to generalize about all crocodiles, and whether she already has some knowledge about crocodiles.

The process of grasping the picture-word relationship is quite complex. In order to show this in more detail, we take *apple* as an example, because pictures of apples seem to be standard pictures in early-concept books. In a more systematic and elaborate fashion, the relevant aspects of the word *apple* may be illustrated in Figure 1:

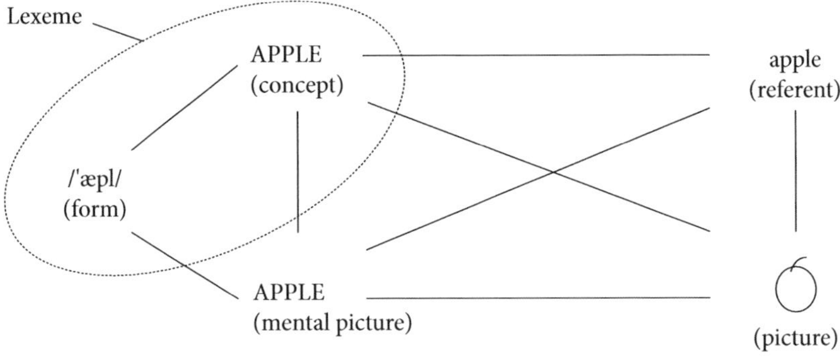

Figure 1. Relevant dimensions of the lexeme *apple*

We assume that children know a word when they have acquired a consistent mapping between form and concept. A form-concept mapping is called a lexeme, i.e. an element that is permanently stored in the child's mental lexicon (there are other elements in the lexicon besides words, e.g. idioms). A concept is the set of properties of a lexeme that makes reference to a referent possible. The referent is the entity that a speaker refers to, while uttering a certain lexeme. Thus, when saying *This is an apple*, the speaker refers to a specific apple. Part of the concept APPLE is that an apple can be eaten, is a fruit, round, has a stem, grows on trees and is red, yellow or green. In general, conceptual knowledge allows us to categorize things, e.g., to decide whether a given object is correctly referred to with the lexeme *apple* or not. It is important to note that conceptual knowledge gradually develops, as several studies on conceptual development have shown (Clark 1995; Murphy 2002).

Pictures are two-dimensional visual representations of referents. Photographs depict a concrete referent, while drawings depict a prototypical referent. Moreover, one has to distinguish between a picture and a mental picture (or image), the latter being a mental pictorial representation. For example, a picture displays a red apple, but an individual may mentally imagine a yellow apple. Knowledge of a concept and knowledge of a mental picture are independent of each other. On the one hand, there is conceptual knowledge without pictorial knowledge, for example in pictureless cultures, or, when children have not yet come into contact with pictures of referents they already know. On the other hand, it is possible to have a mental picture without the knowledge of a referent. This is true for many entities exclusively represented through pictures, for example the unicorn. Hence pictorial knowledge has an impact upon conceptual knowledge, and early literacy involves bringing together acquisitional processes in both domains.

It is worth emphasizing that the child may learn something from looking at early-concept books. With regard to the relation between the referent and the picture, the following four learning situations may be distinguished: First, the child already knows the referent, and is able to recognize the referent in its visual representation. The referent-picture relation is thus strengthened. Second, the child already knows the referent, but is *not* able to recognize the referent in its visual representation. This may happen when the picture is highly abstract, or when untypical colors are used. Thus the child learns that pictures need not to depict referents in a unique way and that there may be an opaque relation between the referent and its depiction. Third, the child knows the picture (or the pictorially mediated mental picture) before seeing the fitting referent. This is the typical case with exotic animals, such as crocodiles, elephants, giraffes, etc. In this case, the picture guides the child into the exploration of the world. Fourth, the child only knows the picture (or the pictorially mediated mental picture), but, on the basis of this knowledge, is *not* able to recognize a certain item. Even in this case the child experiences that not all pictures have a simple and easy-to-detect correlate in her surrounding world.

Moreover, early-concept books tell children that there is a conventional, adult usage of words and pictures that they should adopt (for instance, *telephone*, not *phone*). This observation is supported by the fact that we find early-concept books where a single word denoting the depicted object is given in addition to the picture. Similarly, most illustrators strive at prototypical pictures (but there is, of course, a great deal of artistic variation). Nodelman (1988: 27) observes that stereotypical pictures "operate somewhat like dictionary definitions of objects –

they express the essence of the type of object represented rather than the specific nature of any given one such object". If this is correct, there is a correspondence between the prototypicality of the depicted object and the prototypicality of the way the object is depicted.

Early-concept books focusing on verbal concepts: An overview

In contrast to the many early-concept books focusing on nominal concepts, early-concept books that display actions appear to be rare. Our study is based on the analysis of 16 early-concept books from different countries (Denmark, Germany, Israel, Sweden, UK, US), published between 1931 and 2010. In a broad sense, two different categories are discernible. The first category concerns the appearance of text, since the corpus contains 4 early-concept books focusing on verbal concepts without text and 12 books with text. The second category refers to the presentation of characters. Surprisingly, eight picturebooks show a young child which does something with objects, such as eating porridge or pulling a pull-toy, while the other picturebooks do not show characters at all. In this case, the reference to verbal concepts is only expressed in the accompanying text which either uses a first-person narrator ("I like ...") or a third-person narrator ("Baby likes...").

Nevertheless, in order to facilitate the understanding of the pictures, a young child is always depicted on the book cover, thus indicating that this child obviously is the character/subject referred to in the text.[1] By contrast, all those early concept-books without text invariably show on each page a young child that handles an object.

Let us first turn to examples for the first category. We suspect that the first early-concept book focusing on verbal concepts is Mary Steichen Martin's and Edward Steichen's *The Second Picture Book* (1931). Steichen was influential in the development of photographic books for young children and stimulated similar books. The photographs reflect the purity of style typical of New Realism, which dominated photography at that time. Moreover, *The Second Picture Book* is exceptional, because it constitutes a pendant to Steichen's *The First Picture Book*, published in 1930. Whereas *The First Picture Book* is conceived as an early-concept book presenting objects from the young child's surroundings, *The Second Picture Book* demonstrates what could be done with these objects. In a series of twenty-four black-and-white photographs young children are shown in action: a boy standing before a washing basin brushes his teeth with the toothbrush shown in

1. An exception to this rule is Nash's *My First Picturebook* (1959) which shows a pull-toy on the book cover.

The First Picture Book, another boy is sitting at a table, eating a slice of bread and butter, a girl looks at a picturebook, and so forth. The photographs are shown on the right pages, the left pages are empty. The situations are arranged artistically, often the children are shown from behind or from different perspectives. Sometimes the viewer is at eye level with the child; sometimes the children are presented from a bird's eye view or a worm's eye view.

Besides the preface written by Mary Steichen Martin, this photographic book has no text. One might assume that the correct choice of the verb describing the presented situation is left to the adult who is supposed to stimulate the young child in the production of short sentences by asking questions like "What is the child doing with the toothbrush/bread/picturebook?" (presupposing prior knowledge of *The First Picture Book*), or "What is the child doing?" (eliciting full descriptions of the photographs). Although it is possible to use this picturebook on its own, only the juxtaposition of *The First Picture Book* and *The Second Picture Book* reveals the well-considered concept of these works.[2]

Helen Oxenbury's *Working* (1981) and *Playing* (1981) present further examples of early-concept books without text. These picturebooks contain fourteen double spreads with watercolor illustrations. The simplicity of the objects is stressed by Oxenbury's reduced cartoon-like style, which becomes most obvious in the simplified representation of the young child's face with two dots for the eyes, a small circle for the nose, and a bigger circle for the mouth. In order to draw the viewer's attention to the objects and the young child, the artist frames the objects and the figure with a subtle black outline, and places them almost in the middle of the page and against a white background, thus representing a negative space.

In contrast to Steichen's work, Oxenbury's picturebook is characterized by showing on each double spread an object on the left side, and an activity that could be done with the object on the right side, as for example a teddy bear on the left side, and a young child hugging this teddy bear on the right side (see Figure 2). By this arrangement a certain sequence of actions is demanded: first, the viewers shall focus their attention on the object depicted on the left page, then, they should turn to the right page that presents a situation where the respective object is used by a child. In this case viewers have to identify the object before they are stimulated to acknowledge the action done with the object. The pointing and naming game moves on from noun concepts (presented by the depicted object) to verbal concepts (describing the action).

2. Comparable to *The Second Picture Book* is the Danish photobook *Se hvad vi kan* (Look What We Can, 1964) with photographs by Bernt Klyvare, where young children are shown in different actions, such as bathing, painting, drinking, and playing.

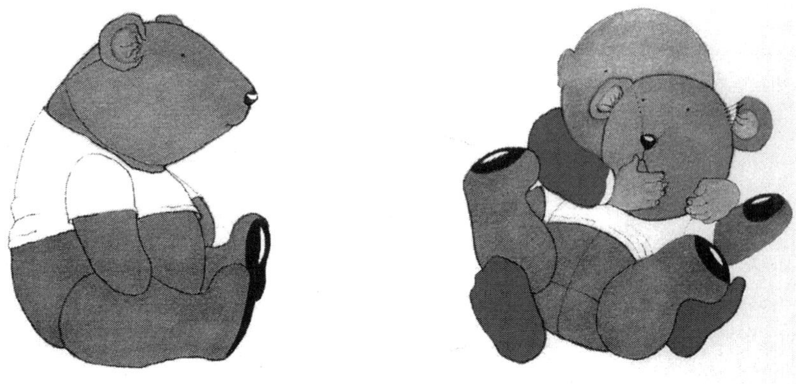

Figure 2. Image from *Playing* (1981) by Helen Oxenbury

Figure 3. Image from *Baby's First Book* (1953) by Annette Edwards and Helen Schad

The second category, early-concept books with text, is characterized by the combination of pictures and text, as well as the complexity of the latter. The simplest type is represented by the German picturebook *Antons ganze Welt* (Anton's Whole World, 2010) with pictures by Judith Drews. On the right pages the protagonist Anton, a little rabbit, is shown, brushing his teeth, bathing in a tub, hiding behind a curtain, building a snowman, and so forth. On the left pages the text refers to the depicted action, always starting with the protagonist's name, followed by a verb and sometimes an adverbial supplement or an object.

However, it is noticeable that in most cases, the left-right-succession of pictures has been changed to a top-bottom-sequence of pictures and text, as for example in Annette Edwards' and Helen Schad's *Baby's First Book* (1953). On the top half of the page, an object, such as a ball, is depicted, while on the bottom, a young child is shown that handles the respective object. While the sentence referring to the object always starts with the deictic particle "here", followed by the naming of the object and the object's owner ("Here is baby's ball"), the text on the bottom describes the action done with the object ("Baby plays with the ball"). This structure is strictly kept throughout the whole book that consists of 18 pages. Striking are the empty white background and the objects' proportions. On the top picture, the object is depicted quite larger than in the bottom picture, thus stressing the shifting focus of attention that shall pass from the object to the young child in action (see Figure 3).

F. R. Schaare's *First Picturebook* (1945) represents another example. In this cardboard book, up to three common objects are shown on each page, such as a potato, an egg, and an apple, arranged from top to bottom. These objects are connected by a text printed on the top of the page, starting with the name of the owner (baby) and a verbal construction, such as *Baby likes.* This text should be completed by the notions of the objects printed next to respective illustrations, so that up to three sentences can be constructed ("Baby likes potato"; "Baby likes egg"; "Baby likes apple"). In this picturebook, in comparison to the aforementioned early-concept book, the baby is never depicted.

Still another variant is E. M. Dawson's *The Picture Book for Baby* (1955) that depicts a scene on the right page and an arrangement of objects related to this specific situation on the left page. On one double spread a young child sitting in her high chair is depicted that is going to eat breakfast. The first sentence printed on the top of the left page describes the situation: "I eat my breakfast". Further short sentences referring to the depicted single items are printed beneath the illustration: "Here is my plate", "Here is my egg", and so forth. On some double spreads the accompanying sentences use another verbal construction, replacing *here is* by *I see.*

Rachel Isadora's *I See* (1985) already indicates the sentence structure with the book title. On each double spread a little girl is shown that is occupied with different actions, such as stroking a cat, drinking milk from a bottle, watching a bird in the tree, and throwing a ball. The text always starts with the phrase "I see" followed by the object presented in the illustration. However, the subsequent sentence either consists of a verbal description of the action displayed in the illustration ("I drink", "I throw") or by an onomatopoetic expression, such as "tickle", "whee", "meow").

Another strategy is used in Mirik Snir's and Zofia Langer's Hebrew picturebook *In My House* (1984)[3]. The first half of the picturebook consists in a sequence of objects. On each double spread a couple of common objects are depicted, such as a spoon and a chair. The accompanying text consists of a long sentence starting with the phrase "In my house I have" and followed by an enumeration of the objects. In the second half a child is seen that is handling the objects. The assigned text begins with the phrase "And I use everything I have", followed by short sentences describing the depicted action, such as "I eat with a spoon, I sit on the chair", etc.

Finally, the combination of *wh*-questions and answers dominates Leonard Weisgard's *My First Picture Book* (1953) and the Danish photobook *Trine kan …* (Trine can …, 1964). While in *My First Picture Book* a *wh*-question is followed by approximately 5–6 answers that repeats the sentence pattern and the verb, but always changes the object referred to, the text in *Trine kan …* firstly describes actions performed by the protagonist Trine, supplemented by a question directed at the child viewer, asking her what she can do with her mouth, nose, hands, and feet.

As this overview already indicates, noun-focused early-concept books have some properties in common with verb-focused early-concept books. The most eye-catching aspect is the depiction of objects themselves which dominate even early-concept books focusing on verbal concepts. Eight picturebooks just show objects. The visual features, such as black outline, neatness, eye-level, wholeness, negative space, and so forth, are the same as in early-concept books focusing on nominal concepts. The main difference consists in the accompanying text that emphasizes the action that can be done with the depicted object. Although these specific picturebooks do not show a deviation from the noun-focused early-concept book type at first sight, they reveal some minor distinctions on closer consideration. While in noun-focussed early-concept books usually one single item is presented, the verb-focused early-concept books show two to five objects per page, either grouped together as scenery or presented as single objects in a top-bottom-sequence. Another point in case is the depiction of the background. While some verb-focussed early-concept books still have a negative space, others depict the objects in a clearly distinctive location, such as a room, meadow, or beach.

3. We would like to thank Mirik Snir for the translation of the Hebrew text.

Oxenbury's *Playing* and *Working* may be analyzed as an intermediate type of early-concept book, because in these cases we see the child as an agent who is handling the respective objects while the object is shown on the verso and the child handling the object on the recto. However, all the early-concept books displaying a young child as an agent either employ a negative space or a reduced background with just some details, such as a carpet, table, sofa, sink, or doorsteps, in order not to distract the young child's attention from the depicted characters. In this regard early-concept books focussing on verbal concepts are clearly connected to early-concept books focussing on nominal concepts and should be regarded as a further development of the latter.

Moreover, as these early-concept books with text have demonstrated, not only the text-picture-relationship is varying, but also the grammatical structure of the text, ranging from simple sentences to a combination of two sentences and rather complex sentences. This calls for a closer analysis of the linguistic aspects of this book type.

Linguistic aspects of early-concept books focusing on verbal concepts

To begin with, let us point out some differences between nouns and verbs and show how they are connected. The main connection, of course, is that sentences, as basic units of language, are built up from nouns and verbs. This is shown in Table 1:

Table 1. Some properties of nouns and verbs

Properties	Nouns	Verbs
Syntax	• nouns/noun phrases (NP) are the arguments of verbs	• verbs take nouns/noun phrases as their arguments, e.g. *Baby pull+s the toy.*
	Agreement between the subject NP and the finite verb in the full sentence.	
Semantics	• common nouns (*apple, child*), proper nouns (*Max, mummy*), abstract nouns (*love, dream*)	• action verbs (*to pull*), event verbs (*to sleep*), state verbs (*to lie*), 'light verbs' (*to make*), modals (*can*), …
Acquisition	• Nouns and verbs coexist already in the early lexicon. • Generally, nouns are acquired before verbs ('noun bias').	
	Composition of types in early (German) lexicon according to Kauschke (2000)	
	13 months: 10%	13 months: Ø
	15 months: 15%	15 months: 3%
	21 months: 27%	21 months: 12%
	36 months: 16%	36 months: 23%
	• preference for basic level nouns: *animal – dog – poodle*	• preference for hyperonyms: *to speak – to murmur*

Note that this table gives only a first impression of the acquisitional relation between noun and verbs. Numerous studies have been undertaken in order to explore this relation, as the recent review by Golinkoff & Hirsh-Pasek (2008) impressively shows. According to them, "relational terms (verbs, prepositions and adjectives) often lag behind nouns in both studies of natural vocabulary acquisition (…) and in laboratory research on verb comprehension (…)" (p. 397). The order of acquisition in the nominal domain appears to be Proper Nouns (*Sue*) > Concrete Nouns (*ball*) > Relational Nouns (*uncle*) > Abstract Nouns (*hope*), while in the verbal domain the order of acquisition appears to be Instrument Verbs (*eat*) > Action Verbs (*jump*) > Path Verbs (*exit*)> Intention Verbs (*pour*), Mental Verbs (*think*) (Golinkoff & Hirsh-Pasek 2008: 400). These processes overlap, i.e. some verbs appear before some nouns.

Our hypothesis is that early-concept books by and large should reflect these properties and tendencies. (This presupposes that authors and illustrators are not totally naïve with respect to the general picture of language development, although it is clear that they impose *their* idea of how language acquisition works upon their child readers.) The first question then is what kinds of verbs we find. The most frequent verbs – based on an analysis of 12 picturebooks (the other 4 from our corpus being textless) – are: *to be* (39), *to see* (17), *to play* (12), *to look* (9), *to eat* (8), *to drink* (7), *to put* (6), *to sit* (5), *to like* (4), *to have* (4), *to pull* (4), *to push* (4), *to ride* (4), *to go* (3), *to hug* (3), *to love* (3), *to open* (3), and *to sleep* (3). The majority of these verbs belongs to the child's early lexicon and can therefore be classified as denoting early concepts. It is interesting to note that almost every early-concept book that displays verbal concepts contains complete sentences with the syntactic form: subject (noun or pronoun) – verb – object (noun), sometimes complemented by possessive pronouns ("my") or deictic references ("here"). The only case of an adjective-noun combination we have found is "new shoes". Just one early-concept book, *Sommar* (Summer, 2010) by the Swedish artist Sara Lundberg, contains infinite verb forms, such as "hoppa högt" (to jump high), "sitta stilla" (to sit still) or "bygga slott" (to build a castle).

The copula *to be* is a verb that shows up early in the child's lexicon. Here is one example where it is used in the context of an enumeration of things being salient in the bathing scenery (Dawson, *The Picture Book for Baby*, 1955):

(1) I have my bath.
Here <u>is</u> my duck.
Here <u>is</u> my sponge.
Here <u>is</u> my comb.

Verbs of vision like *to see* and *to look at* are also quite prominent. Obviously, this has to do with the situation of joint looking at the pictures, where the sentences refer simultaneously to an imaginary child as well as the individual child that looks at the pictures (Isadora, *I See*, 1985).

(2) I see my spoon. I eat.
I see my book. I read.

Note that in (2), the child is invited to construct sentences like *I eat with my spoon* and *I read my book*. Hence, what is left out in the second, intransitive occurrences of the verb may be taken from the first sentences to form a full sentence.

Moreover, the texts in our corpus show sensitivity to the acquisition task. One strategy to focus on syntactic objects as arguments of the verb is substitution of the objects (Schaare, *First Picturebook*, 1945):

(3) Baby has new shoes/socks.
Baby loves the Teddy bear/rabbit.

Interestingly, there is one book in our corpus that displays in a number of sentences firstly the syntactic objects of the verb *to have*, before going on to present complete verbal phrases that contain an already introduced noun as a syntactic object (Snir & Langer, *In My House*, 1984):

(4) In my house I have a spoon and a chair / a pillow and a toilet
And I use everything I have: eat with a spoon / sleep on the pillow

Sensitivity to the acquisition task can also be perceived in (5) (Weisgard, *My First Picture Book*, 1953):

(5) All around the kitchen, what do you see?
I see something big made of wood.
I see some little furry animals (…).

Here, a *wh*-question is posed, followed by the answers. In these answers, a full sentence is given that repeats the sentence pattern. Note that in adult language, an elliptical answer like *something big made of wood* would suffice. Thus, the child learns not only to understand and actively participate in a question-answer-sequence, but is also trained in detecting the relation between the question words and the nominal phrases that are related to them.

Children are not satisfied with isolated words or simple sentences, they strive for complexity, as demonstrated in the following examples taken from two different early-concept books (a. and b. taken from Nash, *My First Picture Book*, 1959; c. taken from Dawson, *Picture Book for Baby*, 1955):

(6) a. Teddy tries to ride my trike, but he is too small to pedal.
b. My doll's house has four rooms and is full of furniture.
c. Here are the baby lambs, I give one of them a drink.

In (6a), the conjuncts are connected by the adversative conjunction *but*, in (6b) by the coordinative conjunction *and*, and in (6c), we find a juxtaposition. Complex sentences such as these are quite demanding for the young child. It is telling, however, that subordinated sentences (e.g., with *that, whether,* or *because*) lack in our corpus altogether.

Typically, narrative texts consist of sentences which display cohesion (syntactic connectedness) and coherence (semantic connectedness). One important means to create connectedness certainly is the use of anaphors. In (7), we have some examples for anaphoric relations; for instance, the anaphor *she* in the second sentence refers back to the noun phrase *my dolly* (Nash, *My First Picture Book*, 1959):

(7) a. Every night I bathe my dolly$_i$. **She**$_i$ has her own towel and soap.
b. This is my lorry$_i$. I load **it**$_i$ with bricks right to the top.
c. The bag$_i$ belongs to my sister$_j$. I call **it**$_i$ her$_j$ dog bag.

These books contain certain schemata or constructional elements that can also be found in narratives for older children. Compare the following sentences (Nash, *My First Picture Book*, 1959):

(8) Teddy tries to ride my bike, but he is too small to pedal.
These sweets are Mummy's, but she lets me eat some.

These two complex sentences show no cohesion. But in (9), all sentences contribute to a single description, namely to the description of the things a child does in the morning (Williams, *Baby's First Book*, 1955).

(9) "Get up, sleepy-head!" says Teddy Bear.
"Tick tock, get up!" says the clock.
I hang up my pyjamas. I help make my bed.
I take a bath. I brush my teeth, I brush my hair.

While this text is descriptive in nature, it is quite obvious that by introduction of a complication the text could turn into a proper narrative. This should have consequences for the accompanying sequence of pictures.

Of the many other intriguing properties of these short texts, at least deixis (indexicality) and the concept of possession should be mentioned. For instance, the sentences in (6) have two deictic expressions: the personal pronoun *I* referring to the speaker, and the local adverb *here*, referring to the place of the speaker. Note that it is not clear for the child at first sight to whom *I* really refers. In general, children, as long as they do not properly master the deictical system, refer to themselves with their proper names or just with *baby* (Gressnich & Meibauer 2010).

In (10), two devices that express possession are discernible, namely a noun with a prenominal genitive, and a noun phrase containing the possessive pronoun *his* (*Baby's Things. A Real Cloth Book*, 1955)

(10) Baby's wagon. Baby pulls his wagon.

Obviously, this will help the child in learning that these two expressions of possession are related. The focus on possession within that picturebook is nicely summarized in the final sentence "Baby has many things!".

In sum, then, it is evident that in these early-concept books pictures representing actions and text containing sentences with verbal construction go hand in hand. Furthermore, these little texts – with a focus on actions that refer to the experience of children – are sensitive to the developmental stage and needs of young children, thereby preparing them for the understanding of the concept of story (see Nachtigäller & Rohlfing, this volume).

Paratexts in early-concept books

It is interesting to note that those early-concept books focusing on verbal concepts without text have a preface or epilogue instead. One might assume that especially this book type needs some explanation from the part of the author-illustrator in order to give a sort of guidance for the adult viewer. Adults might suspect that these early-concept books only have the function of grammatical teaching, thus stimulating the young child both to apply the appropriate words and to build grammatically correct sentences. However, while this book type indeed contributes to the young child's language acquisition by enlarging her early lexicon and her grammatical knowledge, it also contributes to visual literacy and literary competence as well.

This approach is strongly stressed in the preface to Steichen's *The Second Picture Book*, written by Mary Steichen Martin, and the epilogue to the Danish *Se hvad vi kan* (Look What We Can) by Bernt Klyvare. Both photographic books have a similar structure. The right page shows various activities of young children, whereas the left page is empty. These books have no text and the artists obviously felt obliged to explain the intention and concept of their work. Mary Steichen Martin draws on the physical, cognitive and linguistic development of young children. According to her, when young children are still not able to walk around, but are intensively observing their surrounding, picturebooks focusing on the depiction of static objects like *The First Picture Book* appear to be adequate.

Later in their development, when they are able to walk and begin to explore their environment, their interest in pictures depicting actions grows:

> In just the same way his interest in pictures becomes more and more dynamic, until his desire to have something happen will cause him to go beyond the simple but passive recognition of objects, and demand a story. First, "Cup!" Later, "What is the cup for?" (Steichen, *The Second Picture Book*, 1931)

The physical ability to walk and run around is thus connected to the cognitive interest in the function of objects, i.e. how to move and handle them. Moreover, while *The First Picture Book* urges the young child to at least pronounce a single word, such as *Cup*, at a further stage of development, when looking at the photos in *The Second Picture Book*, the child has learned to produce simple sentences, such as the question "What is the cup for?", thus urging the adult to give an adequate answer. But Mary Steichen Martin goes a step further, insofar as she claims that children at this age are not acquainted to listen to a volume-length story. For this reason the pictures do not form a connected story, they should be looked at separately. Nevertheless, the author indicates that the pictures stimulate a question-answer game as a step to a preliminary concept of story.

In addition, Mary Steichen Martin gives an explanation for the lack of text. She claims that reading aloud a story to young children will reduce, even destroy, their creative ability to provide their own story to pictures. While she rejects the passive situation of listening to a story, she strongly insists on the importance of imagination and interactive exchange between adult and child.

Similar ideas are expressed in the epilogue to the Danish *Se hvad vi kan*. In contrast to Steichen, the author draws a clear distinction between different age groups. When thoroughly reading Mary Steichen Martin's preface, one might assume that she is speaking about children aged approximately 2 to 3 years. Klyvare, instead, differentiates between two age groups: young children who are 12 to 24 months old and children in their third year of age. The first group is characterized by an interest in pictures that show everyday objects. The second group is characterized by an increasing interest in simple picturebook stories, this developmental stage going together with the child's acquisition of the concept of "action". Furthermore, the young child learns to control her bodily functions and is gradually able to pursue actions like eating, washing, or putting on clothes autonomously. When children have acquired these abilities, they are, according to the author, deeply interested in pictures that depict children of the same age. The contemplation of these images is supposed to stimulate the child to compare herself with the children on the photos and to describe the presented situation.

By contrast, the early-concept books focusing on verbal concepts with text do not have a paratext (preface or epilogue). An exception to the rule is the Danish photobook *Trine kan…*, where the photographer and the author explain their intention on the last page. This paratext emphasizes the young child's interest in the depiction of everyday situations which stimulate her recognition of already known cognitive schemata. By joint picturebook reading, the adult shall trigger the child viewer to retell the situations presented in the images, thus challenging her to demonstrate her ability both to decode the picture's meaning and to verbally express her impressions. Although this epilogue stresses the learning situation stimulated by this book type, the authors additionally claim that the book's narrative and aesthetic quality is able to satisfy the demands of young children and adults as well.

In sum, these paratexts acknowledge the child's growing physical, cognitive, and linguistic abilities, and stress the importance of picturebooks for even very young children. While some views may appear too simplistic from today's point of view (thus Katharina Rohlfing, p.c., reminds us that early concepts are not acquired by simple observation but through interaction), they nevertheless show a modern, anti-romantic approach to child development and the role of picturebooks therein. The purpose of early-concept books, whether focusing on nominal or verbal concepts, is therefore not restricted to grammatical teaching or the enlargement of the early lexicon. Also they largely support the child's developing visual and literary literacy, thus taking her changing cognitive and aesthetic interests seriously. Although these paratexts are not written by academics, we do not only agree with their main points, but we would like to additionally stress that these are quite modern insights, albeit from an intuitive point of view.

Early-concept books and related picturebooks for young children

Nouns and verbs surely play an important role in the early lexicon, but children aged 12 to 18 months already know other word categories as well; for example adjectives (*hot, high*), personal-social words (*yes, hello, thanks*), relational words (*there, again*), pronouns (*you, my*) and onomatopoetic words (*bow-wow*) (Barrett 1995; Dromi 1987; Kauschke 2000; Kauschke & Hofmeister 2002: 737–740). However, these word categories as well as abstract concepts connected with nouns (such as LOVE) are not easily depictable. Nevertheless, since the 1970s, early-concept books focusing on adjectives and onomatopoetic words come to the fore. In Tana Hoban's *push/pull – empty/full* (1973), the properties are arranged according the contrast principle (big – little; dark – light) and illustrated by objects that prototypically present the respective properties, such as a stone for "heaviness" or a feather for "lightness". Onomatopoetic words expressed by noises turn up in the French *Le livre des bruits* (The Book of Noises, 2004) by Soledad Bravi.

The common feature of these book types consists in the visual presentation of adjectives and onomatopoetic words. Interestingly, in order to depict these word types, the presence of objects is essential. You play with a ball, the telephone is red, the cat meows; activities, properties and noises are usually depicted with respect to objects, since it is hard if not impossible to depict them as such.

Since many words depicted in these picturebooks still belong to the child's early lexicon, these books present a transition from the early-concept book to another book type that might be called "concept book". In contrast to early-concept books displaying common objects from different conceptual classes, concept books go a step further in that they depict objects that belong to conceptual classes or conceptual domains, such as toys, animals, vehicles, food, or clothes. Typical examples for this book type are Elena Eleska's *I eat* (1945), Paul Stickland's *Trucks* (1986), and Chez Picthall's *farm animals* (2008). Picturebooks displaying abstract concepts, for example colors, shapes, numbers, or letters, can also be assigned to this book category. Prominent examples are Tana Hoban's *Red, Blue, Yellow Shoe* (1986), Keith Haring's *Ten* (1998), and Bruno Munari's *ABC* (2006). Although these picturebooks also depict objects that refer to nominal concepts, the words expressing the respective concept for the most part do not occur in the child's early lexicon, but are acquired later, when children are about 24 to 36 months old, and perhaps even older.

This short overview is not complete; however, it should at least illustrate that early-concept books are not an isolated phenomenon, but that they are related to other picturebook types targeted at young children (see Kümmerling-Meibauer 2006). In this way, young children might be gradually introduced to more complex book types and narrative structures that correspond to their cognitive and aesthetic interests.

Early-concept books and emergent literacy

How does joint looking at an early-concept book support literary competence? This book type has neither plot nor dialogue, and usually a complex text-picture-relationship is missing. Moreover, the sequence of pictures does not necessarily tell a story, which is typical for wordless picturebooks. Therefore the joint reading of early-concept books does not represent a typical reading-aloud situation, but a situation that is determined by intensively looking at the pictures, thus encouraging a pointing and naming game. While the impact of early-concept books on language acquisition and the development of visual literacy is obvious, the importance of this book type for the acquisition of emergent literacy has been put in question (Apseloff 1987; Nodelman 1988). This evaluation should be revised.

Generally, the engagement with early-concept books supports the young child's acquisition of at least three basic abilities which are relevant for literary literacy.

First, by turning pages and by attentively looking at the pictures on a double spread, children are introduced to the principle of sequentiality. This aspect is essential for an understanding of literature, because texts must be read successively. During the process of pageturning and viewing children learn that each book has a beginning and an ending, often emphasized by the adult's interjection "the end" or "the book is finished". These are just some important aspects that constitute the basic "rules of book behaviour" (Lewis 2001: 135), including sitting still, turning the pages, looking and pointing at the picture.

Second, the idea that pictures and sentences in picturebooks are connected is covertly conveyed as well. It is striking that the objects presented on a double spread are not chosen haphazardly, but arranged thematically. Usually the objects are arranged according to a pattern of similarity, i.e. the objects belong to the same conceptual class, such as spoon and mug, banana and roll, comb and brush, or spade and bucket. Children are introduced to an understanding of conceptual classes, preparing them for more complex books.

Furthermore, other patterns of object arrangements emerge through contrast and relation. The contrast pattern offers pictures from opposite conceptual classes, such as dog and car, ball and shoes, stimulating the viewer's imagination to find out the reasons for the particular combination. For example, there is a contrast between animate and inanimate. The relation pattern comes into play when related objects, for example doll and pram, or tree and apple are shown. In this case, children have to figure out how the objects belong to each other. This procedure surpasses a typical naming situation insofar as a relationship is established between the depicted objects which might stimulate a specific sort of communication (such as a question-answer sequence) or a short narrative.

These three organizing patterns – similarity, contrast, and relation – confirm a sequential structure of early-concept books. Sticking to one pattern evokes a sense of anticipation in the viewer. By turning the page, the young child expects to look at a double spread that follows the same pattern established in the book's beginning. However, many early-concept books change from one pattern to another, for instance from the similarity pattern to the contrast pattern. In some early-concept books the pattern of similarity determines more or less the whole book until the last double spread, where the relation pattern is used, thus creating a sort of climax. Through oral storytelling that hints at the relation between an image and a real object or builds up a connection between pictures, young children will be introduced to a form of narrative.

Third, young children learn that words and images represent objects, in the case of early-concept books objects from their immediate surroundings. When naming depicted objects such as *apple*, *ball*, or *teddy*, young children gradually comprehend that both real objects and images of these objects can be denoted by these words. This process is accompanied by a growing ability to produce mental images of the objects, an ability that appears to be essential to a full appreciation of literature. People who have not acquired this ability or have difficulties in this respect probably also have difficulties to understand fictional texts, since the latter require the possibility to mentally imagine the relevant characters, actions, and locations.

The findings of this article, then, would indicate that early-concept books convey basic skills which play an important role in the acquisition of literary competence, contributing to visual literacy, language acquisition, and emergent literacy (Goswami 1998; Jones 1996:25–27; Lancaster 2003; Nikolajeva 2003). Consequently, we propose to systematically correlate a child's growing abilities with further properties of early-concept books as well as related books types for children up to three years old. Although picturebooks intended for this age group reveal an astonishing variety in topics, styles and themes, a systematic overview related to the young child's developing cognitive abilities is still lacking.

Children's books cited

Ahlberg, A. & J. 1981. *Peepo*. Harmondsworth: Penguin.
Anonymous. 1905. *Baby's Object Book*. London: Dean's Rag Book.
Anonymous. [c. 1910] *Mim Chindli. Es neus Bilderbuech für die ganz Chline*. Zürich: Rascher and Cie.
Anonymous. [c. 1910]. *What Is It?* London: Dean's Rag Book.
Anonymous. 1955. *Baby's Things. A Real Cloth Book*. Racine WI: Whitman.
Bravi, S. 2004. *Le livre des bruits*. Paris: L'école des loisirs.
Bruna, D. 1964. *Miffy*. London: Methuen.
Dawson, E. M. [1955]. *The Picture Book for Baby*. London: Sampson Low, Marston & Co.
Drews, J. 2010. *Antons ganze Welt*. Weinheim: Beltz.
Edwards, A. & Schad, H. 1953. *Baby's First Book*. New York NY: Wonder Books.
Eleska, E. 1945. *I Eat*. New York NY: Eleska Books.
Haring, K. 1998. *Ten*. New York NY: Hyperion Books for Children.
Hoban, T. 1973. *Push/pull – empty/full*. New York NY: Macmillan.
Hoban, T. 1986. *Red, Blue, Yellow Shoe*. New York NY: Greenwillow Books.
Isadora, R. 1985. *I See*. New York NY: Greenwillow Books.
Jensen, T. B. & Lund-Hansen, L. 1955. *Trine kan …* Copenhagen: Høst & Sons Forlag.
Klyvare, B. 1964. *Se hvad vi kan! Pegebog for de mindste*. Copenhagen: Gyldendal.
Lundberg, S. 2010. *Sommar*. Stockholm: Alvina.
Munari, B. 2006. *ABC*. San Francisco CA: Chronicle Books (first published 1960).
Nash, A. A. 1959. *My First Picture Book*. London: Juvenile Productions.
Oxenbury, H. 1981. *Playing*. London: Walker Books.
Oxenbury, H. 1981. *Working*. London: Walker Books.
Picthall, C. 2008. *Baby sees farm animals*. Bromley: Picthall & Gunzi.

Schaare, F. R. 1945. *First Picturebook*. New York NY: Hampton.
Snir, M. & Langer, Z. 1984. *In My House* [Hebrew title]. Tel Aviv: Shva.
Steichen Calderone, M. & Steichen, E. 1930. *The First Picture Book. Everyday Things for Babies.* New York NY: Harcourt, Brace and Company.
Steichen Martin, M. & Steichen, E. 1931. *The Second Picture Book.* New York NY: Harcourt, Brace and Company.
Stickland, P. 1986. *Trucks.* Yeovil: Matthew Price.
Weisgard, L. 1953. *My First Picture Book.* New York NY: Grosset & Dunlap.
Williams, Garth. 1955. *Baby's First Book.* New York NY: Golden Press.

References

Apseloff, M. 1987. Books for babies: Learning toys or pre-literature? *Children's Literature Association Quarterly* 12: 63–66.
Barrett, M. 1995. Early lexical development. In *The Handbook of Child Language*, P. Fletcher & B. MacWhinney (eds), 362–392. Oxford: Blackwell.
Bloom, P. 2000. *How Children Learn the Meanings of Words.* Cambridge, Mass.: MIT Press.
Bornstein, M. H. 1975. The qualities of color vision in infancy. *Journal of Experimental Child Psychology* 19: 401–419.
Bornstein, M. H., Kessen, W. & Weiskopf, S. 1976. The categories of hue in infancy. *Science* 191: 201–202.
Bowerman, M. & Levinson, S. (eds). 2001. *Language Acquisition and Conceptual Development.* Cambridge: CUP.
Clark, E. V. 1993. *The Lexicon in Acquisition.* Cambridge: CUP.
Clark, E. V. 1995. Later lexical development and word formation. In *The Handbook of Child Language*, P. Fletcher & B. MacWhinney (eds), 393–412. Oxford: Blackwell.
Deloache, J. M., Strauss, M. & Maynard, J. 1979. Picture perception in infancy. *Infant Behavior and Development* 2: 77–89.
Dromi, E. 1987. *Early Lexical Development.* Cambridge: CUP.
Fassbind-Eigenheer, R. & Fassbind-Eigenheer, B. 2002. *Was sagt der Text? Was zeigt das Bild? Vom Orbis Pictus zum Photobilderbuch. Text und Bild in der historischen Entwicklung des Sachbilderbuches.* Zürich: Schweizerisches Jugendbuchinstitut.
Gelman, S. A. 2006. Early conceptual development. In *Blackwell Handbook of Early Childhood Development*, K. McCartney & D. Philipps (eds), 149–167. Oxford: Blackwell.
Goldsmith, E. 1984. *Research into Illustration.* Cambridge: CUP.
Golinkoff, R. M. & Hirsh-Pasek, K. 2008. How toddlers begin to learn verbs. *Trends in Cognitive Science* 10: 397–403.
Goswami, U. 1998. *Cognition in Children.* London: Psychology Press.
Gressnich, E. & Meibauer, J. 2010. First-person narratives in picturebooks: An inquiry into the acquisition of picturebook competence. In *New Directions in Picturebook Research*, T. Colomer, B. Kümmerling-Meibauer & C. Silva-Díaz (eds), 191–204. New York NY: Routledge.
Jones, R. 1996. *Emerging Patterns of Literacy: A Multidisciplinary Perspective.* London: Routledge.
Kauschke, C. 2000. *Der Erwerb des frühkindlichen Lexikons.* Tübingen: Narr.
Kauschke, C. & Hofmeister, C. 2002. Early lexical development in German: A study on vocabulary growth and vocabulary composition during the second and third year of life. *Journal of Child Language* 29: 735–757.

Koerber, S. 2007. Welche Rolle spielt das Bildersehen des Kindes aus Sicht der Entwicklungspsychologie? In *Neue Impulse der Bilderbuchforschung*, J. Thiele (ed.), 31–47. Baltmannsweiler: Schneider Verlag Hohengehren.

Kress, G. & van Leeuwen, T. 1996. *Reading Images: The Grammar of Visual Design*. London: Routledge.

Kümmerling-Meibauer, B. 2006. Preschool Books. In *The Oxford Encyclopedia of Children's Literature*, Vol. 3, J. Zipes (ed.), 288–291. Oxford: OUP.

Kümmerling-Meibauer, B. & Linsmann, M. (eds). 2009. *Literatur im Laufstall. Bilderbücher für die ganz Kleinen*. Troisdorf: Bilderbuchmuseum Burg Wissem.

Kümmerling-Meibauer, B. & Meibauer, J. 2005. First pictures, early concepts: Early concept books. *The Lion and the Unicorn* 29: 324–347.

Lancaster, L. 2003. Moving into literacy: How it all begins. In *Handbook of Early Childhood Literacy*, N. Hall, J. Larson & J. Marsh (eds), 145–153. London: Sage.

Lewis, D. 2001. *Reading Contemporary Picturebooks: Picturing Text*. London: Routledge Falmer.

Markman, E. 1989. *Categorization and Naming in Children: Problems of Induction*. Cambridge MA: The MIT Press.

Meibauer, J. 1995. Neugebildete *-er*-Derivate im Spracherwerb. Ergebnisse einer Langzeitstudie. *Sprache & Kognition* 14: 138–160.

Meibauer, J. & Rothweiler, M. (eds). 1999. *Das Lexikon im Spracherwerb*. Tübingen: Francke.

Moerk, E. L. 1985. Picture-book reading by mothers and young children and its impact upon language development. *Journal of Pragmatics* 9: 547–566.

Murphy, G. L. 2002. *The Big Book of Concepts*. Cambridge MA: The MIT Press.

Nikolajeva, M. 2003. Verbal and visual literacy: The role of picturebooks in the reading experience of young children. In *Handbook of Early Childhood Literacy*, N. Hall, J. Larson & J. Marsh (eds), 245–248. London: Sage.

Ninio, A. 1983. Joint book reading as a multiple vocabulary acquisition device. *Developmental Psychology* 19: 445–451.

Nodelman, P. 1988. *Words about Pictures. The Narrative Art of Children's Picture Books*. Athens GA: University of Georgia Press.

Rakison, D. H. & Oakes, L. M. (eds). 2003. *Early Category and Concept Development. Making Sense of the Blooming, Buzzing Confusion*. Oxford: OUP.

Snow, C. & Goldfield, B. A. 1983. Turn the page please: Situation specific language acquisition. *Journal of Child Language* 10: 551–569.

Taylor, J. R. 1995. *Linguistic Categorization. Prototypes in Linguistic Theory*. 2nd edn. Oxford: Clarendon Press.

Tucker, N. 1990. *The Child and the Book: A Psychological and Literary Exploration*. Cambridge: CUP.

Wagner, K. R. & Wiese, S. (eds). 1996. *Teilkorpus KATRIN (1;5) im Dortmunder Korpus der spontanen Kindersprache*. Essen: Verlag Die Blaue Eule.

CHAPTER 7

Reading as playing

The cognitive challenge of the wimmelbook

Cornelia Rémi

Wimmelbooks are wordless picturebooks which display a series of panoramas teeming with an immense number of characters and details. They constitute a narrative threshold genre with the potential to accompany children a long way on their path to literacy and to introduce them to different strategies of coping with the world and to telling of stories. In contrast to puzzle or search books, wimmelbooks rely on their readers to find their own way through the rich material they present and do not direct their attention by phrasing explicit search tasks. They allow for manifold reading options and encourage a highly active response from children and adults alike, which rightfully might be described as a form of playing.

Reading ought to be fun and books ought to be loved. Although literature and the act of reading may take many different forms, a frequently recurring term to describe them has been that of playing (Anz 2003: 470f.). But the alleged analogies between play and literature have been criticised as blurry, inconsequent, and confusing, despite their stimulating potential (Matuschek 1998: 1–23; Wilson 1981: 79–84; Wilson 1990: 8–12). The longevity of such discussions suggests that they touch essentials of literary communication, but also fail to grasp them with absolute clarity.

This essay contributes to an analysis of the relation between literature and play by focusing on an area where the use of the term "playing" is indisputable: like many other activities, even literacy begins in and as play, creating intrinsic motivation. Infants and toddlers – children at the beginnings of literacy – are frequently described as the most universal and intense players (Mogel 2008: 9, 16). Although children and adults play differently (Morgenstern 2009: 69), children's playful discovery of literacy might anticipate patterns of adult reading behaviour and therefore contribute to a better understanding of the distinct qualities of fictional texts.

The notion of 'reading as playing' will be explored by analysing a specific genre of wordless picturebooks that has not been covered by literacy research yet: *Wimmelbücher*, 'wimmelbooks', as they are called in the German-speaking countries. Since these books accompany children from their first year of life to elementary school and beyond, they offer valuable insights into the long-term development of literacy competence.

Whereas early concept books focus on single everyday objects isolated from their context, advanced wordless picturebooks of greater visual complexity serve as primers for the development of narrative skills (Arizpe & Styles 2003: 39–52; Jalongo et al. 2002; Hughes 1998: 121–125; Richey and Puckett 1992). Since they encourage intense observation and invite the beholder to create verbal stories about their pictures, such books can be experienced as both extremely challenging and rewarding (Graham 1998: 26–31). Wimmelbooks are a very complex example for such advanced wordless picturebooks.

While books for young children usually are grouped in a progression of different types with increasing difficulty (Nikolajeva & Scott 2001: 6–11), wimmelbooks are hard to place on this scale, since their reception is highly variable and not limited to a specific target age. This hypothesis is based on a six-week online survey conducted in early 2009 among German-speaking parents and other caregivers who had used wimmelbooks to introduce small children to literacy.[1] The 115 participants were asked to define what they considered as a wimmelbook, to assess it and describe their reading experiences. Although this sample is too small to claim a statistically relevant outcome, the results were surprisingly consistent, particularly since most sections of the questionnaire required the participants to phrase their answers in their own words. It is hard to tell, however, inhowfar their social or educational background might have influenced the results, since these data were not collected in the survey.

Asked to determine the appropriate target age for wimmelbooks, a third of the participants considered them suitable for children from one year onward, while another third named 18 months as the lower age threshold, although the publishers usually recommend the books for far older readers. This corresponds to observations the participants sent in about their own children: almost two thirds of them began occupying themselves with wimmelbooks when they were between one year and 18 months of age; 96% of all children described in the survey had their first wimmelbook contact before they turned two. This contact tends to be long-ranging and rarely ends before the children enter school, sometimes even far later. For picturebooks these numbers are remarkable. They indicate that wimmelbooks are a threshold or bridge genre, varied enough to accompany children through many stages of their path to literacy.

These books will be examined in three sections here: the first section introduces key characteristics of the genre, the second derives central challenges and reading options from these features, and the third discusses what readers actually *do* with wimmelbooks.

---

1. I am indebted to Karin Gstöttmayr and a number of other blogging parents for spreading the link to the survey via their weblogs.

Not another puzzle book: General genre characteristics

The German term 'wimmeln' could be translated as 'to teem', or 'to swarm with something' (DWb, 219–221).[2] Hence, a *Wimmelbuch* is a book of a plenitude. Due to its popularity this term has become a sort of quality brand in recent years, so that even books which would not be considered wimmelbooks by most consumers are merchandised with *Wimmel*titles.[3] Such titles suggest an abundance of characters and an inexhaustibly rich source of material, but also a certain degree of disorder and chaos. Ali Mitgutsch is usually credited with having started the genre in the late 1960s (Palluch 1998: 6–8; Schröder & Weber 2005), although there are earlier examples of very similiar books (Müller-Firgau 1955). In Dowhower's typology of wordless picturebooks, the genre most closely related to wimmelbooks are visual game books "that invite the reader to interact with the pictures, find hidden objects, compare changes from one picture to another, match, predict ahead, create stories, or visually play with illusions and transformations on the page" (Dowhower 1997: 61). But wimmelbooks defy a classification as typical 'game books' because they are lacking clear rules or instructions.

Constitutive genre characteristics: The caregivers' definition

Since wimmelbooks have not been the subject of closer scholarly analysis yet, any reasonable attempt at defining the genre must start from its public perception. Their essential characteristics, as named by the participants in the online survey, can be grouped in six categories: (1) the size and material; (2) the amount of text; (3) the graphic style; (4) the subject of the pictures; (5) the book's overall structure; (6) the reading behaviour stimulated by the book.

(1) A wimmelbook is robust, preferably made of cardboard, and large enough to allow for richly detailed illustrations. Most wimmelbooks are printed in quarto or even folio format, so that their massive physical appearance adds a material dimension to the reading experience.

(2) The book does not contain any verbal texts, apart from its cover, the preliminary matter and short texts integrated in the pictures.

2. Mitgutsch disapproves of the term because it reminds him of the similarly sounding 'abwimmeln', 'to get rid of' (Mitgutsch and Heller 2008).

3. Such as search books with accompanying texts (Scholbeck 2004), panoramas of German cities (Rieken 2008), graphic sightseeing guides (Ganther 2008), or mnemonic condensations of biblical stories (Rausch 2005).

(3) Each double-page spread presents a panorama, usually in a top-down perspective without major spatial distortions, drawn in a naively realistic style characterised by clear lines and colours. The pictures are extraordinarily rich in characters and detail, "pluriscenic" landscapes composed of various scenes (Thiele 2000: 59f.).

(4) Many of the situations depicted are familiar to young readers from their own daily life. Several participants in the survey criticised "alleged wimmelbooks" with overly kitschy or fanciful settings, populated by fairy tale characters or teddy bears instead of human beings, and dismissed them as violating what they considered an unwritten rule of the genre.

(5) The different panoramas usually form separate, independent units. Some books, however, connect them to form a continuous narrative.

(6) Wimmelbooks activate readers of all ages, invite many different modes of reception and offer new insights with each reading.

Two comparisons may help to sharpen the genre profile sketched in this general definition: a synchronic look at the related, yet distinct genre of puzzle books and a diachronic look at the tradition of wimmelpictures in western art.

Wimmelbook vs. puzzle book

Readers in the English-speaking world are familiar with search or puzzle books, like Martin Handford's *Wally* or *Waldo* series (Handford 2007); they resemble wimmelbooks in their outward appearance, although their essential concept is a rather different one. While Handford squeezes an overwhelmingly huge mass of tiny characters into each of his pictures, a classical wimmelbook double spread looks far less cramped (see Figure 1). Ali Mitgutsch's pictures are densely crowded as well, but his characters are far larger in relation to the whole. Not only does this make the scene more realistic, it also allows the characters to develop more individual features.

Besides, Mitgutsch's panorama is clearly segmented, which reduces the beholder's confusion: lake, brook and trees serve as visual markers partitioning the picture into smaller units. But most importantly, his picture is not accompanied by any texts – no one is telling you what to do with it. While Handford provides his readers with long lists of search tasks, Mitgutsch offers no such guidance. Therefore his pictures require another reading strategy than Handford's.

For puzzle pictures privilege a hierarchic mode of reception. Their search tasks name a small selection of elements as the beholders' chief cognitive priority, while all the remaining elements are designed as distractors, intended to deviate them from their search mission. Only in a second step can these distractors be

Figure 1. Image from *Mein Wimmel-Bilderbuch: Frühling, Sommer, Herbst und Winter* by Ali Mitgutsch

appreciated as elements of their own right. While puzzle pictures are organized hierarchically, with the search object as their hidden centre, wimmelpictures are remarkably open; search options can be added to them, but they are never central to the pictures themselves. Puzzle pictures may be regarded as wimmelpictures if they can be separated from the instructions surrounding them, but their wimmel qualities might rather contradict their puzzle aptitude than support it.[4]

The wimmel tradition in the history of western art

Reviewers frequently point out that wimmelbooks stand in the tradition of an art form represented most prominently by 16th-century painters Hieronymus Bosch and Pieter Brueghel the Elder, who in their turn refer back to even older examples of composing sceneries teeming with characters. Such works of art provide plenty

4. A growing sense for the distinct character of these book types is suggested by the new edition of a puzzle book which – originally characterised as a "wimmel picturebook" – is now marketed as a "search and wimmel picturebook" (Wandrey 2001 and 2008).

of material for pious contemplation or sophisticated reasoning (Silver 2006: 122, 81f.; Vandenbroeck 2002: 213). Their richness often has theological implications and points to the chaotic state of the world (Silver 2006: 78).

While Bosch impresses the beholder with the fantastic ingenuity of his inventions, Brueghel's 'encyclopaedic' paintings, such as *Children's Games*, appear more realistic, since they comprise recognizable extracts of the contemporary world. Its plenitude, visual structure and realistic style mark *Children's Games* as a prototype for later wimmelpictures and suggest a mode of reception that might be applied to wimmelbooks as well: since there is "no real focal point of the action", we are "thrown into a game of trying to figure out which of the games we want to focus on; in other words, the very act of looking at the painting becomes a game" (Bonn 2006: 35). The disordered complexity of wimmelbooks invites a similarly playful and therefore pleasurable response.

What wimmelbooks have to offer: Possible reading options

When Ali Mitgutsch's first wimmelbook was awarded the prestigious Deutscher Jugendbuchpreis (Mitgutsch 1968) and its two successors were shortlisted for the same prize, the jury emphasized the many possibilities of dealing with their rich material. The following section discusses the elements contributing to this impression and outlines the spectrum of possible reader response to a basic and a more advanced type of wimmelbooks.

Abundance of material

Any attempt at grasping a wimmelpicture exhaustively is doomed to fail, for this would require not only an extensive account of its overall structure and details, but also an explanation how its numerous elements might act together. To phrase a coherent analysis, one is inevitably forced to mix analytic descriptions with mere assumptions about the characters' motivations, thoughts and feelings and the events preceding or following the moment captured in the picture. Moreover, each picture simultaneously presents so many single elements that the number of their possible combinations is immense.

This plenitude reflects the complicated composition of the world in general, which demands certain strategies for coping with its wealth. Learning how to handle the demanding abundance of a wimmelpicture therefore implies learning how to cope with a complex world, and mirrors "the child's fundamental need to make sense of the large, the looming, and the loud in her world by forming manageable units and exploring these strange objects over and over again" (Singer 1994: 9). This means that wimmelbooks can be described as models of the world and vice versa: "For children who cannot read yet, the world resembles a picturebook without text" (Ludwig 2008: 7). They encourage curiosity and support their readers in making the world readable and meaningful (Gelberg 2005: 14).

Perspective

Picturebook readers are not clueless when confronted with textless images. If there is nothing else to guide them, a picture at least exhibits "directed tensions", patterns which draw the beholder's attention to certain details (Nodelman 1988: 125–257). In wimmelpictures, however, such visual instructions are usually rather limited, for their perspective does not privilege a particular part of the picture. It is rather unsophisticated and usually remains constant throughout a book.[5]

Ali Mitgutsch's wimmelbooks show each scene from a point of view high above it, which grants the beholder a seemingly omniscient overview (Hann 1977: 486; Palluch 1998: 4). But despite the elevated standpoint, this overview is more confusing than helpful in gaining access to the picture, because it indicates next to no visual hierarchy.[6] Seeing more therefore does not imply understanding everything, although the bird's eye view seemingly grants the beholder a god-like position: it is impossible to determine what happens inside the characters, what they are thinking or feeling (Nikolajeva & Scott 2001: 118).

But wimmelbooks use other means to suggest that there is something worth exploring behind each face. Some authors for example confront their readers with cross-sections through the rooms of a building (Mitgutsch 1968; Müller-Firgau 1955). Not only does the resulting grid of small cells help to segment the page into meaningful units, it also refers to the potential of such looks behind the facade. For even if the minds of the characters remain closed to our perception, these open house fronts suggest that there is more to be discovered beyond the surface. Combined with such clues, the strangely unsophisticated staging of wimmelbooks turns out to be a deliberate artistic feature supporting their overall visual effect: since the pictures have no clear centre, figuring out what to look at becomes an essential step in the process of exploring them.

5. With only few exceptions, like Suess (2007).

6. This remains true even for those authors who vary Mitgutsch's model, e.g. by adding layers of elements to the foreground, which remind the observer of the picture's depth (Regener 2008).

Challenges

These visual qualities open many reading options. Children and adults might focus on single elements, try to agree upon objects to observe together and establish some way of communicating about them, by pointing and labelling, by asking for particular objects, by explaining their characteristics or by adding acoustic elements: a cow mooing, a running woman breathing heavily. To determine an object of shared interest, the beholders need to structure and segment the page into significant scenes and decide which components deserve further exploration. After the separate elements have been examined in detail, one might also try to establish relations and connections between them.

In an even more advanced step, child and adult may speculate about the stories behind the picture and discuss causes and consequences which are not presented explicitly, but might help to understand the portrayed situation: why do the characters behave like this, and what might be the results of their actions? Such speculations may finally evolve into independent stories about any of the characters, objects or places in each picture. The child is challenged to engage in symbolic play, to juggle with visual and verbal symbols (Singer 1994: 13–15; Largo and Benz 2003: 69f.).

Discovering new details in every encounter with the pictures might also trigger thoughts about one's own perceptual capacity. Why haven't I noticed that squirrel, that car, that gesture before? The readers are constantly encouraged to question their own impressions and former hypotheses about a wimmelpicture because there is simply too much to consider about it. Just like the primary observations and speculations even such critical reflexions may serve as narrative seeds for new stories.

While they provide a treasure of elements that may be combined to stories, classical wimmelpictures do not tell stories themselves and cannot be more than starting points for actual narrative constructions. But a group of more complex wimmelbooks anticipates this narrative activity and adds a temporal dimension, which makes it all the more demanding to analyse the relations within them (Berner 2006a: 27; Berner & Weinkauff 2004: 52f.). Instead of constituting separate entities, the double spreads in these books form a successive narrative.

In some cases, the storyline may appear quite unobtrusive and connect the pictures only loosely, often giving the impression that a simultaneous wimmelscene has been expanded to fill an entire book. The backdrop landscape can be designed as a continuous whole (Baumann 2000), with recurring elements suggesting discreet continuity, like heart-shaped balloons that float through an entire book after a wedding party has released them on the first double spread (Regener 2008). The temporal dimension turns dominant and formative as soon as some characters remain present throughout the book, engaged in a sequence of causally connected events constituting one or several plotlines. Such books introduce their readers to the particular challenges of interpreting a sequence of pictures as a story (Bornens 1990: 194f.; Nodelman 1988: 187).

Multiple narratives I: Thé Tjong-Khing

Thé Tjong-Khing's two *Cake* books centre on the adventures of a diverse group of animals moving through a landscape, tracking down a stolen cake and going out for a picnic. While their movements are rather straight and linear in the first book (Thé 2006), the spatial structure of the second is more astute (Thé 2008): here the backdrop reflects an entire dramatic arc the build-up of tension, the peripety and denouement – and also mirrors the forward and backward movements of a reader working his way through the pages.

The pictures are to be decoded as a sequence of snapshots representing a coherent series of events, always involving the same characters. To understand their connections, the beholders must make sense of the signals encouraging them to combine the separate scenes, and fill the gaps and undefined spaces in and between them (Iser 1994: 283–315). The books stimulate narrative creativity by challenging their readers to contemplate change, predict the outcome of events and form hypotheses about their causes (Jones 1996: 141–188; Whitehead 2004: 111–128). Since they do not offer a "clean" story with distinct main characters and clear plot priorities, the reader first of all must determine what is to be considered as a relevant story element.

Therefore, basic decisions about how to organize one's perceptions become even more important here than in books with separate pictures. To establish a plot thread, one must keep a consistent focus on one particular element and try to follow it throughout the book. While the titles of Thé's books suggest focusing on the eponymous cake, any other element catching one's attention may serve as a starting point as well;[7] but even following just one detail proves difficult and almost inevitably triggers an entire series of follow-up questions, because the movement in the foreground is far from orderly, despite the continuous backdrop. Most characters do not follow linear trajectories, but rather seem to dance across the pages, so that their crossing paths become intricately interwoven. All these

7. It is symptomatic that both the original Dutch and the English title of the first *Cake* book are phrased as explicit search tasks, assigning the book to the puzzle book genre ("Where is the cake?"), while the German publisher chose to replace this question with an exclamation ("The cake is gone!"), which leaves more room for open speculation.

additional factors must be taken into account if one is to reconstruct the logic of a character's progression.

Once you reach the end of the book, you will notice that even seemingly marginal details turn out to be at least as important as your original focus elements; a re-reading is required to appreciate their meaning. You are therefore challenged to expand your focus more and more to explore the intertwining of the numerous narrative branches. Following one plotline, one is permanently tempted to investigate a completely different chain of events intersecting the story arc one is focusing on, and might end up leafing back and forth over and over again. Such investigations can develop into a rhizomatic, poly-directional reading all across the book.

When, for example, the animals in Thé's second *Cake* book return home from their adventurous outing, all their houses have been decorated with colourful happy faces. Skimming back, one will notice that various trees and stones in the neighbourhood have been garnished with similar drawings. After stumbling across the culprit – a little fox –, one might follow the trail of his crayons to Mr. Dog's knapsack, which has been slashed open by another malefactor. This delinquent, a rabbit boy, can be spotted on the cover of book, where he threatens the menacing face printed on the knapsack with his toy sword. He even fights many other opponents throughout the book, but a diligent observer will perceive that all these enemies suddenly vanish in the second half of the story, exposing the monsters of the first half as mere products of the rabbit's imagination. In other words: Thé confronts his audience with a modal narrative, where the visible elements represent an individual perception rather than the bookworld's actual reality (Kress and van Leeuwen 2006: 154–174). The turning point of this story arc is reached when the rabbit boy faces a real opponent – a teenage rabbit bully – and suffers a defeat against him. But even this actual monster is finally outplayed, when all the harassed animal children unite and manage to overcome their previous quarrels. On this and countless other reading paths, the dense texture of Thé's book can be explored in many variations.

Multiple narratives II: Rotraut Susanne Berner

In Rotraut Susanne Berner's books, the potential complexity of the reading process is even higher. Between 2003 and 2008 she has published a series of five wimmelbooks, forming one gigantic picturebook project that has brought the interplay of constancy and variance between wimmelpictures to a new level. Like Thé she presents a panoramic sequence of pictures linked by different plot threads (Berner & Weinkauff 2004: 53). Each of her wimmelbooks, set during the four seasons and during a summer night, follows the same route through the town of Wimmlingen, chronicling the activities of its numerous inhabitants. Since the sequence of locations remains the same throughout the series, Berner's wimmel-pictures can be linked not only horizontally within each book, but also vertically between the books, so that even buildings and places are equipped with stories of their own. While the space remains constant, time is passing both between the books and within each of them: the clockfaces in different parts of the town indicate that each book's plot covers about one hour, while the overall chronology of the series is signalled by evidence like the slowly progressing construction of the kindergarten building. Each book ends with a game and party scene at the lake, which provides a distinctive closure similar to the notorious party scenes ending the *Astérix* albums or the picnics in Thé's *Cake* books.

But before this finale is reached, there is ample room for the characters to interact and become involved in different events. Some of them follow rather steady paths across the pages and are easy to spot, thus granting continuity, while others move from the background to the foreground or vice versa, appear or vanish. In the autumn book, two such connecting elements are the children's lantern procession and a flock of bird crossing the sky (see Figure 2 and 3). Other characters are relocated to more unexpected positions. Just take some of the persons in the foreground, i.e. near the bottom of the first scene. The girl next to the sign post in the centre can be spotted inside the bookshop in the next picture, while the two ladies in the lower right corner have been separated in the marketplace: one is queuing at a sales cart in the background, while the other one is dancing next to the fountain. And the woman and man talking on their mobile phones far away from each other in the first scene turn out to be talking to each other.

Decisive for this density of Berner's fictional world is not just her attention to detail, but the countless cross-references strengthening Wimmlingen's coherence. One prominent example are the advertising posters spread throughout the town, many of them referring to certain scenes by means of iconic representation. Posters announcing events at the cultural centre, for example, show a poet reading from his works (Berner 2004) or a violinist giving a concert (Berner 2003a) in exactly the same poses in which those two characters actually appear on stage. These posters are among the many elements illustrating the delights of literacy in Berner's books. They encourage the beholders to occupy themselves with books and reading: there are shops signs, kiosks selling magazines and newspapers, a bookshop, a public library, and a little girl who is never seen without a book. Reading children may find their own situation reflected in such scenes.

It is the inherent quality of Berner's pictures that invites the beholder to explore them, not any explicit search tasks immediately attached to them. Although Berner supplies her readers with stimuli that might serve as such tasks, these are never presented as imperative challenges, but simply as invitations to explore

Figure 2. Wimmlingen's kindergarten and cultural centre.
Image from *Herbst-Wimmelbuch* by Rotraut Susanne Berner

Figure 3. Wimmlingen's marketplace.
Image from *Herbst-Wimmelbuch* by Rotraut Susanne Berner

certain details a little further. Some of these stimuli are integrated into the pictures themselves, like the already mentioned posters referring to events in the town. When Wimmlingen for example is covered with placards asking for the whereabouts of an escaped parrot (Berner 2005b), the reader is confronted with a search task that is presented to the inhabitants of Wimmlingen as well and thus forms an integral part of the fictional world.

Some other search stimuli are clearly separated from the pictures, but even these elements are far from phrasing explicit search tasks like those of typical puzzle books. Berner gathers a small selection of noteworthy characters and objects on the back covers of her wimmelbooks, each of them accompanied by a brief description, which often specifies a character's thoughts or feelings: "Daniela is looking forward to her piano lesson." Only very few of these comments are phrased as direct questions, and even those refer to narrative connections rather than simply prompting the reader to find a specific element, e.g. "Who has lost this wallet?", "What is the fox doing in the town?"

It is characteristic for the different genre conventions of German and Anglo-American picturebook cultures that the marginal position of these elements was changed considerably in the US edition. *In the Town All Year 'Round* unites the first four Wimmlingen books in one single volume, thus eliminating the chance of a vertical reading (Berner 2008a). More than that, the US version separates the four season wimmelbooks by inserting their original cover illustrations between them. Since the original back covers are placed at the very beginning of each seasonal section, their non-committal search suggestions turn into a preset cognitive requirement, which changes the entire character of the books and their reception process.

Even another element which emphasizes the fundamentally open nature of the books has changed significantly in the US edition: each of the original front covers shows a recurring character in its lower left corner, a mysterious woman in green clothes, whose body transgresses the border between the cover illustration and its frame, namely the vertical colour stripe marking the book's spine. Since she protrudes from the inner world of the book, she might be interpreted as the reader's representative on the border between fiction and reality. In some cases she even appears inside the books and can be spotted in the department store (Berner 2005b) or at the kiosk near the marketplace (Berner 2003a and 2005a). But since she always turns her back towards the observer, her face remains hidden and it is impossible to decide what she is looking at. Thus she guides the readers' attention towards the world of Wimmlingen, but does not instruct them to focus on a specific part of this world. She represents the free and open view at the copiousness of Berner's wimmelpictures. *In the Town All Year 'Round,* however, erases this thought-provoking character from all but one of the inserted seasonal title illustrations, and even in this single case integrates her into the picture instead of having her cross its frame.

While the US edition adapts Berner's series to the puzzle book type and tones down its open nature, her German publisher leaves the readers at liberty to decide for themselves what to focus on and therefore makes a point of separating the wimmelworld from external reading instructions. A series of spin off stories printed in a smaller book format, the Wimmlingen chronicles (*Wimmlinger Geschichten*), presents some examples of how to develop individual stories out of the large wimmelbooks, but simultaneously provides more building bricks for the reader's imagination and thus enhances the overall complexity of the Wimmlingen world. Each of these books highlights one or two particular characters familiar from the main series, picks up motives from the larger-sized books and turns them into independent stories by isolating them from their original crowded surroundings and adding simple rhyming couplets.[8] This furnishes the focused characters with background stories, which in their turn influence the perception of events in the wimmelbooks and invite the readers to invent similar stories even for other characters.

Certainly such additional information is not imperative for enjoying Berner's wimmelbooks. But the crucial point is that they provide their readers with many options without imposing a fixed approach on them. The decision which of the many layers to explore remains entirely that of the individual reader, which makes it easy to adapt the books to each child's developmental status. One may focus on single characters and their immediate proximity or on the increasingly complex texture of their further surroundings, even experiment with various narrative techniques. By exploring different ways of transforming the pictures' simultaneous presence into linear narrative discourse, children can develop a sense of central parameters of storytelling.

Core skills for wimmelbook readers

Despite this broad range of possible reading options, most participants in the wimmelbook survey agreed upon a set of essential skills which are challenged and practised through such books. However, the transition between prerequisites and newly acquired skills is a fluent one: as long as the adult caregiver provides sufficient help and support, already children around one year of age may savour the encounter with wimmelbooks.

The children should be able to sustain a high degree of attentiveness and concentration for some time. They should be patient and persistent enough not to be satisfied with a quick glance, but willing to focus on the pictures for a longer

8. Most of the Wimmlingen chronicles are linked to one or two specific books in the main series, e. g. *Petra* to the autumn and *Niko* to the winter book (Berner 2009a, b, 2005b, 2003a).

period of time and explore their details. It is helpful if their conversational skills are advanced enough to allow for some basic exchange about the book. When confronted with the overabundance of a wimmelpicture, they need to filter and structure its mass of information, to memorize selected observations and to combine them, which requires a basic understanding of causal relations. Finally, the children need imagination and creativity to develop possible explanations around the depicted situations.

Most survey participants presumed that the skills a child might enhance through wimmelbooks do not differ fundamentally from these requirements: perceptivity and patience, attention and concentration; hermeneutic competence, language and communication skills. Language promotion was considered particularly important; wordless picturebooks in general stimulate a high degree of verbal input and are therefore assumed to support or diagnose linguistic development (Whitehead 2004: 80–84; Tuten-Puckett & Richey 1993; Kalender & Klimaszyk 2007: 68; Dowhower 1997: 71f.; Demirkaya & Gültekin 2008: 70).

Playing the book: What readers actually do with wimmelbooks

Listing the challenges of wimmelbooks may seem to ignore their aesthetic qualities and reduce them to mere didactic catalysts. But didactic benefits and aesthetic achievement are closely related in this case, because the creative commitment wimmelbooks seek to inspire is a form of entertainment, as long as it is fuelled by a genuine passion for the process of learning itself (Arizpe & Styles 2003: 224). Reading a wimmelbook thus becomes an intrinsically rewarding act of experiencing oneself and the world.

Immersion and cooperation: The roles of child and adult readers

The descriptions of reading situations submitted for the survey confirm this union of pleasure and usefulness and prove that wimmelbook readers indeed carry out the manifold reading options inherent in the pictures. Some participants even sketched how their children had progressed through different stages of dealing with such books, gradually mastering their challenges. Again, the question asking for this actual reading behaviour was phrased deliberately open, yet aimed at distinctive qualities of wimmelbook readings: “What does your child do with wimmelbooks? Are they treated differently to other books?”

About three quarters of the participants reported such notable differences. They described their children’s occupation with wimmelbooks as longer, more frequent, more active or interactive and more intense than that with other books.

While children below three years of age have been observed to become deeply immersed even in other reading situations (Whitehead 2002), this behaviour seems particularly frequent with wimmelbooks: 90% of all participants noticed that their children not only read wimmelbooks together with adults, but all by themselves as well.

This confirms the programmatic idea that wimmelbooks support children in dealing with books all on their own, independent of expert readers (Wildeisen 2009: 9), and thus help them to develop self-confidence (Sutton-Smith 1994: 146). As Mitgutsch has pointed out, he wants his books to represent a world that children can influence and improve, a world enhancing their imagination and problem-solving skills (Mitgutsch & Heller 2008; Palluch 1998: 6). This might even result in a complete levelling or reversal of the usual hierarchy in reading situations: the otherwise seemingly omnipotent adults turn into mere listeners, while the children become authors and storytellers in their own right (Berner 2006a: 26; Berner & Weinkauff 2004: 53; Fein, Ardila-Rey & Groth 2000: 28; Mol et al. 2008: 8f.). Since neither party can make sense of wimmelpictures spontaneously, an adult reader's cognitive advance is radically reduced, which fuels an intense collaboration between adult and child (Rau 2007: 176; Jones 1996: 117–140; Arizpe & Styles 2003: 223).

But this strong position of the child reader does not disqualify the adult companion, who contributes to enhancing the child's status. Asked to specify their own role while reading wimmelbooks with a child, the survey participants described a wide range of activities: they demonstrate their own love for books (Sonnenschein et al. 2000: 123f.), act as motivators and partners, as helpers or just silent observers. Their role therefore extends far beyond the simple task of pointing at different elements and labelling them. With their descriptions and explanations, they help their young companions to structure the confusing multitude of details. By voicing different characters, they create dramatic exchanges that increase the children's emotional commitment. Moreover, they encourage them to become active analysts and interpreters themselves, to search for certain objects, explore the implications of the scenes and connect the pictures with their own experiences. By listening and reacting to the children's utterances, they affirm the importance of their contributions. All these activities are aimed at diminishing the adult's own role in the wimmelbook reading until the child is in full control of the conversation: "I am allowed to hold the book, but nothing more," as one participant remarked.

Provided that the adult partner possesses some communicative talent (Bus 2003), wimmelbooks form an ideal foundation for the technique of dialogic reading, which involves parents encouraging active responses from their children (Whitehurst et al. 1988: 553; Valdez-Menchaca & Whitehurst 1992). Like other positive interactions between child and caregiver, this may aid cognitive development in general and language development in particular (Mol et al. 2008; O'Reilly & Bornstein 1993: 61) and even affect the child's social competence (Galda & Liang 2007: 133f.).

Double address: Motivating adult readers

Dialogic reading is particularly demanding for the parents in their various roles. Many wimmelbooks offer additional rewards to them for immersing themselves in their world. Since their dual address supports both adults's and children's strengths of perception and organisation, it advances their keen collaboration (Nodelman 2008: 206–214).

Berner addresses her adult readers with small elements of verbal humour and many allusions which tie the world of Wimmlingen to a fictional cosmos outside her books (Berner & Weinkauff 2004: 52). Puns and witty remarks on shop signs, door plates or posters challenge the literate reader to approach the world of words just as playful and open-minded as that of pictures: the dentist, for example, is named "S. Eirak" – which nicely illustrates his professional activity, since this name is a reverse anagram of "Karies", tooth decay.

The bookshop at the marketplace is a centre of intertextual references in all five Wimmlingen volumes. Its owner, Armin, is obviously an affectionate portrayal of Berner's husband Armin Abmeier, a learned bookseller himself. Already in her very first wimmelbook (Berner 2003a), the shop window provides surprising intertextual insights, since all the books displayed there are actually existing titles (Bauer 2003; Jacoby & Berner 1999; Berner 2001, 2003b).[9] Motives from one of these, Berner's own *Apfel, Nuss und Schneeballschlacht*, are even quoted twice on the first double spread, in the shape of a poster and a toy polar bear in a nursery: the book eradiates a fascination that extends into Wimmlingen's reality. Even the border between this reality and the reader's own extratextual world is blurred, for the woman leaving the bookshop is holding none other than the winter book itself, the book containing this scene.

Several other examples of such mise-en-abyme interrupt the aesthetic illusion and remind us of Wimmlingen's fictional status. In the spring book, the book itself is on display at the bookshop, while the nursery on the first double spread now features a poster of the winter book's cover (Berner 2004). Even the summer book is depicted inside the book itself and combined with other familiar covers

9. Many of the featured illustrators are personal acquaintances of Berner's, like Bauer, Heidelbach, Erlbruch, Buchholz, Scheffler, or Könnecke (cf. their contributions in Abmeier 2008).

in the bookshop's window (Berner 2005a; Könnecke 2004; Donaldson & Scheffler 2004), similar to the night book (Berner 2008b). Only in the autumn book is the book's own cover missing from the shop display (which shows Andersen 2004 and a detail from Berner 2006b), but instead this book continues another elaborate thread of mise-en-abyme. For the final double spread of the summer book had shown a painter, capturing the whole party scene at the lake on his canvas. In the autumn book his painting resurfaces on the wall of Dr. Eirak's dental practice (Berner 2005a, b). These intricate connections invite the beholder to examine Wimmlingen's fictional status more closely and wonder about how books may mirror and shape our worldview.

Intertextual allusions are not limited to reproductions of book covers; some of them disrupt that frame and merge into the Wimmlingen world, which might spawn reflections about how fictional experiences shape our reality. In the autumn book, a poster illustrating the fable "The Fox and the Raven" (Phaedrus 2006: I.13) turns real when a raven steals a bit of cheese in the marketplace and is then confronted by a fox (Berner 2005b). Earlier on both animals are shown following a flock of wild geese, lead by one single white bird – a clear reference to several animal characters from Selma Lagerlöf's *Nils Holgersson*: Smirre the fox, Bataki the raven and Mårten Goosey-Gander. The latter makes another appearance on a poster in the subsequent night book, including the minute Nils on his back (Berner 2008b). The characters are flexibly changing their affiliation to different fictional worlds, sliding from Phaedrus to Lagerlöf to Berner, and thus illustrate how all parts of Wimmlingen can serve as poetic building blocks at the reader's own command.

The intertextual fabric is densest in the night book, the final volume of the series, which is littered with references to night-themed children's classics (Berner 2008b), ranging from the single book in the nursery on the first double spread (Bassewitz & Baluschek 1915) to the bookshop's broad selection (Rathmann 1994; Michels & Michl 1985; Berner 2008b; Kopisch & Heidelbach 2007). An exhibition of "night pictures" at the cultural centre even offers looks *into* some books (Donaldson 2004; Nöstlinger & Heidelbach 1993; Sendak 1963 and 1970; Buchholz 1993), while the library one floor below is holding a reading night for the children of Wimmlingen and has arranged an additional assortment of relevant books on its shelves (Storm & Pantner 2002; Berner 2001; Bauer & Kantelhardt 2007; Erlbruch 1999). This implies an instruction how to handle the vast amount of references: the night book offers nothing less than an expanded version of the exhibition at the cultural centre and the reading night at the library, a visual encyclopaedia of night books for children. One may delight in the collection of familiar covers and feel encouraged to get back to them, or follow the book's recommendations when stumbling across still unknown books in a library or a bookshop. The massive presence of other books within just the night book is a gesture of approval, but also points to the close relation of artistic invention and fiction to nighttime, the time of dreams, which opens a space for philosophical reflections extending far beyond the scope of a single wimmelbook. Adult readers may therefore feel entertained on many additional levels, apart from enjoying how children reacts to Berner's wimmelbooks; this ensures their commitment to the reading situation.

Conclusion: Playfulness and the joy of reading

Despite their vastly different perspectives, children and adults can act as equally motivated partners when reading wimmelbooks together, because these books offer many "opportunities for playing", as Berner has phrased it (Berner & Weinkauff 2004: 53). Her evaluation echoes that of scholars who have described children's early book encounters in general as essentially playful experiences (Whitehead 2004: 133–136). This close relationship between play and literacy development is frequently emphasized in literacy research (Roskos and Christie 2007; Whitehead 2002: 286), though seldom examined critically (Sutton-Smith 1997: 38–51, 123–125).

When literature is to be related to playing, it is usually described as a 'game' (Wilson 1990; Suits 1985), a term that represents a narrower concept than 'play' and refers to game theories modelling strategic social interaction in the behavioural sciences (Gintis 2009: 48). But applying their strict game concepts to literature is problematic (Wilson 1990: 83–88, 98f.). Even the broad definition that "playing a game is the voluntary attempt to overcome unnecessary obstacles" (Suits 2005: 55) fails to grasp the essence of wimmelbook readings, as it is hard to define a goal behind them that could be blocked by such obstacles. My survey suggests that wimmelbook readings are experienced less as an orderly structured activity than as a manifestation of spontaneous, unstructured playfulness (Caillois 1958: 52–62), which might confirm a fundamental difference in the playing behaviour of adults and children: "whereas children play, adults play games" (Morgenstern 2009: 67).

Playing is an intrinsically rewarding activity (Suits 2005: 149), which absorbs its player completely without any apparent material payoff. As a deeply satisfying mental state, play transforms reality into a play world, where the inner imagination outrules outer circumstances (Olofsson 1992: 31–33). Children's play in particular creates such a reality of its own, which remains in a state of permanent change, since the focus and aim of children's play behaviour may fluctuate continuously (Mogel 2008: 11, 235).

Due to the dynamic nature of such play worlds, playing can be interpreted as a cognitive training mode supporting the emergence of adaptive variability (Sutton-Smith 1997: 217–231; VanderVen 2006: 405–407): players develop a vast repertoire of behaviours, which help them to handle the contingencies of life. In play, behavioural sequences are decoupled from their immediately vital functions and recombined in other contexts, to help the human brain to organise itself in the best way possible (Tooby & Cosmides 2001: 13–17). Our fascination with works of fiction can be interpreted as a motivational system rewarding such adaptive training (Tooby & Cosmides 2001: 19f.); by constructing play worlds, we reassure ourselves that our inborn patterns of cognitive processing can master the chaos of the actual world (Eibl 2009: 20f.). Since wimmelbooks comprehend a far larger world sample than most other picturebooks, they provide children with lots of material for playful experiments with such fictional world constructions. Their plenitude supports the incessant dynamics and ever shifting focus of playing children and encourages divergent thinking (Singer 1994: 22–26; Pepler 1982: 75). By experimenting with them, their young readers gain competence in facing both the actual world and its fictional counterparts.

It is not only the diversity of wimmelbooks that invites their readers to play, but also their portrayals of playing characters; entire wimmelbooks have been dedicated to the theme of playing (Scherbarth 1974; Mitgutsch 1983). This may inspire the beholders to drop the book and recreate the playful situations in immediate physical action (Nodelman 2008: 190–198), but also to translate the depicted physical activites into mental commitment and understand them as a reflection of their own reading behaviour. Just as the characters immerse themselves into their play, wimmelbook readers immerse themselves into the book world for sheer pleasure – they practice "ludic reading" (Nell 1988: 7–10, 256–266). The numerous representations of play situations in wimmelbooks strengthen this play experience and support the formation of motivational loops, which perpetuate the activation circle of playing (Heckhausen 1964).

Reading a wimmelbook can therefore turn into a play fuelled by the idea of discovering new ways of playing (Kafai 2006: 38). The readers' intense and durable relation to these books also suggests that reading wimmelbooks is an "open game", lacking a final goal that might end the game when achieved (Suits 2005: 122–124): the challenge is to prolongate the book experience and create a potentially endless, joyful reading activity from the limited resources of one book. Readers who master this challenge are ready to conquer other literary playgrounds as well – and prepared to motivate themselves for all the other book challenges expecting them.

Children's books cited

Andersen, H. C. 2004. *Märchen*. Translated by Albrecht Leonhardt, with illustrations by Nikolaus Heidelbach. Weinheim: Beltz und Gelberg.

Bassewitz, G. von & Baluschek, H. 1915. *Peterchens Mondfahrt*. Berlin-Grunewald: Klemm.

Bauer, J. & Kantelhardt, A. 2007. *Es war eine dunkle und stürmische Nacht*. 2001. Hildesheim: Gerstenberg.

Bauer, J. (ed.). 2003. *Ich sitze hier im Abendlicht: Briefe*. Hildesheim: Gerstenberg.

Baumann, S. 2000. *Das große Wimmelbilderbuch. Durch Stadt und Land*. Würzburg: Arena.

Berner, R. S. (ed.). 2001. *Apfel, Nuss und Schneeballschlacht: Das große Winter-Weihnachtsbuch*. Hildesheim: Gerstenberg.

Berner, R. S. 2001. *Gute Nacht, Karlchen*. München: Hanser.

Berner, R. S. 2003a. *Winter-Wimmelbuch*. Hildesheim: Gerstenberg.

Berner, R. S. 2003b. *Karlchen-Geschichten*. München: Hanser.

Berner, R. S. 2004. *Frühlings-Wimmelbuch*. Hildesheim: Gerstenberg.

Berner, R. S. 2005a. *Sommer-Wimmelbuch*. Hildesheim: Gerstenberg.

Berner, R. S. 2005b. *Herbst-Wimmelbuch*. Hildesheim: Gerstenberg.

Berner, R. S. 2006a. "Die Herrscherin der Wimmelwelt." *1000 und 1 Buch* 22.1: 26f.

Berner, R. S. 2006b. *Karlchen vor, noch ein Tor!* München: Hanser.

Berner, R. S. 2008a. *In the Town All Year 'Round*. San Francisco CA: Chronicle Books.

Berner, R. S. 2008b. *Nacht-Wimmelbuch*. Hildesheim: Gerstenberg.

Berner, R. S. 2009a. *Petra* [Wimmlinger Geschichten]. Hildesheim: Gerstenberg.

Berner, R. S. 2009b. *Niko* [Wimmlinger Geschichten]. Hildesheim: Gerstenberg.

Buchholz, Q. 1993. *Schlaf gut, kleiner Bär*. Aarau: Sauerländer.

Donaldson, J. & Scheffler, A. 2004. *The Gruffalo's Child*. London: Macmillan Children's.

Erlbruch, W. 1999. *Nachts*. Wuppertal: Hammer.

Ganther, A. 2008. *Romantischer Rhein: Rhein – Mosel – Lahn – Nahe* [Bachems Wimmelbilder]. Köln: Bachem.

Handford, M. 2007. *Where's Wally?* 1987. London: Walker.

Jacoby, E. (ed.) & Berner, R. S. 1999. *Dunkel war's, der Mond schien helle: Verse, Reime und Gedichte*. Hildesheim: Gerstenberg.

Könnecke, O. 2004. *Anton und die Mädchen*. München: Hanser.

Kopisch, A. & Heidelbach, N. 2007. *Die Heinzelmännchen von Köln*. Köln: Emons.

Lagerlöf, S. 1906–1907. *Nils Holgerssons underbara resa genom Sverige*, 2 Vols. Stockholm: Bonniers.

Michels, T. & Michl, R. 1985. *Es klopft bei Wanja in der Nacht*. München: Ellermann.

Mitgutsch, A. 1968. *Rundherum in meiner Stadt*. Ravensburg: Otto Maier.

Mitgutsch, A. 1983. *Wir spielen Abenteuer. Mit Anregungen für Eltern & alle die fröhliche Kinder mögen*. Ravensburg: Otto Maier.

Mitgutsch, A. 2007. *Mein Wimmelbilderbuch. Frühling, Sommer, Herbst und Winter*. Ravensburg: Ravensburger Buchverlag Otto Maier.

Müller-Firgau, S. 1955. *Benjamins Bilderbuch*. Freiburg: Herder.

Nöstlinger, C. & Heidelbach, N. 1993. *Der neue Pinocchio*. Weinheim: Beltz (originally published in 1988).

Rathmann, P. 1994. *Good Night Gorilla*. New York NY: Putnam.

Rausch, S. 2005. *Das Bibel-Wimmelbuch*. Hamburg: Sankt Ansgar.

Regener, O. 2008. *Wir reisen durch das ganze Land. Mein Wimmelbilderbuch.* München: cbj.
Rieken, A. 2008. *Wer schnarcht da hinterm Roland?* Bremen: Schünemann.
Scherbarth, E. 1974. *Komm heraus und spiel mit uns,* 4th edn. Ravensburg: Otto Maier.
Scholbeck, S. 2004. *Wo steckst du, Mäxchen?* 2nd edn. Würzburg: Arena/Edition Bücherbär.
Sendak, M. 1963. *Where the Wild Things are.* New York NY: Harper & Row.
Sendak, M. 1970. *In the Night Kitchen.* New York NY: Harper & Row.
Storm, T. & Pautner, N. 2002. *Der kleine Häwelmann.* Bindlach: Gondolino.
Suess, A. 2007. *Weihnachts-Wimmelbuch.* Köln: Schwager & Steinlein.
Thé Tjong-Khing. 2006. *Die Torte ist weg! Eine spannende Verfolgungsjagd.* Frankfurt am Main: Moritz (Originally published as *Waar is de taart?* Tielt: Lannoo, 2004).
Thé Tjong-Khing. 2008. *Picknick mit Torte.* Frankfurt am Main: Moritz (Originally published as *Picknick met taart.* Tielt: Lannoo, 2005).
Wandrey, G. 2001. *Folge der Spur … durch die Stadt: Ein Wimmelbilderbuch.* Esslingen: Esslinger.
Wandrey, G. 2008. *Folge der Spur … durch die Stadt: Ein Such- und Wimmelbilderbuch.* Esslingen: Esslinger.

References

Abmeier, A. (ed.). 2008. *Alphabet & Zeichenstift. Die Bilderwelt von Rotraut Susanne Berner.* München: Hanser.
Anz, T. 2003. Spiel. In *Reallexikon der deutschen Literaturwissenschaft: Neubearbeitung des Reallexikons der deutschen Literaturgeschichte,* Vol. 3, J.-D. Müller, W. Oesterreicher & F. Vollhardt (eds), 469–472. Berlin: de Gruyter.
Arizpe, E. & Styles, M. 2003. *Children Reading Pictures: Interpreting Visual Texts.* London: Routledge Falmer.
Berner, R. S. & Weinkauff, G. 2004. Geheimnisse in Bildern und Texten. Kinderliteratur im Gespräch. Zu Gast: Rotraut Susanne Berner. *Lesezeichen. Mitteilungen des Lesezentrums an der Pädagogischen Hochschule Heidelberg* 15: 25–56.
Bonn, R. L. 2006. *Painting Life. The Art of Pieter Bruegel, the Elder.* New York NY: Chaucer Press.
Bornens, M.-T. 1990. Problems brought about by 'reading' a sequence of pictures. *Journal of Experimental Child Psychology* 49: 189–226.
Bus, A. G. 2003. Joint caregiver-child storybook reading. A route to literacy development. In *Handbook of Early Literacy Research,* S. B. Neuman & D. K. Dickinson (eds), 179–191. New York NY: Guilford Press.
Caillois, R. 1958. *Les jeux et les hommes (Le masque et le vertige),* 3rd edn. Paris: Gallimard.
Demirkaya, S. & Gültekin, N. 2008. Die Begleitstudie der Bielefelder vorschulischen Sprachfördermaßnahme. In *Auf neuen Wegen. Deutsch als Fremdsprache in Forschung und Praxis. 35. Jahrestagung des Fachverbands Deutsch als Fremdsprache an der Freien Universität Berlin 2007,* C. Chlosta, G. Leder & B. Krischer (eds), 65–82. Göttingen: Universitätsverlag.
Dowhower, S. 1997. Wordless books: Promise and possibilities, a genre come of age. *Yearbook of the American Reading Forum* 17: 57–79.
[DWb] *Deutsches Wörterbuch von Jacob und Wilhelm Grimm,* Vol. 30. 1999. Fotomechanischer Nachdruck der Erstausgabe 1854–1984. München: Deutscher Taschenbuch Verlag.
Eibl, K. 2009. Vom Ursprung der Kultur im Spiel. Ein evolutionsbiologischer Vorgang. In *Literatur als Spiel: Evolutionsbiologische, ästhetische und pädagogische Konzepte,* T. Anz & H. Kaulen (eds), 11–25. Berlin: de Gruyter.

Fein, G. F., Ardila-Rey, A. A. & Groth, L. A. 2000. The narrative connection: Stories and literacy. In *Play and Literacy in Early Childhood. Research from Multiple Perspectives*, K. A. Roskos & J. F. Christie (eds), 27–43. Mahwah NJ: Lawrence Erlbaum Associates.

Galda, L. & Liang, L. A. 2007. Reading aloud with young children. In *Literacy for the New Millenium*, Vol. 1: *Early Literacy*, B. J. Guzzetti (ed.), 129–140. Westport: Praeger.

Gelberg, H.-J. 2005. Die Welt ist voller Geschichten, man muss sie nur erzählen. In *Ali Mitgutsch. Ein Chronist der Welt im Kleinen. 12.6.2005 bis 11.9.2005 Museum Burg Wissem, 23.9.2005 bis 30.10.2005 Internationale Jugendbibliothek*, M. Linsmann & B. Scharioth (eds), 10–16. Troisdorf, München: Bilderbuchmuseum Burg Wissem; Internationale Jugendbibliothek.

Gintis, H. 2009. *The Bounds of Reason: Game Theory and the Unification of the Behavioral Sciences*. Princeton NJ: Princeton University Press.

Graham, J. 1998. Turning the visual into the verbal: Children reading wordless books. In *What's in the Picture? Responding to Illustrations in Picture Books*, J. Evans (ed.), 25–43. London: Chapman.

Hann, U. Ali Mitgutsch. 1977. In *Lexikon der Kinder- und Jugendliteratur. Personen-, Länder- und Sachartikel zu Geschichte und Gegenwart der Kinder- und Jugendliteratur*, Vol. 2, K. Doderer (ed.), 486–488. Basel: Beltz.

Heckhausen, H. 1964. Entwurf einer Psychologie des Spielens. *Psychologische Forschung* 27(3): 225–243.

Hughes, P. 1998. Exploring visual literacy across the curriculum. In *What's in the Picture? Responding to Illustrations in Picture Books*, J. Evans (ed.), 115–131. London: Chapman.

Iser, W. 1994. Der Akt des Lesens. Theorie ästhetischer Wirkung, 4th edn. München: Fink.

Jalongo, M. R., Dragich, D., Conrad, N. K. & Zhang, A. 2002. Using wordless picture books to support emergent literacy. *Early Childhood Education Journal* 29(3): 167–177.

Jones, R. 1996. *Emerging Patterns of Literacy. A multidisciplinary perspective*. London: Routledge.

Kafai, Y. B. 2006. Playing and making games for learning. Instructionist and constructionist perspectives for game studies. *Games and Culture* 1(1): 36–40.

Kalender, S. & Klimaszyk, P. 2007. *Schritte international 5. Lehrerhandbuch. Deutsch als Fremdsprache*. Ismaning: Hueber.

Kress, G. & van Leeuwen, T. 2006. *Reading Images: The Grammar of Visual Design*, 2nd edn. London: Routledge.

Largo, R. H. & Benz, C. 2003. Spielend lernen. In *Spiel und Kreativität in der frühen Kindheit*, M. Papoušek & A. von Gontard (eds), 56–75. Stuttgart: Pfeiffer bei Klett-Cotta.

Ludwig, E. 2008. Die Bernerin. *Bulletin Jugend & Literatur* 39(11): 6–8.

Matuschek, S. 1998. *Literarische Spieltheorie: Von Petrarca bis zu den Brüdern Schlegel*. Heidelberg: Winter.

Mitgutsch, A. & Heller, U. 2008. Ali Mitgutsch. Er lässt's in seinen Kinderbüchern wimmeln. *Eins zu Eins. Der Talk*. Bayerischer Rundfunk, Bayern 2 Radio, Munich, July 3.

Mogel, H. 2008. *Psychologie des Kinderspiels: Von den frühesten Spielen bis zum Computerspiel*. 3rd revised edn. Heidelberg: Springer.

Mol, S. E., Bus, A.G., de Jong, M. T. & Smeets, D. J. H. 2008. Added value of dialogic parent-child book readings. A meta-analysis. *Early Education and Development* 19(1): 7–26.

Morgenstern, J. 2009. *Playing with Books: A Study of the Reader as Child*. Jefferson NC: McFarland.

Nell, V. 1988. *Lost in a Book: The Psychology of Reading for Pleasure*. New Haven CT: Yale University Press.

Nikolajeva, M. & Scott, C. 2001. *How Picturebooks Work*. New York NY: Garland.

Nodelman, P. 1988. *Words about Pictures. The Narrative Art of Children's Picture Books*. Athens GA: The University of Georgia Press.

Nodelman, P. 2008. *The Hidden Adult. Defining Children's Literature*. Baltimore MD: The Johns Hopkins University Press.

Olofsson, B. Knutsdotter. 1992. Lek för livet. In *Leka för livet*, H. Medelius (ed.), 28–57. Stockholm: Nordiska museet.

O'Reilly, A. W. & Bornstein, M. H. 1993. Caregiver-child interaction in play. In *The Role of Play in the Development of Thought*, M. H. Bornstein & A. W. O'Reilly (eds), 55–66. San Francisco CA: Jossey-Bass.

Palluch, A. 1998. Ali Mitgutsch. In *Kinder- und Jugendliteratur. Ein Lexikon*, Teil 2: *Illustratoren. Begründet von Alfred Clemens Baumgärtner und Heinrich Pleticha*, K. Franz, G. Lange & F.-J. Payrhuber (eds), 5th suppl. Feb. 1998. Meitingen: Corian, 1995-. Loose-leaf collection.

Pepler, D. J. 1982. Play and divergent thinking. In *The Play of Children: Current Theory and Research*, D. J. Pepler & K. H. Rubin (eds), 64–78. Basel: Karger.

Phaedrus. 2006. *Liber Fabularum. Fabelbuch*, transl. F. F. Rückert & O. Schönberger, ed. by O. Schönberger. Stuttgart: Reclam.

Rau, M. L. 2007. *Literacy: Vom ersten Bilderbuch zum Erzählen, Lesen und Schreiben*. Bern: Haupt.

Richey, V. H. & Puckett, K. E. 1992. *Wordless/Almost Wordless Picture Books: A Guide*. Englewood: Libraries Unlimited.

Roskos, K. & Christie, J. 2007. Play and early literacy in these times. In *Early Literacy*, B. J. Guzzetti (ed.), 201–211. Westport: Praeger.

Schröder, G. & Weber, J. 2005. Auswahlbibliographie. In *Ali Mitgutsch. Ein Chronist der Welt im Kleinen. 12.6.2005 bis 11.9.2005 Museum Burg Wissem, 23.9.2005 bis 30.10.2005 Internationale Jugendbibliothek*, M. Linsmann & B. Scharioth (eds), 30–39. Troisdorf, München: Bilderbuchmuseum Burg Wissem, Internationale Jugendbibliothek.

Silver, L. 2006. *Hieronymus Bosch*, Transl. I. Hacker-Klier. München: Hirmer.

Singer, J. L. 1994. Imagination play and adaptive development. In *Toys, Play, and Child Development*, J. H. Goldstein (ed.), 6–26. Cambridge: CUP.

Sonnenschein, S., Baker, L., Serpell, R. & Schmidt, D. 2000. Reading is a source of entertainment: The importance of the home perspective for children's literacy development. In *Play and Literacy in Early Childhood. Research from Multiple Perspectives*, K. A. Roskos & J. F. Christie (eds), 107–124. Mahwah NJ: Lawrence Erlbaum Associates.

Suits, B. 1985. The detective story: A case study of games in literature. *Canadian Review of Comparative Literature* 12: 200–219.

Suits, B. 2005. *The Grasshopper: Games, Life and Utopia*. Peterborough: Broadview. (Originally published by the U of Toronto P, 1978).

Sutton-Smith, B. 1994. Does play prepare the future? In *Toys, Play, and Child Development*, J. H. Goldstein (ed.), 130–146. Cambridge: CUP.

Sutton-Smith, B. 1997. *The Ambiguity of Play*. Cambridge MA: Harvard University Press.

Thiele, J. 2000. *Das Bilderbuch. Ästhetik – Theorie – Analyse – Didaktik – Rezeption*. Oldenburg: Isensee.

Tooby, J. & Cosmides, L. 2001. Does beauty build adapted minds? Towards an evolutionary theory of aesthetics, fiction and the arts. *SubStance: A Review of Theory and Literary Criticism* 30(1): 6–27.

Tuten-Puckett, K. E. & Richey, V. H. 1993. *Using Wordless Picture Books: Authors and Activities*. Englewood CO: Teacher Ideas Press.

Valdez-Menchaca, M. C. & Whitehurst, G. J. 1992. Accelerating language development through picture book reading: A systematic extension to Mexican day care. *Developmental Psychology* 28(6): 1106–1114.

Vandenbroeck, P. 2002. *Jheronimus Bosch: De verlossing van de wereld.* Gent: Ludion.

VanderVen, K. 2006. Attaining the protean self in a rapidly changing world: Understanding chaos through play. In *Play from Birth to Twelve: Contexts, Perspectives, and Meanings,* 2nd edn, D. Pronin Fromberg & D. Bergen (eds), 405–415. London: Routledge.

Whitehead, M. R. 2002. Dylan's routes to literacy. The first three years with picture books. *Journal of Early Childhood Literacy* 2(3): 269–289.

Whitehead, M. R. 2004. *Language and Literacy in the Early Years,* 3rd edn. Thousand Oaks CA: Sage.

Whitehurst, G. J., Falco, F. L., Lonigan, C. J., Fischel, J. E., DeBaryshe, B. D., Valdez-Menchaca, M. C. & Caulfield M. 1988. Accelerating language development through picture book reading. *Developmental Psychology* 24(4): 552–559.

Wildeisen, S. 2009. Am Anfang war das Bild. *Bulletin Jugend & Literatur* 40(2): 7–9.

Wilson, R. R. 1981. Three prolusions: Toward a game model in literary theory. *Canadian Review of Comparative Literature* 8: 79–92.

Wilson, R. R. 1990. *In Palamedes' Shadow: Explorations in Play, Game, & Narrative Theory.* Boston MA: Northeastern University Press.

CHAPTER 8

Metaphors in picturebooks from 0 to 3

Marie Luise Rau

The study focuses on metaphorical uses in a wide range of picturebooks for children younger than four and links them to scientific findings in cognitive psychology and language acquisition. Prototypical situations and familiar grounding make it possible for children to form (rough) concepts of abstract notions otherwise difficult to comprehend, e.g., IMAGINATION, ANGER, FRIENDSHIP, NATURE, DISCRIMINATION. Conceptual metaphor theory is useful for this multimodal approach and allows for the role of metaphors as vehicles for knowledge acquisition. The relationship between pictorial and textual metaphors and their interplay varies from close correspondence between pictures and words to a (much) greater weight in the pictures. These picturebooks introduce young children to non-literal language and will support the process of acquiring comparative structures.

Overview

From reading to preschoolers and research we know that 4- and 5-year-olds do not only comprehend pictorial metaphors, but are even capable of explaining or reasoning about them and that particularly younger children feel encouraged to use metaphorical language when talking about picturebooks (Arizpe & Styles 2003; Kiefer 1995: 29–32). Such observations raise two questions: firstly, what kind of pictorial and linguistic metaphors do we find in children's books for the age group younger than four years? Secondly, what do we know from research, experimental and naturalistic data, about metaphor production and comprehension in particular in this age group and how do these findings tie in with picturebooks for very young children?

Exploring metaphor capacities at this age level poses problems, although some learning process can be expected from early on. Traces of metaphoric abilities are observed with 3- to 4-week-old infants, who spontaneously make *cross-modal* matches of intensity between light stimuli followed by sound stimuli and are later on capable of perceiving links between dotted lines and discontinuous sounds (Lewkowicz & Turkewitz 1980; Wagner et al. 1981; Marks & Bornstein 1987).

Research in cognitive sciences has given new insight into the role of metaphor in everyday speech. Relevant results from cognitive psychology will be related to picturebooks to prove close correspondences. In terms of language acquisition metaphors must be distinguished from misused words, overextension and simple renaming in pretend play in early speech data. Starting point for our analysis is the second half of the second year (ca. 1;9) for three main reasons: First, by then children have learned the symbolic function of words and their vocabulary is growing rapidly. Second, pretend play is developing, and third, learning how to read images is in full progress. There is evidence of increasing literary experience because children begin to identify with book characters and to act them out at the age of two and a half years or a little later. Words and phrases from book reading pervade their language quite suddenly and influence storytelling (Lowe 2007: 11, 137ff; Wolf & Heath 1992, passim). At the same age picture drawing develops. Young children are very creative and versatile in naming and making inferences from visual images.

They are sensitive to other perspectives and – as tests show – even two-year-olds have some idea that the painter's intent is relevant to how a picture is named and this idea can be swayed by intentional cues (cf. Bloom 2000: 183). They draw what they *know* rather than what they *see.* When asked to draw a man, Aidan aged two and a half years (2;7) starts with a circular scribble and adds three other spirally scribbles overlapping the first, calling them Mummy, Daddy, and Angela (Cox 1992: 19).

Research on metaphor competence

Since the 1920s up to the 1970s Piaget's concept of metaphor had dominated cognitive psychology. As he made metaphor comprehension dependent on the verbal explanation of proverbs, he did not find evidence of metaphoric competence until children were 9 years and older (1968/1972: 168ff). In the 1970s Ellen Winner analysed the tapescript data from a longitudinal study of the child Adam from age 2;3 to 4;10.15. She found that the majority of unconventional word uses proved to be metaphors, but later ruled out perceptual metaphors in Adam's early utterances at the age of two and three years as cases of *undifferentiated similarities* and made metaphorical use dependent on "evidence that the child knows the appropriate, literal name for the metaphorically named object" (1988: 101, 92). This seems at least controversial when we look at the following examples, where we can identify metaphorical use although we do not expect the child to know the literal name of the object: a 26-month-old child pointed to a yellow plastic baseball bat, and running up to one of his parents exclaimed with a look of delight: "Corn! Corn!" Another called a folded crisp a "cowboy hat" and a 15-month-old looking at his big toe sticking out of a hole in his sock pointed to it and said, with a laugh, "Turtle" (Winner et al. 1979: 33).

With experimental tasks becoming less demanding than Piaget's, the age for metaphor competence was lowered, although results are still extremely experiment-related and are more likely to underestimate than overestimate young children's abilities. Whenever three-year-olds were included in the tests and a lack of metaphor competence was verified, the experimental design was called into question, in the 1970s as well as in recent studies (cf. Winner et al. 1976; Özcaliskan 2005). One act-out experiment suggests that embedding metaphor in stories scaffolds comprehension: When children were asked to enact a sentence containing a metaphor at the end of a story, a predictable ending of a story made the task easier for them than an unpredictable ending (Winner 1988: 52).

Distinction of metaphor from anomalous use and overextensions

Research on metaphor capacity also involves the difficulty of distinguishing metaphors from misused words, i.e., anomalies and overextensions. Anomalous use, e.g., moon for "piano", is relatively easy to identify. Experiments show that even 3-year-olds prefer metaphorical to anomalous use, e.g., "a river is a snake" to "a river is a cat" (Vosniadou & Ortony 1983; similarly Winner et al. 1980). Simple renamings like calling a block a "cup" or a banana a "telephone" in pretend play do not range under metaphorical use (Vosniadou 1987).

The distinction between overextension and metaphorical use, however, can often be a matter of controversial interpretation, because it depends on the observer's familiarity with the child's lexicon, knowledge of the context and the affective components involved. Overextensions appear most commonly in children's speech from about age 1;6 to 2;6. The child overextends a word like "ball" to refer to other round objects like doorknobs, lamps, pieces of soap, apples and oranges. Overextensions are most often based on similarity of shape, but also on one of movement, sound, taste, size, or texture, like "candy" for cherries and just anything sweet, or "sizzo" for scissors and any other metal object. Some overextensions may last one day, others weeks and months. Eve Clark gives two explanations: either children do not know the difference between a doorknob and a ball, or they resort to the next best word in their lexicon for communicative reasons (Clark 2003: 88). By contrast, Gunther Kress insists that this should not be seen as an issue of lexical availability. A child using "*heavy* hill" instead of "*steep* hill" expresses what is the critical aspect to him at that moment (1997: 94f). Interestingly, Virginia Lowe discovers overextension in reading pictures as well. Her son Ralph interpreted all closed or nearly invisible eyes as 'cry' from 2;0 years on for some period and open mouths or beaks as 'speaking' from 2;11 on (Lowe 2007: 130f.).

Metaphor in spontaneous utterances

The above examples from literature show how very young children use metaphors in their spontaneous speech. Metaphors with verbs of motion seem to crop up first (Özcaliskan 2005). This is supported by personally collected data. Searching for lost objects the just-three-year-old suggested that the book might have flown away or the slippers slurred off.

Cognitive development in the first three years

Between their second and fourth birthdays children make important cognitive progress. Three developing capabilities matter in metaphor comprehension and will be linked to picturebook reading.

Animate / inanimate distinction

Antje Damm (2006) *Was ist das?*
The development of the categorical distinction between *animates* and *inanimates* starts earlier, but not until the second half of their second year have children acquired a general notion of the *animate/inanimate* distinction, which includes purpose of action and state of mind (intention) in addition to motion-based characteristics (Rakison & Poulin-Dubois 2001). Personification catches children's interest early and picturebooks exploit it.

Was ist das? by Antje Damm is the favourite picturebook of Sebastian and his friend right around their second birthday when the first metaphors are discovered in their spontaneous speech. Antje Damm gives the boring labelling game a new creative form and encourages the child reader to participate in the process of producing metaphors by means of a riddle, a form which stimulates children to make inferences (Winner 1988: 50). The stereotyped question "Was ist das?" (= What's that?) is written on the left-hand page, background and material of the lettering give clues to the answer which is revealed overleaf, e.g., feathers on a blue background hint at a swan. The photo of an object is complemented by some painted details on the following page.

In our example the fixing of a washbasin turns into a swan with the original familiar object still visible (Figures 1a and b). The sight of an everyday object

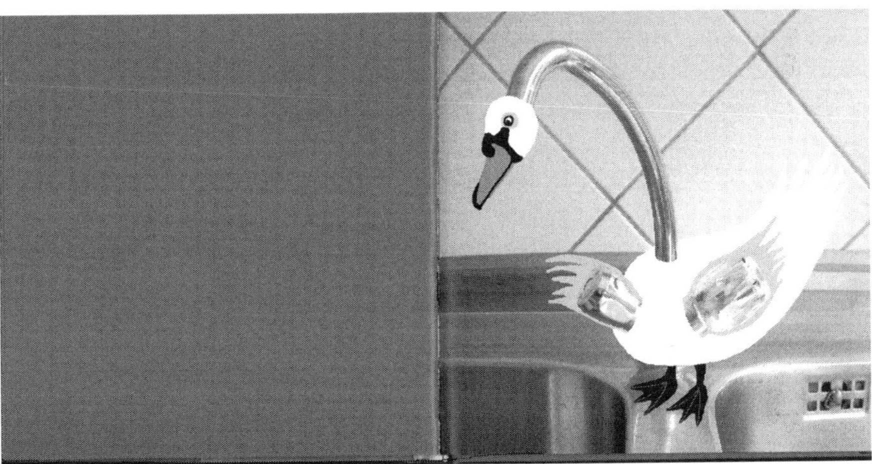

Figures 1a and 1b. Images from *Was ist das?* by Antje Damm

triggers a mental picture. It is the same process when a child recognizes a crocodile in a piece of toast (Kress 1997:49) or puts raisins back into a fluffy bun while singing a lullaby (Philipp 1;9.24). In these cases metaphorical thinking involves the transfer from inanimate to animate.

With a view to the learning process we can expect young children to understand personifications as we find them in the story of *Little blue and little yellow* by Leo Lionni (1959) where spots represent characters. The story *What's That?* by V. A. Jensen and D. W. Haller (1977) for blind and sighted children personifies geometrical forms with different surfaces for the different characters.

Reality and knowledge vs. imagination

Around their second birthday children begin to distinguish between reality and imagination. Shortly before their third birthday they are able to contrast reality with various alternatives (Woolley & Wellman 1990; for a survey cf. Woolley 2002). At the end of their third year of life children talk and understand a lot more about the mind, about imagining, dreaming, thinking, and knowing. The older they get the better they perform. Yet, young 3-year-olds do not draw a clear line between imagination and reality, but as young as age three years they do understand the fictional nature of dreams and imagination. In another study Woolley and Wellman (1993) tested 3- and 4-year-olds on their understanding of things based on experience and perception in contrast to things made up, which can take place independently of perceptual input and do not purport to represent the world. The 3-year-olds' responses to questions at the end of stories showed a rudimentary understanding of the distinction, which will develop substantially in the year between their third and fourth birthdays (1993: 11; Lowe 2007: 45).

In the laboratory, in a warm-up test, experimenters made children shut their eyes and asked what they saw in order to explain to them the meaning of *imagine* (Woolley & Wellman 1993: 4). We find that this can be achieved in a much more attractive way by reading a picturebook, e.g., *Frederick* by Leo Lionni (1967). Pictorial metaphors illustrate words from the semantic field of theory of mind, making the meaning of *dream*, *imagine*, *see* (cognitive denotation), *mind* visible. Frederick's words inspire his fellow mice to imagine colours, which fill thought bubbles, the imaginings make them feel the warmth of the sunbeams depicted through diffuse yellow colouring in the picture.

Conceptual metaphor theory

Contemporary conceptual theory has long dispensed with the notion of metaphor as figurative language. Metaphors pervade everyday language and influence "a good deal of how people think, reason and imagine in everyday life" (Gibbs 1997: 145). George Lakoff and Mark Johnson laid the groundwork of conceptual metaphor theory in their book *Metaphors We Live By* in 1980. The definition of metaphor involves two conceptual domains, A = target (or topic) and B = source (or vehicle) and a mapping of properties from source onto target domain. In Lakoff's and Johnson's words: "The essence of metaphor is understanding and experiencing one kind of thing in terms of another" (1980: 5). In general, conceptual metaphors are rooted in everyday experience and can be culled from everyday expressions. The underlying conceptual metaphors of *in high spirits*, *elevated* and the opposite *feel low, depressed* are HAPPY IS UP and SAD IS DOWN (conceptual metaphors will be written in capitals). They seem to be universally understood and frequently used in picturebooks. One of the most studied conceptual metaphors is ANGER. Forceville (2005) analysed how it is expressed visually in the Asterix album *La Zizanie*. Apart from striking parallels in the picturebook *Angry Arthur*, a detailed analysis will show what opportunities the two modalities of the picturebook, verbal and pictorial, offer and how creatively they are used by Oram Hyam and Satoshi Kitamura in presenting the stages of ANGER in a way a small child might experience it.

Metaphorical uses

Metaphors are usually unidirectional, i.e., the two terms cannot be changed around without making the sentence nonsensical, e.g., *Cigarettes are time bombs* is different in meaning from **Time bombs are cigarettes* (Glucksberg & Keysar 1993: 415ff). Since the same is true for comparative structures with *like*, the term *metaphor* also includes similes. In developmental studies comparative structures with *like* and pure metaphors are classified as "metaphorical uses". This is of some relevance in our picturebook context. Levorato & Cacciara (2002) find in their tests on 7-year-old and older children that the comparative structure (*is like* ...) is preferred by younger children. It obviously facilitates the search for cross-domain matching. In the picturebooks *My Mum* by Anthony Browne (2005), or *Swimmy* by Leo Lionni (1963) the illustrations present the pure metaphor, whereas in the linguistic modality the author is free to choose between comparative structures and metaphors. Comparative structures are most likely to support the acquisition process that starts in the second half of their second year.

Although Lakoff's and Johnson's theory allows for a wider interpretation, almost for a decade research was limited to linguistic metaphors. Since the 1990s pictorial metaphors have been studied in art, film, advertising, and comic books (Forceville 2008). The multimodality of picturebooks has been completely ignored. The study of gestural metaphor is an expanding field of research (Cienki & Müller 2008). The significance of gestures in picturebook reading sessions seems to be worth studying.

Conceptualizing ANGER

Hiawyn Oram, illustrations by Satoshi Kitamura (1982) *Angry Arthur*
The underlying metaphor of ANGER can be construed from everyday expressions like *boil with anger, hit the ceiling, burst, let off steam*. The majority of American English expressions are covered by the underlying metaphor ANGER IS HEATED

FLUID IN A PRESSURIZED CONTAINER. Heat, internal pressure, and agitation are important elements of the source domain. To control one's anger is to keep the fluid inside the container; exploding brings about social dysfunctionality. Other underlying metaphors can have the same or similar entailments, among them ANGER IS A NATURAL FORCE (Lakoff & Kövecses 1987).

In their picturebook *Angry Arthur* Oram and Kitamura transform the conceptual metaphor ANGER IS A NATURAL FORCE into ANGER IS A NATURAL CATASTROPHE. This hyperbole opens a fantastic dimension and has a humorous effect, which are both likely to attract a child's interest.

The boy is not allowed to watch a western on TV after bedtime. His anger becomes a "stormcloud, exploding thunder and lightning and hailstones". Four words denoting terrifying weather phenomena and the motion verb *exploding* emphasise how suddenly und powerfully anger soars. The double spread shows chaos and debris (Figure 2). Jagged lines correspond with *lightning* in the text and express Arthur's irrational way of thinking just as jagged contour lines of speech bubbles or jagged lines pointing to the mouth of the speaker in comic books. Arthur's posture and facial expression signify the first stage, when anger is still under control. The pictorial signs are those used in the comic book (Forceville 2005): eyes fixed, mouth tightly shut, arms folded over one's chest, knees drawn up. The text does not characterize Arthur or describe details of the havoc, but concentrates on action expressing the escalating stages of anger. When his anger

Figure 2. Image from *Angry Arthur* by Hiawyn Oram and Satoshi Kitamura

is out of control Arthur is shown as its victim desperately holding on to the branch of a tree. Anger grows into a hurricane, a typhoon, an earth tremor, a "universe-quake", each stage taking up a double spread. In this way Kitamura makes the most of Arthur's devastating anger. "That's enough" is the simple recurrent phrase of the grown-ups with a familiar ring for the child reader and the equally simple narrator's comment: "But it wasn't." In the end Arthur can't remember what the reason for his anger was, as it often happens when it is over. We see him lying in his bed on a rock from Mars. The pictorial metaphor adds how isolated someone feels after anger has abated.

The first impression might be that the book was too sophisticated for very young readers, but children often surprise us. The book arose a three-year-old's interest on the spot and he even chose to read it by himself. In fits of anger children at that age experience a stressful existential situation. Humorous elements offer a kind of relief. The story highlights salient properties of the concept ANGER such as loss of control, destruction, isolation, but also provides familiar grounding such as strict bedtime rules and authoritative phrases used by family members, parents and grandparents.

Conceptualizing IMAGINATION

Leo Lionni (1970) *Fish is Fish*

Fish is Fish by Leo Lionni is an example of a picturebook where close correspondence between the pictorial metaphors and words support children in acquiring (part of) the concept IMAGINATION and relating it to lexical items at an age when they can be expected to be particularly perceptive.

The story is about a minnow and a tadpole who became best friends. After the tadpole developed into a frog and left the pond, he comes back one day to tell his friend about the extraordinary things he saw. His words inspire his friend's imagination. The fish's longing to see this "wonderful world" becomes so strong that he decides to jump out of the pond and would have suffocated if the frog had not pushed him back into the water.

The story is carefully built up for a young child to understand the fish's final state of mind. It develops in three steps. Each double spread depicts the dialogue situation: the frog is talking to the fish, which is signalled by the frog's open mouth, his eyes are fixed on the fish, who, with his mouth shut, is imagining the things, transforming the words into pictures, which are represented in a thought bubble pointing to the fish's head and whose background is white. In other words, his mind is filling with pictures triggered by the frog's story of the world outside the pond.

In terms of Lakoff's and Johnson's theory this is in accordance with the conceptual metaphor MIND IS A CONTAINER, which is conveyed in verbal expressions such as *in the fish's mind, the picture in the fish's mind was full of lights and colors…, his friend saw the birds fly through his mind.* How do pictorial and verbal metaphors interrelate? In the first dialogue scene the two modalities, pictorial and verbal, are used symmetrically, which makes comprehension easier for the child. The text accentuates talking and imagining as simultaneous activities. In the following double spread the frog describes cows; the thought bubble stretches beyond the surface of the water; there is no textual reference to the fish's reaction. In the third scene the fish's mental picture appeals to the child reader's personal experience: it shows a man accompanied by a small child holding a lolly in her hand. Compared to the first scene the text has become more abstract and vague about the content of his imaginings. The fourth scene forms the climax: it unifies and enhances the fish's imaginings in a vivid wordless scene and the text overleaf explains how the pictures obsess him. Pushed back into the pond he sees and feels the beauty of the world where he belongs. Lionni makes the young child reader participate in the process of imagining and realising its effect on feelings. In the final scene the weight of expression is again in the picture evoking the reader's empathy, whereas the poetical linguistic metaphor will be understood only much later.

In *Fish is Fish* imaginings are false and cause anxiety, whereas in *Frederick* they make the mice forget hardship just as in real-life experience where imaginings can have a positive or negative effect. In Lakoff's terms Lionni chooses "prototypical scenarios" in the two picturebooks.

Conceptualizing NATURE

Malachy Doyle, paintings by S. Johnson & Lou Fancher (2005) *The Dancing Tiger*
The concept NATURE has many facets or properties. The picturebook *The Dancing Tiger* is about MYSTERY in nature, the CYCLE of seasons, and the LIFE CYCLE. The central metaphor is BEING-AT-ONE-WITH-NATURE as a joyful experience. In contrast to the preceding picturebooks metaphors are poetic throughout. The story is about a girl who, from her dormer window, spots a tiger dancing in the wood when the moon is full.

The perspective shifts page by page from the girl's point of view in an extreme close-up of the tiger's face with his friendly eyes that take away the girl's fright and likewise the reader's, to a long shot of the two in profile, where the full moon in the background directs attention to the tiger speaking with a warning gesture to make the girl promise to keep him secret. Overleaf, the two are seen from behind disappearing into the wood, which draws the reader into the action by evoking his curiosity. After they have disappeared into the wood the shift from *I-* to *we-*perspective verbally signals the beginning of their joint adventure depicted in the following double spreads. The tiger and the girl always dance together when the moon is full. The four dancing scenes set in spring, summer, autumn, and winter form the centre of the book. At the end of her life she passes on the tradition to her great-grandchild.

NATURE IS MYSTERY is conveyed by moonlight. Throughout the book it is present through shadows and light effects. In the endpapers tree trunks similar in colour and shape to the stripes of a tiger imply that they might cause the vision of the dancing tiger in the wood. Linguistic metaphors will be understood later, yet some words might have a familiar ring even for a very young child, watchwords like *tiptoe, still, whisper,* promising secrecy as part of the tiger's contract. In the central dancing scenes onomatopoeia reinforces the illustrations. Trochaic and iambic metres and vowel quality alternate according to the rhythm of dancing. The text functions as sound track accompanying and enhancing action expressing harmony and delight.

Their dancing is enthusiastic, graceful and creative. The camera position changes scene by scene from medium shot to close-up and long shot. The girl and the tiger are seen from various angles, from below and from above, the figures move from right to left and in the opposite direction signifying movement towards and away from the reader respectively. Ascending and descending movements are rendered by the diagonals from bottom left to top right and vice versa (cf. Lewis 2001: 110; Kress & van Leeuwen 2006). In each double spread there is a single line with a verb denoting motion: *skip, circle, high-kick,* and *waltz.* Despite so much activity we keep looking into the girl's happy face, from which we can tell how this experience makes her feel happy and free: in metaphorical terms: NATURE IS UP with dancing as the appropriate accompanying behavioural expression (Kövecses 2000: 33). From very early on in life, even before they learn to walk children enjoy rhythmic movements immensely. Other experiential knowledge which even small children have already acquired is woven into the pictures, such as kicking leaves, making prints in the snow, skipping in bluebells in spring. Small children find moon and moonlight fascinating.

NATURE AS A LIVING ENTITY and MYSTERY like the dancing tiger is what the imaginative girl finds out and cherishes all her life. NATURE IS A CYCLE is shown in the phases of the moon, the sequence of the seasons and the life cycle. With adults the pictures evoke the dynamic mental imagery of nature at its most beautiful; they evoke memories of childhood days and corresponding positive feelings. With small children they support the development of such imagery. At an age when they have become sensitive to the distinction between reality and non-reality this picturebook links imagination with the inspiring power of NATURE.

Coherent metaphors: LONELINESS vs. FRIENDSHIP

Madeleine Floyd (2005) *Cold Paws, Warm Heart*
In the picturebook *Cold Paws, Warm Heart* the author/illustrator focuses on the coherent metaphorical structuring of LONELINESS and FRIENDSHIP by coordinating and interrelating commonplace textual and pictorial metaphors. Such diverse domains as colour, temperature, sound, activity and feeling are linked and contrasted simultaneously. The associations COLD/SAD and WARM/HAPPY are created in the pictures and are paralleled in the text.

Hannah, a small girl, makes friend with a polar bear named Cold Paws. The story describes the gradual shift from feeling lonely, cold and sad to being with a friend and feeling warm and happy. Boundaries between the outside world and the inside world remain vague in both modalities. Negative and positive emotions are expressed in simple language: *troubles, miserable, poor Cold Paws, feel cold vs. smile, laugh, warm glow.* The white and greyish colours of the polar bear's environment and his lonely place behind an iceberg is paralleled by *cold, ice,* and *snow*, and the bear's *shivering* in the text. The young reader is well prepared to share Hannah's empathy, which is clearly expressed: "Now Hannah knew how miserable it was to feel cold". Hannah's home village in vivid colours and the eye-catching red colour of her coat, cap and scarf accentuate the contrast between her and the polar bear in colour, temperature, and feeling. She gives him her scarf, makes him jump up and down, and offers him a steaming mug of hot chocolate. Step by step he feels less cold inside, which is metaphorically expressed in the two modalities, visual and linguistic, by making the shivering sound "Brrrrrrrr" shorter and the letters smaller. In the final scene Hannah gives him a very big hug. Cold Paws has closed his eyes, which is a cue for switching to the inner world. The picture is static, but the verbal modality allows the reader to overlook the dynamic process by expressing what "wonderful thing" has happened, pointing out the change from cold to warm including the textual metaphor that Cold Paws feels "a warm glow all over", where the word *glow* refers to colour as well as to fire/temperature. The underlying premise draws on young children's general experiential knowledge that they have gained by the age of three or two years or even earlier, namely that when you feel cold, a scarf, jumps, hot chocolate and a big hug will make you feel warm and cosy. The layout of the pictures varies page by page, from long shots rendering the story line to close-ups focusing on facial expression and body language. The front and final endpapers illustrate the two poles, from loneliness to friendship, i.e., long shots show Cold Paws first alone and then together with Hannah. The compound *warm-hearted* is a conventional metaphor. Someone warm-hearted is open, altruistic, caring like Hannah. The title is based on a popular saying ("Cold hands, warm heart"), slightly changed to characterize the polar bear. Madeleine Floyd makes the child reader participate in the emerging pattern of a common metaphor FRIENDSHIP IS WARMTH.

Synaesthesia and metaphor

Satoshi Kitamura (2005) *Igor, the Bird Who Couldn't Sing*
In linguistic terms synaesthesia is a case of cross-sensory mapping. Everyday language has many synaesthetic metaphors in which two senses are involved, e.g., *cold silence, a stony flavor* (Cacciari 2008: 426), *loud colours, etc.* and there is evidence of this multimodal competence in early childhood. Experiments show that there is no clear-cut boundary between the senses (for a survey cf. Cacciari 2008). Brain imaging techniques brought to light a neural basis of synaesthesia, which might explain that such transfers are not at random and that certain cross-modal associations are preferred (433); e.g., the pairing of sight and sound is much more frequent than any other. Like other metaphors synaesthesia is usually unidirectional: if a sound induces a colour experience, this does not automatically go for the other way round (428f). The picturebook *Igor, the bird who couldn't sing* makes sound visible in shape and colour and links both to bodily movement.

It is spring and the crow Igor has been longing to sing for the first time in his life. A double spread with the picture of a tree shows birds sitting in the tree and singing their conventional undulating tunes depicted as strings of beads, ribbons, and garlands in yellow, orange and light green. They are contrasted with Igor's music as a bunch of multi-coloured wild zig-zag shapes. The pictorial metaphor expresses their different songs perceptibly and comprehensibly, whereas the textual metaphors, e.g., *quiet winter*, spring as *time of music* and *dawn chorus* for the polyphony at daybreak are beyond the young readers grasp. Igor's song – though spontaneous and creative – causes alarm and laughter. After his music is generally rejected and music lessons with Madam Goose do not improve him, he settles in a remote place, determined never to do music again. One evening, however, there is such a beautiful sunset that he cannot help singing. The beauty of nature inspires him. The double spread forming the climax of the story shows the space above the horizon filled with sharp-edged shapes of various bright colours, more or less similar, contrasting beautifully with the dark blue sky and making Igor's singing visible. Igor himself is singing with his beak wide open, his wings spread, and his whole body up in the air. In the pictorial modality colour and sound are combined with the spatial metaphor HAPPY IS UP (cf. Gardner 1974; Marks 1975; Osgood 1980: 207–212; Lakoff & Johnson 1980: 15–21). He feels "free" and "easy", which is duplicated in the text to bring home the main point. However, the text expands the pictorial metaphor by incorporating volume, sound WAVES and the sensation of bodily VIBRATION: "And as he sang, he felt his music ripple and jolt the evening air", which requires world knowledge acquired much later. But Kitamura gives the child reader enough cues to draw inferences and to comprehend (some of) the meaning of the concept SINGING / MUSIC from the pictures. Finally he finds someone who admires his style; together they will tour the world.

A striking example for this link between colour, space, and mood is Dr. Seuss' picturebook *My Many Colored Days* for "very young children" (inside flap). A bear painted in shades of dark brown with drooping posture, closed eyes, and passive behaviour illustrates what it means to feel *down*. The meaning of *down* is accentuated graphically by a downward line of the words reinforcing the metaphor SAD IS DOWN. By contrast, upward action, flying bees and the colour yellow correspond with the underlying conceptual metaphor: HAPPY IS UP.

The fact that boldface letters cue loudness and often nearness can be classified as the generic metaphor MORE OF FORM IS MORE OF CONTENT (Lakoff & Johnson 1980: 17f) or EMOTION IS FORCE. The meaning of large letters varies, depending on the context (Forceville 2005: 84), e.g., boldface letters might express nearness/loudness, emotion, or emphasis on key words. As to synaesthesia in general, picturebooks make children familiar with ways of thinking and expressing that are within their scope and personal experience, but are also grounded in our general cultural experience.

Conceptualizing social behaviour

Ei, Ei, Ei! by Eric Battut

On the basis of conceptual metaphor theory Raymond W. Gibbs advocates what he calls the "embodied action" or "embodied simulation" view (Gibbs 1997; Gibbs & Matlock 2008), i.e., action verbs are used to construct the metaphorical meaning of an abstract idea. This is exactly what Eric Battut does in his picturebook *Ei, Ei, Ei!* by creating a link between action and the abstract term DISCRIMINATION. In accordance with Lakoff's and Johnson's observation that SOCIAL GROUPS ARE CONTAINERS (1980: 59f), the spatial metaphors DISCRIMINATION IS OUT, TOLERANCE IS IN (15) are brought across by the persuasive image of the nest.

A white and a black bird have hatched. As soon as they see the speckled egg in the middle they are determined to get rid of it: "Wir wollen kein gesprenkeltes Ei im Nest! Hau ruck! Raus mit Dir!" (= We don't want a speckled egg in the nest. Heave-ho. Out with you!). In a united effort they throw it out of the nest but fall out of the nest themselves and into the water. The speckled egg grows feet and wings and carries them back to their nest. What follows contrasts sharply with the opening scene: the black and white birds address the speckled egg, say thank you, apologize and want to know who the speckled egg really is. This all happens in the absence of their parents and without their interference. In the final picture a little red bird is looking out of the shell, sitting between the black and white birds, their parents behind them, the five of them all in the nest as an image of perfect harmony. It represents the conceptual image TOLERANCE IS IN(SIDE). The picturebook links DISCRIMINATION with discriminatory activities which are well understood even by small children (Ausdale & Feagin 2001). Text and illustrations concentrate on the crucial actions and words expressing the metaphor. In order not to distract from the theme details of the scenery are reduced to a minimum, background and camera position remain the same throughout the book. The text is presented very prominently on the left-hand page. The empty white background underlines the words and contrasts with the blue background for action on the facing page. The text renders exactly what the black and white birds notice and say. It corresponds with what they do and what happens to them.

Many other picturebooks deal with social behaviours. The story *The Doorbell Rang* by Pat Hutchins (1986) is all about sharing cookies with friends. The text expresses "how nice" this is, but the pictures go beyond that and also highlight other properties of the conceptual metaphor FRIENDSHIP IS IN(SIDE): the picture shows children of different colours sharing chairs. Colour of skin does not matter: friends and company are a higher value than a spick-and-span kitchen just cleaned by their mother. In the old favourite by Leo Lionni (1963) it is Swimmy's idea to teach the small fish how to swim together like one big fish in order to be able to enjoy the wonderful deep sea without fear of the big fish. It is a metaphor of power through COOPERATION and the benefit you get from it.

Conclusion

Our analysis brought to light ample evidence of metaphors in picturebooks for very young readers. Moreover, conceptual metaphor theory, which includes multimodality of metaphors, turned out to be a useful tool to describe metaphors in picturebooks. With a view to results from research in cognitive sciences they are well within the scope of children from one to three years of age. We could see that authors choose characteristic or prototypical situations in their stories and focus abstract terms that are within the experience of a child of this age group. They use metaphors that are conventionalized, even universally understood, such as HAPPY IS UP / SAD IS DOWN.

The relationship between pictorial and textual metaphors and their interplay varies. In *My Many Colored Days* pictures and words are coordinated consistently throughout, introducing metaphors expressing states of minds and relating them to lexical items. Picturebooks like *Was ist das?* by Antje Damm, *Fish is Fish* or *Frederick* by Leo Lionni even make the child reader participate in the process of producing metaphors. In the case of *Angry Arthur* one (comprehensive) metaphor underlying ANGER is chosen and exaggerated. Starting point, escalation and the final state of Arthur's anger are echoed in the text. In the presentation of FRIENDSHIP in *Cold Paws, Warm Heart* and of IMAGINATION in *Frederick* the two modalities, text and picture, closely interact. In *Cold Paws, Warm Heart* the mapping between different domains such as colour, temperature, feelings, and social behaviour is repeatedly established in pictures and words, and makes it easy for a small child to understand salient properties of the terms LONELINESS and FRIENDSHIP. Madeleine Floyd uses the advantage of the verbal modality to finally overlook the whole process of change. The picturebook *Frederick* introduces and explains the meaning of words belonging to the field of theory of mind: *dream, imagine, see, in one's mind*, and the possibly abstract quality of imaginings, such as colour and its effect on feeling. *Fish is Fish* starts with close correspondence between words and pictures, which grows out of proportion when thoughts become an obsession, taking up one double spread without words and the verbal explanation on the following page.

The relationship between pictorial and textual metaphors differs in picturebooks dealing with NATURE and SINGING. The concept AT-ONE-WITH-NATURE is presented in *The Dancing Tiger* through fascinating pictorial metaphors expressing the feeling of harmony with nature. Apart from some keywords the text is little understood by a child at this age level, because comprehension depends on world knowledge acquired much later. It is the prosody of the text in verse that heightens the dynamics of the images, carrying the load of meaning. Similarly, the significance of SINGING / MUSIC and Igor's emotional experience is conveyed in the visual modality. Both, pictures and text are open to deeper levels of interpretation later on.

Peter Stockwell (2002: 108) distinguishes between *explanatory* and *expressive* linguistic metaphors, which I think applies to multimodal metaphors as well and is well suited to explain the difference described above. According to Stockwell *explanatory metaphors* tend not to be very rich and are very clear, as we saw in the picturebooks where the two modalities run more or less parallel. *Expressive metaphors* (often poetic) have a low degree of clarity, but a high degree of richness, as we found in the analysis of *Igor, the bird who couldn't sing* and *The Dancing Tiger*.

In the process of acquiring abstract terms like *imagination, anger, friendship, nature, music* a child might start with comprehending just one salient property, i.e., the feeling that NATURE and SINGING are sources of happiness. They are explained through metaphors that are rooted in a child's personal, even bodily experience, and her cultural knowledge from early on. In the course of repeated reading the child will discover more mappable properties.

The picturebooks under discussion can be considered as the follow-ups of what Bettina Kümmerling-Meibauer and Jörg Meibauer term "early-concept books", those small-sized cardboard books with usually one or a very limited number of objects on one page, which help the child to interrelate word and object (Kümmerling-Meibauer & Meibauer 2005). Our picturebooks are follow-ups inasmuch as they contribute to forming mental concepts of *abstract terms*. Children will acquire linguistic expressions by associating them with pictorial metaphors. The acquisition of comparative structures, which tend to develop around their third birthday, will be supported. In terms of pragmatic development their notion of non-literal language will improve.

Since experimental design poses problems when testing children aged three and younger on metaphor capacities, we suggest using picturebooks in future research. Testing children of various age groups and adults on metaphor comprehension in picturebooks will be interesting for cognitive scientists as well as for those who are interested in how picturebooks work.

Children's books cited

Battut, E. 2005. *Ei, Ei, Ei!* Zürich: Bohem press.
Browne, A. 1992. *Zoo.* New York NY: Farrar, Straus and Giroux, Sunburst Book 2002 edn.
Browne, A. 2005. *My Mum.* London: Random House Picturebooks.
Damm, A. 2006. *Was ist das?* Hildesheim: Gerstenberg.
Doyle, M., Johnson, S. & Fancher, L. 2005. *The Dancing Tiger.* New York NY: Simon and Schuster.
Dr. Seuss, Johnson, S. & Fancher, L. 1996. *My Many Colored Days.* New York NY: Alfred A. Knopf.
Floyd, M. 2005. *Cold Paws, Warm Heart.* London: Walker Books.
Hutchins, P. 1968. *Rosie's Walk.* New York NY: Macmillan.
Hutchins, P. 1986. *The Doorbell Rang.* New York NY: Greenwillow Books.
Jensen, V. A. & Haller, D. W. 1977 1993[8]. *Was ist das?* Frankfurt: Sauerländer Verlag [orig. *What's That?*].
Kitamura, S. 1987. *Lily Takes A Walk.* Bradfield: Happy Cat Books.
Kitamura, S. 2005. *Igor, the Bird who Couldn't Sing.* London: Andersen Press.
Lionni, L. 1959. *Little blue and little yellow.* New York NY: HarperCollins.
Lionni, L. 1963. *Swimmy.* New York NY: Alfred A. Knopf.
Lionni, L. 1967. *Frederick.* New York NY: Alfred A. Knopf.
Lionni, L. 1970. *Fish is Fish.* Alfred A. Knopf. New York NY: Random House:
Oram, H. & Kitamura, S. 1982. *Angry Arthur.* London: Andersen Press.

References

Arizpe, E. & Styles, M. 2003. *Children Reading Pictures. Interpreting Visual Texts*. London: RoutledgeFalmer.

van Ausdale, D. & Feagin, J. R. 2001. *The First R. How Children Learn Race and Racism*. Lanham MA: Rowman & Littlefield.

Bloom, P. 2000. *How Children Learn the Meanings of Words*. Cambridge MA: The MIT Press.

Cacciari, C. 2008. Crossing the senses in metaphorical language. In *The Cambridge Handbook of Metaphor and Thought*, R. W. Gibbs, Jr. (ed.), 423–443. Cambridge: CUP.

Cienki, A. & Müller, C. (eds). 2008. *Metaphor and Gesture*. Amsterdam: John Benjamins.

Clark, E. C. 2003. *First Language Acquisition*. Cambridge: CUP.

Cox, M. 1992. *Children's Drawings*. London: Penguin.

Forceville, C. 2005. Visual representations of the idealized cognitive model of anger in the Asterix album *La Zizanie*. *Journal of Pragmatics* 37: 69–88.

Forceville, C. 2008. Metaphor in pictures and multimodal representations. In *The Cambridge Handbook of Metaphor and Thought*, R. W. Gibbs, Jr. (ed.), 462–482. Cambridge: CUP

Gardner, H. 1974. Metaphors and modalities: How children project polar adjectives onto diverse domains. *Child Development* 45: 84–91.

Gibbs, R. W., Jr. 1997. Taking metaphor out of our heads and putting it into the cultural world. In *Metaphor in Cognitive Linguistics. Selected Papers from the Fifth International Cognitive Linguistics Conference Amsterdam, July 1997* [Current Issues in Linguistic Theory 175], R. W. Gibbs, Jr. & G. J. Steen (eds), 145–166. Amsterdam: John Benjamins.

Gibbs, R. W. Jr. & Matlock. T. 2008. Metaphor, imagination, and simulation: Psycholinguistic evidence. In *The Cambridge Handbook of Metaphor and Thought*, R. W. Gibbs Jr. (ed.), 161–176. Cambridge: CUP.

Glucksberg, S. & Keysar, B. 1993. How metaphors work. *Metaphor and Thought*, 2nd edn, A. Ortony (ed.), 401–424. Cambridge: CUP.

Kiefer, B. Z. 1995. *The Potential of Picturebooks. From Visual Literacy to Aesthetic Understanding*. Englewood Cliffs NJ: Merrill, Prentice Hall.

Kövecses, Z. 2000. *Metaphor and Emotion: Language, Culture, and Body in Human Feeling*. Cambridge: CUP.

Kümmerling-Meibauer, B. & Meibauer, J. 2005. First pictures, early concepts: Early concept books. *The Lion and the Unicorn* 29: 324–347.

Kress, G. 1997. *Before Writing. Rethinking the Paths to Literacy*. London: Routledge.

Kress, G. & van Leeuwen, T. 2006[2]. *Reading Images: the Grammar of Visual Design*. London: Routledge.

Lakoff, G. & Johnson, M. 1980. *Metaphors We Live By*. Chicago IL: University of Chicago Press.

Lakoff, G. & Kövecses, Z. 1987. The cognitive model of anger inherent in American English. In *Cultural Models in Language and Thought*, D. Holland & N. Quinn (eds), 195–221. Cambridge: CUP.

Levorato, M. C. & Cacciari, C. 2002. The creation of new figurative expressions: Psycholinguistic evidence in Italian children, adolescents and adults. *Journal of Child Language* 29: 127–150.

Lewis, D. 2001. *Reading Contemporary Picturebooks. Picturing Text*. London: Routeledge Falmer.

Lewkowicz, D. J. & Turkewitz, G. 1980. Cross-modal equivalence in early infancy: Auditory – visual intensity matching. *Developmental Psychology* 16(6): 597–607.

Lowe, V. 2007. *Stories, Pictures and Reality. Two Children Tell*. London: Routledge.

Marks, L. E. 1975. On colored-hearing synesthesia: Cross-modal translations of sensory dimensions. *Psychological Bulletin* 82(3): 303–331.
Marks, L. & Bornstein, M. 1987. Sensory similarities: Classes, characteristics, and cognitive consequences. In *Cognition and Symbolic Structures: The psychology of metaphoric transformation*, R. E. Haskell (ed). 48–65. Norwood, NJ: Ablex Publ.
Osgood, C. E. 1980. The cognitive dynamics of synaesthesia and metaphor. In *Cognition and Figurative Language*, R. P. Honeck & R. R. Hoffman (eds), 203–238. Hillsdale NJ: Lawrence Erlbaum Associates.
Özcaliskan, S. 2005. On learning to draw the distinction between physical and metaphorical motion: Is metaphor an early emerging cognitive and linguistic capacity? *Journal of Child Language* 32: 291–318.
Piaget, J. 1968/1972. *Sprechen und Denken des Kindes*. Düsseldorf: Pädagogischer Verlag Schwann.
Rakison, D. H. & Poulin-Dubois, D. 2001. Developmental origin of the animate-inanimate distinction. *Psychological Bulletin* 121(2): 209–228.
Stockwell, P. 2002. *Cognitive Poetics. An Introduction*. London: Routledge
Vosniadou, S. & Ortony, A. 1983. The emergence of the literal-metaphorical-anomalous distinction in young children. *Child Development* 54: 154–161.
Vosniadou, S. 1987. Children and metaphors. *Child Development* 58: 870–885.
Wagner, S., Winner, E., Cichetti, D. & Gardner, H. 1981. "Metaphorical" mapping in human infants. *Child Development* 52: 728–731.
Winner, E., Rosenstiel, A. K. & Gardner, H. 1976. The development of metaphoric understanding. *Developmental Psychology* 17(4): 289–297.
Winner, E., McCarthy, M. Kleinman, S. & Gardner, H. 1979. First metaphors. *New Directions for Child Development* 3: 29–41.
Winner, E., McCarthy, M. & Gardner, H. 1980. The ontogenesis of metaphor. In *Cognition and Figurative Language*, R. P. Honeck & R. R. Hoffman (eds), 341–361. Hillsdale NJ: Lawrence Erlbaum Associates.
Winner, E. 1988. *The Point of Words: Children's Understanding of Metaphor and Irony*. Cambridge MA: Harvard University Press.
Wolf, S. A. & Heath, S. B. 1992. *The Braid of Literature. Children's Worlds of Reading*. Cambridge MA: Harvard University Press.
Woolley, J. D. & Wellman, H. M. 1990. Young children's understanding of realities, nonrealities, and appearances. *Child Development* 61: 946–961.
Woolley, J. D. & Wellman, H. M. 1993. Origin and truth: Young children's understanding of imaginary mental representations. *Child Development* 64: 1–17.
Woolley, J. D. 2002. Young children's understanding of pretense and other fictional mental states. In *Pretending and Imagination in Animals and Children*, R. W. Mitchell (ed.), 115–128. Cambridge: CUP.

CHAPTER 9

Early impressions

Paths to literacy

Carole Scott

Six engaging picturebooks for young children are analyzed for their ability to stimulate the physical and cognitive processes involved in the acquisition of visual, musical and language literacies: these include alphabet and music notation, and narrative, word use and grammatical structure. Recognition involving categorization of stimuli and memory formation depends on the development of networks of synapses, and the firing of mirror neurons reinforces the storage of these experiences. Porter's *ABC*, Bataille's *ABC3D*, and Van Allsburg's *The Z Was Zapped* represent innovative alphabet books merging perception, action and experience; Simon's *Mocking Birdies* introduces musical sounds, rhythms and notation; Goffin's *Oh!* and Gravett's *Orange Pear Apple Bear* humorously convey notions of book structure, language convention and word use.

Introduction

"We listen to music with our muscles," Nietzsche tells us, bluntly pointing to aspects of the mind-body continuum that neuroscientists increasingly uncover through painstaking research. They tell us, "Rhythm stirs our bodies. Tonality and melody stir our brains … bridg[ing] our [primitive] cerebellum and our [evolved] cerebral cortex" (Levitin 2006: 263). Like music literacy, visual and language literacy involve not simply an intellectual, but also a physical learning process, as networks of synapses throughout the body develop systems of perceptual and creative configurations which set the body in motion. Ackerman, Nocera and Bargh point out that "sensory and motor processing constitute necessary components of cognition," for "sensorimotor experiences in early life form a scaffold for the development of conceptual knowledge." This scaffolding "describes the process by which higher-order cognition emerges from bodily experience [so that] physical actions and sensations are used to acquire an initial comprehension of more abstract concepts"(Ackerman 2010: 1713).

Because infants' brains are "functionally undifferentiated" unable to clearly distinguish vision, hearing and touch as separate sensory inputs, researchers believe that this "sensory cross talk" puts them in "a state of complete psychedelic splendor" (Levitin 2006: 262). The growing child's brain develops specific regions to manage the different stimuli, and stores memories which begin to make sense of this chaotic world. In language acquisition terms, the child begins to undertake form-concept mapping so that "a lexeme [becomes] permanently stored in the child's mental lexicon" (Kümmerling-Meibauer & Meibauer 2005: 334–5).

This study will explore six works that involve early literacies for young children, including alphabet books of various complexities which provide early letter recognition; musical pitch and notation literacy; basic structures of books and stories which develop understanding of narrative and prepare for reading; and word use and syntax which provide the foundation for reading and writing. Marilyn Apseloff identifies a number of ways in which "Pre-Literature" prepares small children for later learning (Apseloff 1987: 63). I will be analyzing the ways in which the books involve mind and body – sight, hearing, tactility, movement and emotion – to stimulate the acquisition of these literacies, and to categorize and store the memories they provoke. Three are Alphabet books that teach sounds, shapes, and meaning. One focuses on sounds and colors for musical expression and notation recognition; one introduces ideas of stories and books; and one offers fundamental concepts of word use and grammatical structure.

Cognition and memory formation

Researchers intrigued by human memory have for at least a century debated the superiority of two basic approaches used to describe how human beings learn and remember, and several recent works have taken music as the locale in which to conduct their inquiries. I'll make it simple. The first absolute or "record-keeping" theories envision memory as a kind of tape recorder or video camera, preserving detailed experience accurately. The second relational or constructivist theories suggest that "our memory system stores information about the relations between objects and ideas, but not necessarily details about the objects themselves," and that we remember the gist, but may need to create the details when we construct or reconstruct a memory representation (Levitin 2006: 135).

It is not surprising that both approaches have proven valuable. Like theories about light, which use both particle and wave theory to explain and predict behavior, both "record-keeping" and constructivist views appear to be valuable in the investigation of memory. For example, memories of melody in music are defined by pitch relations (a constructivist view) but the melodies are composed of precise pitches (a record-keeping approach). Similarly, in speaking, people are usually better at remembering general content, rather than recreating a word-for-word account.

Nonetheless certain specific phrases and sentences are stored. People "make sense" of bits and pieces of memories, recreating a whole out of precise parts.

The ways in which these processes interact with one another becomes more evident as we examine cognition. To become aware and to understand the world around us we must learn to generalize and to particularize. For example, a single object, say a pear, looks different from different angles or viewpoints, but these differences are simply variant manifestations of the same object. Multiple points of view converge and we amalgamate these into a single, coherent, multi-dimensional perception of the object. Conversely when we have two pears, we can see that they are separate and probably differ in some small way – in size, color, or complexion – but they are basically the same and we learn to categorize them as such.

Thus, "a single object may manifest in multiple viewpoints," and several objects may have nearly identical viewpoints. In other words, we must analyze information into the "momentary circumstances of the manifestation of [the] object or scene," and the "invariant properties." Our record-keeping facility interacts with our constructive energies to marshal our perceptions into understanding and prediction of our surroundings. To make things more complex, it is not simply visual viewpoints that we must incorporate, but aural, tactile, and even taste and olfactory inputs. And the emotions we feel as we touch, see, hear and taste, themselves have enormous impact on the memory. For high emotion causes the release of dopamine, the neurotransmitter that "aids in the encoding of the memory trace" (Levitin 2006: 198).[1] As we learn to read the world, so do we approach the literacies, the words and other notations that capture and record our experiences.

ABC: Touch and memory

I'll begin with a very simple alphabet board-book. Matthew Porter's *ABC* (2006) is truly a board book, in that the book appears to have been constructed from weathered boards of wood. With a distressed paint finish, the original "grain" of the wood shows through both background and figures, and although the texture is not splintery it is uneven to the touch, giving a tactile "reality" to the book. The drawings of animals to illustrate the letters are constructed from simple shapes, and are quite crude, without sophistication, like rough drawings on a fence. Finally, the notion of a block of wood is enhanced by having the leopard's face on the front cover and the back of its head on the back cover, as though one might

1. See also Seitz and Dinse (2007), who explore neurological reconfiguration derived from heightened states of attention and determine that "the key to learning is that sensory stimulation needs to be sufficient to drive the neural system past the point of a learning threshold" (149).

carve the rest of the details into the block. This also introduces, in very simple terms, the notion not only of front and back perspectives, but of the beginning and end of a book, a story or an alphabet.

In addition, the physical act of turning the board pages provides an opportunity of mastery: the child learns to reach out, touch, grasp the edge of the page and move it first just back and forth – as Rhian Jones (1996) points out (25) – and later, more purposefully, to access the next image, initiating the development of higher order concepts such as the progression of events and logical development. Research on speech and gesture has found a connection between hand movements, language, and memories, so that "the very fact of moving your hands around ... help[s] you access memory and language."[2] And the study of "sensorimotor resources to support working memory" has provided evidence that "motor control and language understanding are intertwined with each other." (Anderson 2007: 157)[3] In addition, studies of developing musicians also link movement, the brain and music, as the nervous system develops neural pathways that weave sensory experience and muscular movements together.

The Z was Zapped: Assaulting the alphabet

The cover of Chris Van Allsburg's *The Z Was Zapped* (1987) alerts us to the fact that this will not be just an ordinary ABC book, for it features the letter, poised on a platform before a curtain, being attacked by lightning bolts. It introduces us to the idea that the letters are going to be assaulted, and indeed they are, each one undergoing a different mode of violence, being crushed (F), bound (T), punctured (N), dismembered (B) and cut up (C) just to note a few. For a child being introduced to the letters, these various modes of destruction are both funny and engaging. First, the letters behave as though they can take on the characteristics of various substances: wood (C), candle wax (M), rubber (W), so that the distortions call upon a myriad of external recollections and experiences.

The various methods of distortion, which involve a range of often very physical encounters with the letters, offer bizarre images which stimulate memory not only in visual terms, but in action: for example, the hands grasping K, the foot stomping F, the cutting up of Q. In this way, the involvement triggers a variety of physical paths, including the neuron paths to muscles, which flex arms and hands,

2. Elena Nicoladis (University of Alberta) quoted in LaFee (2009).

3. Anderson (2007) analyses research into Broca's area of the brain exploring the "opportunistic reuse of existing functional components," and finds that "language process and action-related tasks including movement preparation," use the same neural pathways (157).

legs and feet. For so-called "mirror neurons" in the brain's cortex fire "both when performing an action and when observing someone else performing that action" (Levitin 2006: 266). Vilayanur Ramachandran (2010) describes mirror neurons as "perform[ing] a virtual reality simulation," for 20% of these front-brain motor command neurons fire as the observer watches another person's movements, thus "adopt[ing] another person's point of view" as the observers' brains "emulate and imitate other persons' actions." Ramachandran considers this brain action, where seeing is doing, as the source of human empathy and, in a longer view, the basis for the development of civilization. Certainly it provides additional insight into the mechanics of early learning.

In Van Allsburg's book, the theatrical setting for each scene – for the book is presented as a drama with each letter coming on stage as a player – provides observed action tied with emotional affect. Personalizing letters as dramatic characters arouses empathy in the reader, and the vivid actions portrayed provoke reaction leading to the arousal of the mirror neurons. This response offers an alternative viewpoint for the readers. Do they relate to the letter being destroyed, or to the perpetrator of the destruction? Do they waver between the two, according to which letters are favorites or excite more compassion? Or are they simply detached observers? Each situation will stimulate different emotions and different learning paths. And, as is conventional in ABC books, each action exemplifies the letter. Thus the Z is zapped, the P is repeatedly pecked, the S is simply soaked, the U is abruptly uprooted. Here sound is transformed into shape, into action, and into tactile substance.

But Van Allsburg also defies convention to add another element, which tantalizes the reader and contributes to learning. Rather than using the double spread to feature both image and text, the memory is sparked by showing the image first, and offering the text on the reverse of the image to which it refers, in violation of the normal pattern where it is on the facing page. This requires that the page be turned in order to find the written description of what is happening. By delaying the words, and demanding that the reader suspend closure while physically engaging with the book, the organization resembles a flash card which first provokes memory and then satisfies it.

ABC3D: Letters in motion

Marion Bataille's meticulously crafted pop-up alphabet book, *ABC3D* (2008) includes no environmental visual clues. Instead it excites visualization from many angles and multiple viewpoints so that letters are apprehended often three dimensionally and in movement, the letter taking or changing shape as it appears, and sometimes metamorphosing into another. Not only do individual letters appear, but also their relationship to others becomes apparent through this real, not simulated motion that transforms one letter into another. And the three dimensional appearance is not simply visual but tactile. The turning of the page creates the form of the letter so that the reader is eminently involved in shaping it, and the pop-out, like a carved object, invites an inquiring touch.

The cover of this extraordinary book introduces the legerdemain that the presentation will involve, for whether you see A, B, C, or D depends on the angle at which you hold the book. In this way the reader controls the letter according to the angle of the hand and the head, foreshadowing the future as it suggests what one must do to write letters, immersing the reader into the creative act. As the book is opened, a white A moves upward into three dimensionality, stark against a black page with a hint of red shadow in the triangle where the strokes join. It is surprising in its concrete appearance and invites touch. Turning the page produces B, whose redlined curves extend from the downward stroke as the white page is opened. Rather than appearing full-blown like the A, the flat line of the B produces its semi-circular extensions slowly, becoming a full B only when the double spread is fully opened. This sense of developing shape titillates the eye, not as a shape, but as an action, and the reader must track its development. C, a straightforward red letter on a white page suddenly flips over to join its backward self to a straight black line, surprising us by becoming a multicolored D. When E loses its lowest bar to turn into an F, in much the same way, we feel a sense of familiarity, as well as an understanding of how the two pairs of letters resemble each other in their construction.

Watching five-year-olds learning to make their letters, with challenges of what goes forward, what goes back, what goes up and what goes down, suggests that this alphabet book lays an early writing foundation for much younger children, developing visual acuity by interrogating the structure of the letters, and deconstructing them to reconstruct. The movements that are involved in the pop-ups introduce the movements that one must master with one's mind and body in order to reproduce the letters, and eventually to write.

Most of the letters move up into three-dimensionality, and take on a concrete objectivity, but there are many variants in the way they appear and the way they are formed. For example, A, H and L lie down on the page, while M and N stand up on it. G unfolds itself, twisting as it revolves from one ready-formed G into another one double its size. U is one of the most convoluted and extravagantly created forms, shaped from a fan of delicate paper strips as it rises from the page. Some of the letters, like the C, resolve themselves into others, so that the X loses a foot and becomes Y, while O and P gain a tail and become Q and R. V becomes W when its mirrored verso doubles its image; and S involves pinwheels turning within its curves as the page is opened.

The kind of touch that the letters invite varies. In some cases, the hard surfaces and angles of the letters provide a tactility that calls for a simple contact, but others, like the hollow M or the see-through Z, solicit poking a finger into or through, while the intricacy of the U, for example, suggests a very delicate touch. The mirrored V/W wants to be stroked as the reflection slithers across the shiny page, while the spinning effect of the S's pinwheels needs both hands on the book to make it go faster or more slowly. The effect of the touch reminds us that "physical action and sensations are used to acquire an initial comprehension of more abstract concepts and, as such become automatically tied to their activation" (Ackerman 2010: 1713).

Mocking Birdies: Steps to music literacy

Of particular interest, since it addresses musical literacy directly, is Annette Simon's *Mocking Birdies* (2005), which features a red bird and a blue bird sitting on telephone lines, singing the same simple words, and annoying each other because each wants the other to "stop copying me" "stop singing my song!" As they accuse each other of being a "copycat" they first begin variations on the basic words, using scat singing, and rhythmic phrases: "skidoodle/ skidaddle/ skit scat, copycat/ copycat copycat/ copycat cat cat. Stop singing my song/ stop singing my song."

Soon they begin to enjoy singing together: solfege "do-re-mi," onomatopoeic phrases "chipper cheery-cheer cheer," and sounds like "warble whee, whistle whee." It is easy to imagine a parent and a little child making and echoing the words and sounds, and the aural back-and-forths are dramatized visually by the colors used. The blue bird sings in blue letters and hears blue sounds "blue as the noon, when the sun calls to play," while the red bird sings and hears in red print, "red as the dawn, when the sun peeps hello." Together, they "sing purple as dusk, when the sun coos goodnight." Thus they tie together not only the colors on the page, but the colors of the natural world where the birds truly sing.

It is not possible to read this book aloud without being pressed into sounding out the rhythms, rhymes and syncopated repetitions which are certainly more characteristic of music than of regular speech. Thus the development of the voice as a musical instrument engages the reader and the listener. At the early stage, the child will respond to the bright colors and the rhythmic sounds, though one hopes that the parent will introduce musical sounds and simple tunes to enhance the back-and-forth interaction that the birds model. The aural/oral learning also connects with the visual stimulation to suggest that there is a connection between musical sounds and rhythms and the written page.

Joined by a purple bird, they all sing together, and, if one hasn't realized before, it is at this point that the telephone lines on which the birds are sitting to sing are clearly seen as a musical staff, with the birds themselves – with their round heads and upraised tails – as the notes written upon it. Here we see an a, and c and an e, and we realize that the book has introduced us to musical literacy in several forms: in singing sounds and words, in blending voices together, in simple terminology and in music notation. Certainly the small child will not grasp this level of sophistication (I must confess that it took me several readings to discover this for myself!). Nonetheless, the adult mediation in pointing out details can begin the process of recognition that forms the foundation for future understanding of musical notation.

The complex involvement of so many aspects of the mind and body is stimulating and exciting. First it builds upon the young child's game of taunting others by aping their movements and speech, an ironic comment on the role patterning that all youngsters learn. The sense of amusement and aggravation that this play arouses provides an emotional and interpersonal context for the music to interact with. This affective dimension is dramatized by the simple design of the movement of the color shapes: for example the birds' confrontation followed by their rejection, turning tail to tail; and the organization of different pages into almost a narrative form, followed by a double spread of wild activity expressing joyous sound.

OH!: Linear progression

In contrast to the books explored so far, Josse Goffin's wordless picturebook *OH!* (2007) does not involve language and notation literacy, but is rather an introduction to books and to book literacy, communicating many concepts about the ways in which books function. It unfolds events and scenes which develop before the reader's eyes; it introduces notions of linearity; connection between events and scenes; the idea of recurrent themes; and the creation of characters that reappear in different modes. And, of course, it includes the very elementary concept of page turning, leading to the sense of discovery, and focusing upon the delightful surprises that books can keep in store for readers who engage with them.

As appropriate, the book begins with a hand pointing forward – the right direction to read a book in the author's language – and continues to reveal a new simple image each time the page is turned over: a cup of tea or coffee; a fish swimming; a clothes peg/pin; an apple; a shoe; a half moon; a ping-pong bat and ball; a pipe; a toothbrush; a toy jack-in-the-box; and last of all a flower. There doesn't seem to be any particular order in these objects, unless one thinks of an early morning cup of coffee, daytime activities, and later the moon and brushing teeth for bedtime. But I wouldn't like to push this too hard. More significant is that each recto page opens out, and the revealed two-page spread adds to the verso in a different way. Thus the hand at the beginning is no longer pointing – it is holding an alligator's tail; furthermore the alligator has a hat on, and is balancing a cup of coffee on its snout. The simple object has become a complete scene, and a humorous one at that, and the coffee cup on the alligator's snout now connects with the next simple image, as we refold the recto page and turn it over.

By unfolding the cup's recto page, we find that the half cup left on the verso has become the stern of a boat, which is floating in the water together with the fish, which is the next simple image that appears when we refold the page and turn it over. The fish's tail becomes the tail of a goose that has the clothespin fastened onto its beak, and the clothespin's legs become the tail of the next unfolding picture of a fish chasing an apple. The half apple in turn becomes the back of a person trying to catch a shoe, and the shoe the tail of a creature (not an alligator, but certainly a cousin) who is reaching for a moon. Here there is a significant move, for the next simple image of the moon is smiling, where the one chased by the creature was alarmed. The moon becomes a snake reaching for the ping-pong equipment, that becomes a plane smoking a pipe; the pipe becomes a cat looking askance at a toothbrush, the toothbrush an elephant reaching into a box, the box image, with jack now jumping out, becomes a dog driving a horse with a flower in its mouth, and the flower, on the back endpages, completes the book.

The connections between the simple objects and the active scenes in which they first appear are immediately apparent. But other more subtle elements of organization are also included. I mentioned the obvious change on the moon's face, but in each case there is a delicate alteration that takes place between the introductory appearance in the active scene picture and the full, focused image that appears on its own double spread before it is unfolded. Some changes are slight: the apple's stem is straighter; the coffee cup is no longer steaming; the clothes pin is closed instead of open, the pipe, and the ping pong equipment are at different angles. But the toothbrush moves from the cat's hand to the top of the glass, and, more surprising, Jack is hidden in the box the elephant holds, appearing only on his own double spread. We might consider that these changes suggest a book's varying narrative viewpoints on characters and events in a developing story.

There are also thematic recurrences that link characters or events. For example, the fish appears both as the image on a double spread and the action figure on the triplespread, and the alligator and the dinosaur-like creature are clearly related. Furthermore, the relationship between the action figure on each triplespread with the object that appears in the next double spread, is interesting. From balance, co-existence and entrapment in the first three images, the next four all deal with a chase, as the action figure pursues the object, chasing it onto the next page.

The last four images all have to do with mouth sensations of the object which the action figure now possesses: the plane smokes the pipe, the cat considers the toothbrush before or after brushing its teeth, the elephant puts its trunk into the box, and the horse holds the flower in its mouth. This overall progression toward catching, holding and tasting suggests an overall developing plot which reflects a child's consumption of a book in more ways than one, as the chewed corners of many books for young children bear witness!

Orange Pear Apple Bear: Playing with words

Since this study began with learning theories involving pears, I think it is most appropriate to end with an examination of Emily Gravett's *Orange Pear Apple Bear* (2007). The first impression of this apparently simple work is deceptive, for the book introduces some very sophisticated concepts of visual metaphor, word use, word play, rhyme and grammatical structure. It also provides a great example of metamorphosis in image and in referent as nouns merge into adjectives and the image follows suit; and it exemplifies the notions I introduced earlier regarding generalization and categorization.

Like the board book, the front and back covers tell a story. On the front, the bear balances three pieces of fruit – the orange, the pear and the apple – on its head. No bear appears on the back cover, but we can see the result of its interaction with the fruit: apple and pear cores, and orange peel. This progression is reinforced by the front endpapers which depict several pieces of whole fruit, and the back end-papers' images of cores and peel. The endpapers, which depict more than the covers' three pieces of fruit, are also of significant relevance to my earlier discussion of the process of generalization and particularization in the development of cognition. For the fruit neither stays in the same order, nor do all the apples, all the pears, or all the oranges look identical.

This shifting around requires a keen eye, and characterizes the book as a whole. On the front cover, for example, the words of the title, in rhyming verse form,

Orange
Pear
Apple
Bear

do not correspond with their order in the illustration, for the pear is on the top, next the orange, then the apple, and finally the bear at the bottom. On the title page, the bear has taken the three pieces of fruit from his head, and offers them to us: though the verse remains constant, the sequence of fruit in the illustration has changed, for, while the pear remains on top, the apple and the orange have changed places. Once again, the sequence of words does not match the sequence in the illustration.

The narrative of the book then moves from the depiction of relationship to focus on the individual as each is introduced separately on its own page with its name, the first letter appropriately capitalized, printed underneath. Superficially the work appears to be a simple reader, one object to one picture, but the next sequence begins their interplay. First the apple and pear appear together, the pear poised on top of the apple as it was on the title page, and both names beneath, only the first with an initial capital letter, and the two words separated by a comma. On the recto, is just one object, an orange bear. The orange fruit has metamorphosed into a color and furthermore into an adjective, becoming a descriptor of the bear, which has indeed exchanged its brown coat for a red one. And, as appropriate, the words now announce "Orange bear" with no comma.

Figure 1. Book cover from *Orange Pear Apple Bear* by Emily Gravett, New York: Macmillan Publishers Ltd, 2007

The next double spread becomes increasingly complicated: this time the orange, still a color and an adjective, has shifted to join with the pear as "Orange pear" and, amazingly, the apple, which remains as a noun, is also acting as an adjective, "Apple bear" describing the bear. Visually the combination works remarkably well: the bear seems a little surprised at its coloring and shape, but it does clearly resemble an apple, both in color and shape, while losing none of its identity as a bear.

Over the page, the four characters are together again in one image, but it is the pear's turn to merge itself in shape and color with the bear, while the orange and apple are back as individuals, balanced in the pear bear's hand. This time it is the recto page that carries all the words, "Apple, orange, pear bear" with the "sentence" initiated by a capital letter, and the two separate objects divided by commas from the pear bear. Noticeably, this is the first time that the rhyme has been interrupted. It will, of course, be the reader, not the child, who recognizes the significance of commas, but one hopes that the reader will sound out the difference the comma makes between, for example "apple, bear" and apple bear" so that the "sort of visual grammar" (Kümmerling-Meibauer & Meibauer 2005: 333) in the images will prepare the child for later reading.

In a reprise of the cover, the next verso page once again shows the fruit balanced on the bear's head, as they were on the front cover, but in a somewhat different configuration, for this time the words and images appear in the same order. The words "Orange, pear, apple, bear" are set in one line in the center of the page and divided by commas. The shifting process has rendered them accurately presented in appropriate book format, and the rhyme has returned. This recreation of the relationship of each "character" is continued on the following double spread, with the bear taking control in a juggling act. The illustration, which shows the bear tossing the fruit from hand to hand, covers both pages, while the words are included on the recto. Both fruit and words are set in roughly diagonal lines downwards from left to right: the fruit appears in the same order as their names, "Apple, bear, orange, pear" the bear appropriately intervening with his nose and his name in second place.

From this point on, the denouement begins, for the next four double spreads reveal the bear steadily consuming each of the pieces of fruit. The last time that the words orange and bear appeared together, the bear had assumed the qualities of the fruit. This time he has eaten it. The orange is now represented solely by its peel, which sits on a plate in the bear's outstretched hand, and the words "Orange, bear" while they give pride of place to the orange, are clearly separated by the comma. The plot continues logically as the bear eats the pear (only the core remains) and then the apple from which he has as yet taken only one bite. The very last double spread reveals the end of the story: the end of the fruit (peels and cores) on the verso, the back end of the bear on the recto, and the final pronouncement "There!" on the verso which brings in a new word on the penultimate page.

This humorously brilliant work introduces the young reader to so many literary concepts: character and interaction, narrative sequence, rhyme and word play and notions of metamorphosis to name a few. But it also foregrounds the nature of language and word relationships, and – though these are beyond the recognition capability of the youngest children – the formalities of the written word, and punctuation (including the use of capitalization noting the division of sequences) which establish an aural groundwork for later learning.

Conclusion

Gravett's book is especially cogent because it exemplifies the very elements of learning and memory formation noted at the beginning of this study. For it includes the concepts of basic memorization (object and name), as well as the challenges of representing objects in language and language structures. Like the pieces of fruit, the words and their structuring into meaning have a slippery way of slithering around, sparking new interrelationships that demand understanding, organization, and constructive re-creation. The persistent juggling that the Bear must engage in involves balancing, tossing around, ordering and re-ordering before he achieves mastery and can finally consume the words and their referents with pleasure. The "There!" suggests, like the QED in mathematics, the satisfaction in the final achievement. In addition, the gymnastic actions themselves bring an element of physicality to the manipulations, reminding us of the neuroscientists' theories regarding learning theory including the firing of mirror neurons and the way they seem to support the ability of human beings to think and to pass on their ideas to others. In these ways Gravett's work might itself be considered as a metaphor for the early learning process that researchers in many fields continue to explore.

Children's books cited

Bataille, M. 2008. *ABC3D*. New York NY: Holtzbrinck.
Goffin, J. 2007. *OH!* Brussels: Kalandraka.
Gravett, E. 2007. *Orange Pear Apple Bear*. New York NY: Simon and Schuster.
Porter, M. 2006. *ABC*. Vancouver: Simply Read.
Simon, A. 2005. *Mocking Birdies*. Vancouver: Simply Read.
Van Allsburg, C. 1987. *The Z Was Zapped*. New York NY: Houghton Mifflin.

References

Ackerman, J. M., Nocera, C. C. & Bargh, J. A. 2010. Incidental haptic sensations influence social judgments and decisions. *Science* 328 (June 25): 1712–1715.

Anderson, M. L. 2007. The massive redeployment hypothesis and the functional topography of the brain. *Philosophical Psychology* 20(2): 143–174.

Apseloff, M. 1987. Books for babies: Learning toys or pre-Literature. *CHLAQ* 12(2): 63–66.

Jones, R. 1996. *Emerging Patterns of Literacy: A Multidisciplinary Perspective.* London: Routledge.

LaFee, S. 2009. The not-so-simple gesture. *San Diego Union Tribune* January 26: E1.

Levitin, D. J. 2006. *This is Your Brain on Music.* New York NY: Penguin.

Kümmerling-Meibauer, B. & Meibauer, J. 2005. First pictures, early concepts: Early concept books. *The Lion and the Unicorn* 29(3): 324–347.

Ramachandran, V. 2010. The neurons that shaped civilization. TED India, 2009, posted 2010. <http://www.ted.com/talks/us_ramachan_the_neurons_that_shaped_civilization.html> (July 18, 2010).

Seitz, A. R. & Dinse, H. R. 2007. A common framework for perceptual learning. *Current Opinion in Neurobiology* 17(2): 148–53.

CHAPTER 10

Linking behavioral training and scientific thinking

Toilet training picturebooks in Japan

Kyoko Takashi and Douglas Wilkerson

This study demonstrates the continuity between Japanese picturebooks about toilet training for very young children (0–3) and the use of subjects related to toilet training and bodily functions to introduce scientific concepts and ways of thinking about the body and the world to readers of elementary-school age. The authors suggest that knowledge about bodily functions may be used to increase control over those functions in an effort to encourage uniform behavior in young children.

Introduction

Japan is not unique in publishing books, targeted at children under four, which deal with images of the self, play, names for things, colors and shapes, sound and song, and simple stories. However, the number of Japanese books for children of all ages, but particularly those in their first three years, devoted to human excretory functions, seems to be unusually great. According to Mukougawa Mikio, until the late 1970s the purpose of such books, as with books on getting dressed, brushing ones teeth, and using appropriate greetings when required, was "training" or inculcating "proper behavior" (Mukougawa 1998: 53–57). While "discipline" books continue to be published, and books which encourage children to show "proper behavior" during toilet training continue to appear, the marked increase in books dealing with bodily functions over the last thirty years can be attributed largely to a new approach, books which emphasize the universal nature and importance of excretory functions, as epitomized in the widely translated *Everybody Poops* by Gomi Taro. A recent search of a Japanese bookseller's website (*amazon.co.jp*) for current titles of books employing the Japanese equivalent of the words "pee-pee" and "poop" resulted in 34 and 58 titles respectively. The number of books that deal directly or indirectly with these subjects, but do not include these words in the title, is surely much greater.

This study examines the introduction of such topics in books for younger children as a form of preparation for the increasingly popular appearance of these same topics in science books and magazines for older children (6–10 years of age). More specifically, this paper will show how recent Japanese books for infants and toddlers move beyond the treatment of toilet training as merely one step in behavioral training and socialization, to the deployment of excretory functions as the first step in the construction of the foundations for a link which will later be forged between the toddler's experiences in toilet training and a more "scientific" approach to the world around them: a scientific understanding of human anatomy, in particular, and, by carefully planned extension, a more scientific approach to a great variety of natural and social phenomena. This "scientific" approach is then, in its turn, directed back at the child and used to inculcate, in the mind of the child, a more "scientific" approach to the child's own behavior, linked to further exemplars of "proper behavior" through books for toddlers (as well as for older children) which locate this behavior consciously in the wider social and human context.

Linking behavioral (toilet) training to scientific thinking: "Poop" and "poot" (gas) as "prompts" in introducing human anatomy and other scientific topics to older children

Glancing through children's magazines and popular comic books for children published in Japan, a Western reader may be surprised by the frequency of scatological references and allusions, especially in titles and section headings. Titles such as "Carnivorous vs. Herbivorous Dinosaurs from Fossilized Poop" (2007), "How Japanese and French Princesses Pooped: The Development of Sewage Systems" (2007), "Pee-pee and Poop Float About When You Use the Toilet on a Spaceship" (2007), "Would a Poot on a Spaceship Cause an Explosion?" (2007) and "Would a Poot on a Spaceship Be Unbearably Stinky?" (2007) are excellent examples of the introduction of a variety of historical and scientific topics to slightly older children through the agency of "pee-pee", "poop", and "poot." This use of human effluents as a teaching tool is likely a conscious effort to capitalize on the practice, long established in Japan and other parts of East Asia, of observing excrement for indications of ones general state of health and the suitability of ones dietary habits. During the last few years this type of observation has been strongly encouraged from an early age (2–3 years) in many Japanese kindergartens and child-care centers. It makes use of children's universal fascination with their own bodily effluents, but also has a long history of acceptance in Japanese culture. Scatological references are frequently made in popular comic books, and have long been common in fairy tales, children's stories, and the classic comic storytelling (*rakugo*) of the eighteenth and nineteenth centuries.

One might argue that the use of scatological subjects as a teaching tool is not unique to Japan. Sylvia Branzei, American author of such popular books (over 300,000 copies sold) as *Grossology* (1995) and *Grossology and You* (2002), takes advantage of kids' fascination with the "gross" to teach about bodily functions and offer a glimpse of the scientific explanations behind what kids think of as "gross." But the appeal of Branzei's books lies in the thrill of indulging the immature in their fascination for what is generally a forbidden topic, and, more often than not, the pseudo-scientific justification for handling such topics consists of little more than "experiments" in making imitations (out of common household materials) that look or feel like human effluents (excrement, blood, pus, vomit, gas) or that imitate the unpleasant results of accidents (scars, scabs, wounds, etc.). In contrast, Japanese writers demonstrate a marked tendency to use such topics as pedagogical prompts for the introduction of significant scientific concepts such as the history of sewage and human hygiene, or the effects of weightlessness in space.

The difference in these two approaches to bodily functions can be more fully understood by examining the Japanese historical and cultural perspectives on human excrement. Japan has a long history and tradition of religious veneration related to human excrement. According to Japanese mythology, Izanami, one of the divine ancestors of the Japanese emperors and consort of Izanagi, progenitor of many deities, died when giving birth to the fire god Kagutsuchi. Izanami also defecated and micturated; from the bolus came the gods of clay, Haniyasu-biko and Haniyasu-bime; from the urine came the gods of water, Mitsuhanome, and grains, Wakumusuhi. In addition to the veneration of gods produced from (divine) excrement, belief in gods of the toilet is found throughout Japan. These gods are thought to protect women during pregnancy and childbirth. The popularity of these gods of the toilet is evident from their appearance in such fairy tales as "The Three Talismans."

The recent popularity of "Gold Poop" figurines underscores the wide acceptance of images of, and references to, human excrement in Japanese culture. In late 1999 a Kyoto doll maker hit on the idea of producing small gold-covered images of human excrement as symbols of good fortune. *Un* meaning "fortune" or "luck" in Japanese is also the first sound in *unchi* "poop," so the combination *kin'un* "golden fortune" is very close to *kin'unchi* or "gold poop" (Gordenker 2007). Interestingly enough, the figurines were particularly popular among teenage girls. References to human excrement in humorous situations, or as a guide to the physical health of an individual, have not been condemned in Japan, or confined to the medical examining room as they have in many other cultures.

References to flatulence in Japanese culture are also not uncommon or necessarily seen as being in bad taste. Flatulence plays a central role in folk tales such as

"The Farting Bride" (*Heppiri yome-sama*) (Matsutani 2002: 74–77), and in *rakugo* stories such as "A Southerly Wind from Suma" (*Suma no ura-kaze*) and "Perdonosis" (*Tenshiki*)[1]. Generally it is not necessary to avoid mention of natural bodily processes and their effluents; in some cases they can even be seen as heroic virtues. In "The Farting Bride" an unusually flatulent woman goes to great extremes to insure her own rectal continence after marriage, but her health fails as a result. Unburdening herself to her mother-in-law, she receives permission to pass wind, at which point a flatus of astounding proportions blows the mother-in-law out of the house. Seeing his own mother subjected to such violent mistreatment, the husband sends his bride back to her own home. On her shameful journey home she encounters the procession of a nobleman, who makes known to her that he is suffering from an overpowering thirst. Firing off several rounds of flatus the ill-starred bride knocks many juicy pears out of a nearby tree, and is handsomely rewarded for the pears by the nobleman. Reward in hand she returns to her husband's house once more, where they live together happily ever after.

In "A Southerly Wind from Suma" a nobleman plans a visit to the home of a wealthy merchant. To receive his noble guest in a fitting manner, the merchant instructs his servants to take a chest to the seashore at Suma, and there fill it with the cooling sea breezes for which this part of Japan's Inland Sea coast is famed. When his guest arrives, the merchant plans to open the chest and refresh his guest with its contents. Lugging the heavy chest back from the seashore, the servants stop for a rest, and are unable to resist the temptation to refresh themselves with the contents of their burden. Refreshed, but unwilling to take back an empty chest, they make their own wind to refill it, with predictable results when the nobleman arrives for his visit to their master's home. Another classic tale, "Perdonosis," describes a doctor's visit to a learned monk seeking relief from an ailment. In the course of his examination the doctor asks if the monk has had "perdonosis" (intestinal gas) recently. Unwilling to reveal his own ignorance, the monk pretends to understand the question, and the tale goes on to describe how the monk and others use the term in comical ways because they do not realize that it is simply an old Chinese medical term for "fart."

The last century and a half of contact with the West has begun to effect a change in these traditional attitudes. Dr. Fujita Kouichirou, a Professor of Medicine at Tokyo Medical and Dental University, is the translator of the Japanese edition of *Grossology* and *Grossology and You*. In the Translator's Note to both books he states the following:

---

1. *5-Minute* Rakugo *Stories to Read Aloud* (2005) by Osada Sadao is a collection of twenty-three classic rakugo tales rewritten for easy reading aloud by adults or children. Breaking wind plays an important role in these two tales from this collection.

> The Japanese obsession with cleanliness has become even more thoroughgoing of late. I worry that the common belief that a sterile environment is "godly" is robbing our children of their natural defenses against contagion. It was as I became convinced that the only way to restore our children to health was to reduce the repulsion they feel about "dirty things" that I encountered this book [*Grossology*].
> (Fujita 1998; and Fujita & Yanagi 2006)

Through the publication of these books in Japanese Dr. Fujita hoped to undermine this recent obsession with cleanliness, and restore a healthier outlook on natural functions and human hygiene.

It is probably too early to conclude that in recent years children in Japan have come to consider human excrement as repulsive ("gross"), but there is a growing tendency to at least view it as somewhat embarrassing. Murakami Yachiyo, a self-professed "comfort stylist," advises corporations and public organizations on ways to make public facilities more comfortable for their users. In the first book of her *The Book of Poop* series, *Poopy, Pooey, Poo, Poop* (*Unpi, Un'yo, Ungo, Unchi*) she states:

> Poop is nothing to be ashamed of; it is a natural and very important part of living.
> Shall we talk about it together?
> A book to help you feel good about going to the toilet. (Murakami 2000)

Linking scientific thinking to proper behavior: Human anatomy and proper behavior

Having discussed Japanese cultural attitudes toward human excrement, we would now like to discuss the changing nature of "discipline books" for younger children, along with the role which they serve in laying the foundations for a meaningful understanding of the emerging field of "disciplinary comments" for children, and the agency of "poop," and to a lesser extent "gas," in these genres.

Universal nature of excretory functions emphasized

There are many toilet training books for infants (two years or younger) in Japan whose primary purpose is clearly to encourage infants to urinate (or defecate) in appointed toilets because this behavior is considered correct. Examples of this type include *Non-chan Goes "Pee, Pee"* (Kiyono Sachiko, Non-tan o-shikko shii-shii, 1987) and *We Can Wee* (Fuyuno Ichiko, Chii dekita-yo, 2006), both of which stress how much fun and how easy it is to comply with the authoritarian demands of toilet training. However, recent publications in Japan evidence a tendency to play down the obligatory nature of this behavior and in its place to emphasize the universality and natural importance of the excretory functions in a wide variety of humans as well as in a range of non-human animals. This newer type of book is epitomized by *Everybody Poops* by Gomi Taro (1977), widely translated from Japanese into European languages, in which all sorts of animals are depicted together with excrement of distinctive and characteristic shapes and sizes. A German book somewhat similar in nature, W. Holzwarth and W. Erlbruch's *Vom kleinen Maulwurf, der wissen wollte, wer ihm auf den Kopf gemacht hat* (The Story of the Little Mole Who Went in Search of Whodunit, 1989), was translated into Japanese in 1993, and has also been widely read in Japanese translation.

More recent toilet training picturebooks for infants follow this lead, focusing on the universality of the excretory functions. One of the most widely read (by children, and to children) toilet training picturebooks, *Can You Poop by Yourself?* (Kimura Yuuichi, Hitori de unchi dekiru kana? 1989) shows a kitten, a bird, a puppy, a monster, and a little girl one by one using a portable toilet. The text includes comments on what type of stool each of these characters produces (tiny, huge, good, healthy), together with a reminder to flush the toilet and wash ones hands, and concludes with a picture of a mother clapping her hands in approval.

During the last thirty years disciplinary books which encourage very young children to cooperate in toilet training have evidenced several changes in the presentation of the topic: a move toward a new standard for normative behavior, and a nearly simultaneous move from a narrow disciplinary approach towards a wider pedagogical approach, reflecting similar trends in formal education in Japan during roughly the same period. Before this period disciplinary books in general, and books on toilet training in particular, tended to set as their normative standard the approbation of a figure of authority, such as a parent, child-care giver, or instructor. The influence of this approach can still be seen even in the 1989 publication *Can You Poop by Yourself?*, which rewards "performers" at the end of the book with the cheery approval of a mother figure. Voluntary accommodation to the behavioral norms of toilet training is "correct behavior" because it earns the approval of authority, as was usually the case in books published before this period. But the majority of pages in this same book, *Can You Poop by Yourself?*, is devoted to a different approach and appeal to a different standard of correct behavior: the behavioral norms inculcated during toilet training constitute correct behavior now because they are practiced universally; the ultimate justification for the behavior as well as its normative force, as portrayed in these picturebooks, derives, not so much from approval by individual accepted authority figures (parent, care-giver), but from the practice of a normative "(wider) community," bound by some elemental feature held in common, which gives the behavior of this community moral authority over any individual member belonging to it.

The particular nature of the figures chosen to represent and embody this normative "wider community" also reveals a didactic element in these books which lays the groundwork for acceptance of elements which later become essential to a culturally acceptable understanding of animal life, the place of humans in the natural world, and the formation of characteristic Japanese conceptions of morality based on the sanctity of (animal) life. Depictions of older family members in the same act of defecation found in toilet training picturebooks may help the toddler to overcome any sense of isolation or frustration arising from the struggle to control the excretory functions, but they also serve to inculcate not only the behavior modeled there, but also the types (socialized family members) which should serve as models for all types of acceptable behavior. The extension of this community of behavioral models to include non-human animals implies a certain degree of parity with humans in terms of modeling correct behavior. The animals included in depictions of this wider community by different writers are surprisingly similar: with the exception of the bird mentioned above, they are animals or imaginary creatures which defecate in a manner similar to humans, and even the avian exception is portrayed so as to more closely resemble its human counterpart. This normative wider community thus consists largely of the larger animals, predominantly mammals, with the addition of clearly anthropomorphic "monsters" or other imaginary creatures.

Picturebooks which depict the human community as models for the toddler's behavior, such as *Everybody Poops*, often point out that the bolus varies considerably in a number of important characteristics from individual to individual. This might serve to assure the toddler who is attempting to make their behavior better conform to the norm that it is the behavior, rather than the end product, that is to be most closely modeled, but this feature of the picturebooks also serves another pedagogic function: to alert the child to differences in the bolus which will later be identified as significant, and whose significance will be explained in a variety of contexts. Just as one can expect humans of different size and age to produce a bolus of characteristic size, the qualities of the bolus of other animal species also have their characteristic qualities – consistency, shape, color, and size. Quite early in the education of children in Japan (often from the age of two or three) the attention of the child is called to variations in the child's own bolus from day to day. Through simple reflection on the child's recent meals and state of health, a connection is made between the qualities of the bolus, dietary habits, and bodily condition. This conscious observation of distinguishing characteristics in the bolus later serves as the foundation for observations on the relationship between human health and observable variations in excrement, as well as more complex discussions of the relationship between the consistency, shape, color, and size of animal excrement and the dietary habits of animals, both living and extinct.

It is not surprising, in light of the analogy which toddlers are expected to make between their own toilet training and the behavior of non-human animals, that the animals chosen for portrayal in picturebooks for the very young perform their excretory functions in a manner similar to that of humans. Another interesting point of commonality between the animals chosen for this normative community in these books is that the bolus of all animals usually displays a surprising conformity to the archetypical portrayal of the human bolus in popular Japanese culture. This archetypical portrayal roughly depicts the shape formed when a soft semi-solid is extruded from a tube or nozzle in a series of ever narrowing concentric circles, a pyramid or pointed swirl similar to that made when soft ice cream is extruded into an ice-cream cone. With surprisingly little variation this shape represents the human bolus in children's picturebooks, in comics for older children, and in a wide variety of trinkets and souvenirs on sale in Japan, including the hugely popular Golden Poop described above. With some artistic liberty the bolus of the various animals appearing in toilet training books is depicted as quite similar to that of humans, and the representative animals are chosen in part by their conformity to this standard. Usually absent from this normative group are animals whose bolus is not easily recognizable as such, and animals, such as goats with their hard, pellet-like bolus, known to differ significantly from this archetype. Membership in this normative community in Japan is thus largely a factor of the degree of similarity to humans in terms of excretory functions and the resultant bolus, largely limiting membership in the community to larger animals, and the larger mammals in particular. As Japanese children grow older and are introduced to abstract moral concepts, such as the sanctity of (animal) life, both in informal discussions as toddlers, and in formal settings in Ethics classes, it is this same normative community of animal life which is most often invoked.

Becoming health conscious

One writer of toilet training picturebooks, Murakami Yachiyo, who promotes herself as a "comfort stylist," has received the unusual distinction of being chosen by the Japan Toilet Association as one of their facilitators, specially trained to conduct sessions aimed at helping children overcome their reluctance to use toilet facilities outside of the home. This service of the Japan Toilet Association was introduced in June 1998, the year that marked the publication of the Japanese translation of *Grossology*. Murakami has now published three picturebooks in *The Book of Poop* series: *Poopy, Pooey, Poo, Poop* (Unpi, unnyo, unchi, ungo – unko no ehon, 2000), *Poop-pusher Man* (Unko-dasu-man, 2001), and *Can You Go to the Toilet at School?* (Gakkou de toire ni ikeru kana? 2004).

Figure 1. Book cover from *Unko-dasu-man taisou* (Poop-pusher Man Exercises) by Yachiyo Murakami. Tokyo: Horupu, 2008

The first volume begins in this way: "I am Dr. Poop. I know everything about poop. Have you looked at your poop carefully? There are many shapes, colors and smells… Let's see when you have each kind." Dr. Poop goes on to discuss four types that differ according to what one eats. "Everyone, everywhere. We poop at home. We poop at school. We poop around the world. It shows you are alive! Look lively when you go! 'I'll be right back!' Icky poo, sticky poo, healthy poo, rocky poo. What kind will it be today?" The book then encourages children to keep a daily watch on the quality of their bowel movements, and the different stool specimens cry out to be flushed away. The book concludes with a reminder to wash ones hands after all the fun. This book has received the imprimatur of the Japanese Association for the Study of Children's Books, in apparent recognition of its pedagogical value for toilet training. Among the lessons incorporated in this volume we can find the following: bodily functions are not cause for embarrassment; different textures of excrement can be identified and named; your excrement reflects what and how you eat; one should examine ones stools, and make daily observations; don't forget to flush the toilet and wash your hands. The book comes complete with a wall poster showing the different types of stools (life size), to help children make accurate observations and aid in identification.

Murakami's second book was published the following year (2001) under the title *Poop-pusher Man*. Following in the long line of precedents begun by Batman, the main character is dressed as a superhero, complete with tights, mask, and cape. The author asks her little readers if they have a stool every day; she encourages them to imitate the hero by becoming poop-pushers, and having a healthy poop. After mentioning four symptoms of constipation, the villain of the drama, Murakami explains that the daily bowel movement depends on lifestyle and eating habits, and provides suggestions that each child can follow to become a superhero: eat breakfast, eat plenty of fiber-rich vegetables, drink lots of water, exercise, and keep regular hours, early to bed and early to rise. But the path of the budding superhero is fraught with danger. "But suppose that, just when you're ready to go, you don't want to leave the TV … Your poop will get upset, and will refuse to come out! Anywhere, anytime, if you want to go, then GO!" In a separate message to parents and teachers, Murakami claims that an interest in one's stool is the first step toward active health self-management, and for this reason a habit of daily observation should be inculcated, and should later prove invaluable to the child. This publication also provides stickers portraying four types of stool mentioned in the book. The new compact disc (CD) of music for *Poop-Pusher Man Exercises* (see Figure 1) went on sale in 2008. The author states that in some child-care facilities the book and music are combined in a daily training ritual: a teacher reads Murakami's book to children, has each of them don their own hand-made Poop-Pusher mask and perform Poop-Pusher Man exercises to the music provided; the "transformation" to superhero complete, the teacher sends each of them to the toilet with confidence that a successful bowel movement will be the result.

The Japan Toilet Research Center (Lavatory Laboratory), an organ of the Japan Toilet Association, has announced plans to release a recording, in Japanese and English versions, of a "Poopy Song" (*unchicchi no uta*). According to the Center's website, "A child's health starts with its poop." As the song will be recorded in English as well as Japanese, it is a song that "children, not only in Japan, but all over the world, will be able to enjoy singing and dancing to. The booklet explains how to have a healthy (lit. good) poop, provides illustrations detailing the choreography [of the dance for which the music provides accompaniment], and is full of things that will make kids love their poop" (Japan Toilet Research Center 2008). The music and exercises help children to become more aware of their bodies and bodily functions, and begin the process of transforming them into health-conscious members of society. This is very different from the scatological diarrhea song found in *Grossology*, intended for a bit of fun, and to cover the embarrassment occasioned by dashing to the toilet.

Popular science magazines[2] for elementary school students continue to build on this foundation later in the child's life, stressing the importance of a daily bowel movement, and providing tips to help the child exercise control over the timing of their own bowel movement, so as to allow them to choose when and where to use the toilet. Murakami's third volume in *The Book of Poop* series, *Can You Go to the Toilet at School?* attempts to build yet further on this foundation constructed through toilet training picturebooks for infants and toddlers, seeking out ways to use the toddler's experiences in toilet training to ease the troublesome transition from home to school in later years. The earlier emphasis on the universality of animal waste, and the understanding of their own by-products gained by children through these picturebooks is an important part of Murakami's program for older children.

A word about gas

Along with the universality of animal wastes and the general sensitivity toward personal health which this concept has been used to inculcate, recent children's "discipline" books (as well as science books and magazines for older children) have also featured flatus as a means of introducing important concepts. One year after the publication of Gomi Taro's *Everybody Poops* (1977), Cho Shinta's book on intestinal gas was published by the same Fukuinkan Publications. *The Gas We Pass: The Story of Farts* (1978) shows an enormous elephant "farting" and people sitting in bath water doing the same, hinting at the universality of this effluent as well. The book suggests that the air one swallows comes back out as a burp or a fart, and shows a diagram of a human body marked to indicate the various pathways taken by food and air ingested into the system, together with mention of other sources of intestinal gas. Once again the book makes it clear that frequency and volume of gas released varies from individual to individual, and species to species. This is followed by advice on related behavior: "If you try too hard to hold in your farts, your stomach may hurt, you may feel dizzy and even get a headache. Don't hold it in – pass the gas! When a patient begins to fart again after a surgical operation, it shows that their intestines have finally started to work again." The discussion ends with mention of the sources of unpleasant odors in flatus, including that of other carnivorous animals. The final word in the English translation of this book is "FARTHEEWELL," a translation of the Japanese pun (common

2. Examples include *First Grade Challenge: Discovery Book*, Sept. 2005, Science Book, pp. 11–12, and "Feels Great to Get It Out! Discover Body-Helper Men (Body Effluents)" in *Third Grade Challenge: Why!?* Nov. 2007, pp. 12–13.

among children in Japan), *sayo + o-nara* (*sayo* + "fart") on the common parting phrase *sayounara*. The end pages of the book are decorated with a list of nearly one hundred different and distinct onomatopoetic notations for the sound of human flatulence, a rich thesaurus of choice words and noises, of endless fascination to toddlers, and further evidence of the important place which discussions of human effluents hold in Japanese culture.

2007, the year before the debut of *Poop-Pusher Man*'s CD, saw the appearance of a CD and DVD devoted to Farting Exercises, or Gasercises. The DVD contains episodes from an animated series based on a popular, award-winning girl's comic book series, *Nodame Cantabile*, in which the eponymous main character, Nodame, attends a music school and aspires to become a kindergarten teacher. She composes a song, complete with choreography, to encourage her little charges to pass their gas. While there are three songs recorded on the compact disc, pride of place and prominence are given to the song "Gasercises," which is also the title of the album. Unlike Poop-Pusher Man's song the lyrics do not explicitly instruct children to pass gas, but they do convey the message that adults do it often, so children should not be shy. Don't hesitate. Fart with vigor. The sky's the limit. Everyone together now!

> Let it fly, what nice sounds,
> Do re mi fa pu pu pu. Hey!
> Stand up high, squat down low,
> Still the same old fart.
> Hands on hips, everyone!
> Hey, hey, puu.
>
> Let's all do it, do it laughing,
> Do re mi fa pu pu pu. Hey!
> Daddy does it, Mommy does it,
> Eeeverybody does it, now.
> Sky's the limit. Ready, set,
> Hey, hey, puu.
>
> Working at it, … here it comes now
> Do re mi fa pu pu pu. Hey!
> Great big fart? Cutesy fart?
> What kind will it be?
> Everyone together now, Ready, set,
> Hey, hey, puu. (It's out!)

As with picturebooks on toilet training, the message taught to toddlers is later explicitly linked to science education in works for older children. Volume 6 of the *Doraemon's Amazing Exploration* series, *Exploring the Body* (Fujiko F. Fujio,

Doraemon fushigi tanken shiriizu: Karada dai-tanken, 1993) shows a character with mouth tightly closed, using intestinal gasses to "sing a song." In another panel a boy, face red with the accompanying strain, attempts to hold in his gas, only to release it in a tremendous blast which sends him flying out of the window. "It's not good to try too hard to hold in your farts," concludes the writer. A monthly science magazine for third-graders makes the same comment after an explanation of human excretory functions (Third Grade Challenge, Nov. 2007: 14–15).

Conclusion

"Don't hold it in." Whether it is gas or poop, the message in picturebooks, and then again later in books and science magazines for preschoolers and elementary students is loud and clear (e.g., Suda, *Healthy Poo, Gas Smells Good*, 1999). Other books chime in with, "Everyday, check your stool, count your gas, keep a journal, and know your body!" (Murakami 2000). The new line of books on advanced toilet training is in!

The stool can be a good indicator of health, and it seems commendable to keep regular hours. If gymnastic exercises help children visualize the path food takes, and encourages them to have a bowel movement when they feel the urge, perhaps Japanese early-childhood educators can kill two birds with one stone: by teaching about the human digestive system, the origins of intestinal discharges, and what effluents can tell us about our state of health, they also hope to overcome any hesitation or discomfort in dealing with the body's natural functions. But even when one contemplates the recent emphasis on advanced "toilet training" for children (gymnastic exercises, unison singing, and other strategies) in light of Japan's historical lack of discomfort when dealing with natural functions, one cannot but wonder if the newer "discipline books" may not be burdening the younger generation of Japanese with yet another form of pressure to conform socially and "do the accepted thing" at the same time, and in the same way as everyone else in the normative community.

A casual look at "toilet training books" and books on the body in the United States suggests that American books do not carry the same message to conform. In *Body Noises* (1983), authors Susan Buxbaum and Rita Gelman discuss what causes gas, but offer no advice on how or when to dispel it. Interestingly enough, in Japanese translation the title was changed to *Farts, Snores, Sneezes … Body Noises*. Note that, while there are eight other body noises mentioned in the book before the description of gas, flatulence is placed first in the Japanese translation. Likewise, in the section on constipation in *Grossology*, the author merely suggests steps which might be taken to induce a bowel movement without suggesting that this is a daily necessity or that a lack of "regularity" is something to be feared.

In Japan group exercises to music broadcast nationally over the radio have a long history of popularity. Workers, even white-collar workers, often begin their workday with group exercises, using recordings of the original radio music to fit their work schedule when they cannot exercise to live broadcasts. Children often gather early in the morning in neighborhood parks during summer vacation to participate in "radio exercises" in lieu of the physical education classes taken while school is in session. Now younger elementary students and even preschoolers are being encouraged to perform a new type of group exercises by authors, publishers, and "comfort stylists." Perhaps the time will come when the day for children, whether in Japanese child-care centers, local parks, or kindergartens and schools, will begin with exercises for internal health consciousness.

When we began research on this topic we used the provisional title "Linking Proper Behavior to Scientific Thinking," conceiving of these science books for older children as encouraging a quite literally "bottom-up" approach to scientific thinking. However, as the research progressed, and the examples multiplied, we came to realize that these books really represent a "top-down" approach and an extension of toilet training well beyond the pre-school years, even into the later years of elementary schooling. Many toilet training picturebooks purport to empower the child, to impart control over the difficult sphincter muscles, the mastery of which marks an important step toward maturity, and suggest even the possibility of granting control over involuntary bodily processes through a scientific understanding of the digestive system and an informed manipulation of significant life-style factors such as diet, exercise, and rest. They also claim to free the child from physical and social constraints, to grant each individual the full freedom to follow their body's urging at their own convenience, uninhibited by time or place. But in doing so they also work to put these forces under the control of the group and its leader. This last vestige of personal control over one's body's most intimate functions can, through picturebooks, physical training, music, and group exercises, be placed within the control of the child-care worker, parent, or teacher, ensuring that children will not only walk, talk, and eat as instructed, but will also learn to defecate, micturate, and pass gas on command, together with the group, at the convenience of its leader and an impersonal timetable. Thus we have been forced to conclude that the title "Linking Behavioral Training AND Scientific Thinking" will better express the ongoing dialectic between these two aspects of early childhood education in Japan.

Children's books cited

Branzei, S. 1995. *Grossology.* Harlow: Addison Wesley Longman.

Branzei, S. 2002. *Grossology and You.* New York NY: Price Stern Sloan.

Buxbaum, S. & Gelman, R. G. 1983. *Body Noises.* New York NY: Alfred A. Knopf.

Carnivorous vs. herbivorous dinosaurs from fossilized poop. *Third Grade Challenge,* Oct. 2007: 8–9.

Cho, S. 1978. *O-nara* (Farts). Tokyo: Fukuinkan.

Cho, S. 1994. *The Gas We Pass: The Story of Farts.* La Jolla CA: Kane/Miller Book Publishers.

Feels great to get it out! Discover Body-Helper Men (body effluents). *Third Grade Challenge,* Nov. 2007: 12–15.

First Grade Challenge: Discovery Book. September 2005. Tokyo: Benesse.

Fujiko, F. F. 1993. *Doraemon fushigi tanken shiriizu: Karada dai-tanken* (Doraemon's Amazing Exploration Series, Exploring the Body). Tokyo: Shogakukan.

Fujita, C. (transl.). 1983. *O-nara, ibiki, kushami … karada kara deru oto* (Farts, Snores, Sneezes … Body Noises). Tokyo: Sa-e-ra shobo (Translation of S. Buxbaum & R. G. Gelman. 1983. *Body Noises.* New York NY: Alfred A. Knopf).

Fujita, C. 1984. *Ningen no chie 13: Gesui no hanashi* (Human Knowledge 13: The Story of Sewage). Tokyo: Sa-e-ra shobo.

Fujita, C. 1987. *Ningen no chie 30: Dai-sho-ben no hanashi* (Human Knowledge 30: Stools and Urine). Tokyo: Sa-e-ra shobo.

Fujita, K. (transl.). 1998. *Kimi no karada no kitanai-mono-gaku* (Study of the Dirty Things of Your Body). Tokyo: Kodansha (Translation of S. Branzei. 1995. *Grossology.* Harlow: Addison Wesley Longman).

Fujita, K. & Yanagi Y. (transl.). 2006. *Kimi no karada no kitanai-mono-gaku, kimochi waruui hen* (Study of the Dirty Things of Your Body: Repulsive Edition). Tokyo: Kodansha (Translation of Sylvia Branzei. 2002. *Grossology and You.* Harlow: Price Stern Sloan).

Fuyuno, I. 2006. *Chii dekita yo! (0-1-2-saiji shitsuke messeiji ehon)* (Picturebooks for Children Ages 0, 1, 2 with a Disciplinary Message: We Can Wee). Tokyo: Shogakukan.

Gomi, T. 1977. *Minna unchi* (Everybody Poops). Tokyo: Fukuinkan.

Goodman, S. E. & Smith, E. H. 2004. *The Truth about Poop.* New York NY: Puffin Books.

Holzwarth, W. & Erlbruch, W. 1989. *Vom kleinen Maulwurf, der wissen wollte, wer ihm auf den Kopf gemacht hat.* Wuppertal: Peter Hammer.

How Japanese and French princesses pooped. The development of sewage systems. *Third Grade Challenge,* Oct. 2007: 17–21.

Kimura, Y. 1989. *Akachan no asobi ehon 4: Hitori de unchi dekiru kana* (Picturebooks for Babies 4: Can I Go Poo by Myself?). Tokyo: Kaiseisha.

Kiyono, S. 1987. *Akachan-ban Non-tan o-shikko shii-shii* (Baby Book: Non-chan Goes 'Pee, Pee'). Tokyo: Kaiseisha.

Matsutani, M. 2002. *Katari no mukashi-banashi, Mama no hanashi kikasete: Ikiru chikara o sodateru hen* (Folk Tales Told by Matsutani Miyoko: Mommy, Tell Me a Story: "Tales for Living"). Tokyo: Shogakukan.

Maynard, J. & McEwen, K. 1998. *Sam's Science: I Know Where My Food Goes.* London: Walker Books.

Murakami, Y. 2000. *Unpi, unnyo, unchi, ungo – unko no ehon* (Poopy, Pooey, Poo, Poop: The Book of Poop). Tokyo: Horupu.

Murakami, Y. 2001. *Unko-dasu-man* (Poop-pusher Man). Tokyo: Horupu.

Murakami, Y. 2004. *Gakkou de toire ni ikeru kana?* (Can You Go to the Toilet at School?). Tokyo: Horupu.

Murakami, Y. 2008. *Unko-dasu-man taisou* (Poop-pusher Man Exercises). Tokyo: Horupu.

Murkoff, H. & Rader, L. 2000. *What to Expect When You Use the Potty*. New York NY: Harper Collins.

Nakano, H. 2003. *U-n-chi* (P-O-O-P). Tokyo: Fukuinkan.

Nodame Cantabile. 2007. *O-nara taiso CD* (Gasercises CD). Epic Records.

Osada, S. 2005. *5-fun de rakugo no yomikikase* (5-Minute Rakugo Stories to Read Aloud). Tokyo: PHP.

Pee-pee and poop float about when you use the toilet on a spaceship. *Third Grade Challenge*, July 2007: 4–7.

Sekiguchi, H. (transl.). 1993. *Unchi shita no wa dare!* (Who Made This Poo?!) Tokyo: Kaiseisha (Translation of Werner Holzwarth & Wolf Erlbruch. 1989. *Vom kleinen Maulwurf, der wissen wollte, wer ihm auf den Kopf gemacht hat.* Wuppertal: Peter Hammer Verlag).

Suda, T. 1999. *Genki na unchi; o-nara wa ii nioi* (Healthy Poo, Gas Smells Good). Tokyo: Poplar.

Would a poot on a spaceship be unbearable stinky? *Third Grade Challenge*, July 2007: 12–15.

Would a poot on a spaceship cause an explosion? *Third Grade Challenge*, July 2007: 8–11.

References

Gordenker, A. 2007. Gold Poop. *The Japan Times Online*, 20 March 2007, <http://search.japantimes.cojp/cgi-bin/ek20070320wh.html>(24 January 2009).

Japan Toilet Research Center. 2008. Pre-ordering for 'Poopy Song' now available. <www.toilet.or.jp/uta/> (27 January 2008).

Mukougawa, M. 1998. *0-sai kara 3-sai no ehon no hizumi* (The Imbalance of Picturebooks for Children from 0 to 3). Tokyo: Koubundou.

PART III

Child-book interactions

Case studies

CHAPTER 11

Mothers' talking about early object and action concepts during picturebook reading

Kerstin Nachtigäller and Katharina J. Rohlfing

Early picturebooks mostly contain pictures of static objects that are useful in introducing rules of book behavior (Kümmerling-Meibauer & Meibauer 2005). Yet, they do not evolve narratives with a temporal or sequential structure. Our study was motivated by the approach suggested in Mandler (2000) stating that the conceptualization of an object is less complex than of an event, because events involve relations among objects. We therefore raised the question, whether early picturebooks do not provide a verbal organization in form of e.g. a temporal sequence, because they are mostly about single objects and not about events. For the investigation, we observed 10 mother-child dyads longitudinally, while they engaged in two different book-reading scenarios. Our analyses focused on the question whether maternal verbal behavior differed depending on the book content. Results reveal that an early form of narratives, proto-narratives, was elicited more often in books about events.

Theoretical background

In this article, we aim at providing a rather cognitive motivation of book reading to young children. More specifically, we pursue the question of how in the process of book reading, meaningful information is provided to children when looking at books with a different content. Thus, we take the perspective on the *caregivers*, who scaffold the meaningful perception of their children. By following a specific approach to cognitive development that will give us the motivation for the different book contents in our study, we consider, however, also the effects on the child.

Dynamic view on concepts

Our view on concepts and the ability of representing something is inspired by functional approaches, in which the ability to represent something is linked to the ability to recall something (Mandler & McDonough 1997). While recalling means that information that is perceptually not present is brought to conscious awareness, representing means that something not perceptually present needs to be represented. Thus, one cannot bring to mind a past event without having represented it, in the sense of having conceived of it in some way (Mandler & McDonough 1997). But the link seems to be bidirectional in the sense that in the book situation, it is difficult for a child to understand a picture without recalling what she or he knows about this object or event.

This view is different from traditional approaches claiming that forming a concept actually means to generalize from concrete. More specifically, in traditional view, perceptual categories of dogs, cats and other beings and entities are the foundation on which concepts formation builds on. This means that infants first learn about individual instances of e.g. apples from which they generalize to apples as a fruit class. Infants, thus, first learn to identify what an apple looks like and then to associate various properties (such as its shape or color) and behaviors (such as growing on the tree) with these perceptual categories. In this view, conceptual development is assumed to begin at a concrete level and then gradually becomes more abstract.

This is in contrast to our approach, which is in line with dynamic concept theories (Smith & Thelen 2003; Smith 2005). In this view, meaning of entities is formed on the basis of characterization of the roles they play in events (Nelson 1974). Thus, it is not the perceptual appearance but rather the functional core, i.e. what objects and other entities do (which movement they perform) and what is done to them that constitute meanings (Mandler 2000). According to the approach presented in Mandler (2000), representing events is almost always more abstract than representing what an object looks like, because events involve relations among entities. Relations among objects are, in turn, functional in nature.

There is some support for the functional view on concepts from language acquisition data. Nelson (1974, 1996) suggests for example that children overgeneralize a word because they perceive a whole event rather than single entities. And there is also support from research on memory development postulating that children remember events better when they can link them to their own experience and can talk about them (Schank 2000; Reese, Haden & Fivush 1993; Bauer & Wewerka 1995; Boland, Haden & Ornstein 2003; McGuigan & Salmon 2006).

In summary, while in the traditional view, it is important how an apple looks like, what its shape, color and other instantiations are, in Mandler's view (or the functional approaches), it is crucial what is done to an apple and what an apple can do, for example an apple hangs on a branch or one can slice an apple or eat it. These are the essential characteristics on which basis a meaning of an apple is formed. For our study design below, it is important to note that in the traditional view, a picture of a single object appropriately visualizes a concept, while in Mandler's view, a picture of an event or relations among objects are a more appropriate visualization of a concept.

Book contents

When we face early picturebooks, it is apparent that most of them contain static pictures of single objects. Kümmerling-Meibauer and Meibauer (2005) inform us that such content is useful as it is helpful in introducing rules of book behavior. But the authors also state that such content does not constitute verbal input as in a narrative (Kümmerling-Meibauer & Meibauer 2005) that is organized and structured on the one hand and goes beyond the perceptual situation on the other hand. We therefore raise the question, whether the early picturebooks do not provide organization in form of e.g. a temporal sequence and associations that go beyond the given picture because they are mostly about single objects and not about events.

For our study, we hypothesize that early picturebooks containing events rather than static pictures of objects should be more appropriate for a meaningful perception, better recall of events in children and better elicitation of an associative talk in caregivers. This is because events provide already a form of organization, which, in turn, seems to be important for a story or a narrative (Labov & Waletzky 1973; Kümmerling-Meibauer & Meibauer 2005). This organization is achieved by a sequential structure. The aim of our study that we present below is therefore to investigate how the content of a book can change the discourse. Once again, our hypotheses were that books containing objects will elicit less sequentially organized and associative input in caregivers' talk about these books to their children. In contrast, books that contain a relation between objects will elicit more organization and associations in caregivers' talking, as in order to provide a story or a sequential (causal or temporal) structure they only have to describe this event that is already depicted. To investigate these hypotheses, we designed a semi-controlled longitudinal study with two comparable conditions.

Bring-ins

Since in our study we will measure the effect of different book contents on caregivers' discoursive behavior, it is necessary to specify our understanding of organization and associations in caregivers' talk.

An elaborated organization is provided within a narrative. It is characterized by a temporal organization that concerns any sequence of clauses, which contain at least one temporal juncture (Labov & Waletzky 1967). But it also has been proposed that a thematic structure is central to a narrative, because an action sequence on its own is meaningless (Gee 1991). Thus, a meaningful narrative involves not only temporal organization but also thematic content. It seems like time and temporal as well as causal relations are central to the concepts of narrativity (Nelson 1996).

The basis of a narrative structure can then be best described by the following interrogatives "who", "what", "where", "when", "why" and "how". A story involves thus a character in action, with intentions or goals, using particular means.

As the focus of our study lies on caregivers talking to their children that are on their way to acquire language, we cannot expect to find a complete narrative structure in the maternal discourse due to the incomplete status of language development of the children. Coming with linguistic background in discourse analysis, we noticed that a less elaborated form of a narrative – a kind of a proto-narrative – can be observed in caregivers when they talk about something that is perceptually not accessible (Rohlfing 2011; Choi & Rohlfing 2010). These 'proto-narratives' are characterized in terms of background knowledge (about events or keywords) that can be useful in understanding the present. In Rohlfing (2011) or Choi and Rohlfing (2010), this form of a discourse is called "bring-in strategies" (p. 123), because other than perceptually accessible knowledge is brought into this situation: "In the bring-in discourse, the mother evokes a particular event or situation […] which is familiar to the child". Instead of saying "this is a cup", a mother might say "let's have a tea party" suggesting a whole event that can be associated with the perceivable object (Rohlfing 2011). Thus, the mother not only describes the given situation, but also interprets it in the light of past events and experiences. In their study, Ornstein, Haden and Hedrick (2004: 382) described a similar phenomenon, which they called "associative talk". It delineates a particular way of maternal conversations to a child during an ongoing event and refers to mothers that relate aspects of the event to the child's previous experiences.

Because of the semantic elaboration with reference to background knowledge that associates to what is present in the given situation, we consider the 'bring-ins' as a kind of proto-narratives. We attempt to achieve a first step towards a thematic structure along Gee (1991) by conducting our analyses along the concept of 'bring-in' strategies (Rohlfing 2011).

Methods

Our experiment is an excerpt from a longitudinal study that extends over a period of 8 months. The motivation for such a study is to observe developmental processes. More specifically and with regard to our hypothesis, it was of question whether proto-narratives are more applied with the age as children's language abilities improve. Considering age as a process of linguistic and cognitive maturing, we take it as one variable into account that might influence caregivers' input and narrativity. In this respect, one of the leading questions for this study was whether the structure of caregivers' input varies in a quantitatively and qualitatively way under the influence of infants' language capacities.

Procedure

Our team of research assistants visited each family in their home. The mother and her child were then asked to sit down on the ground floor and to read a book together in a comfortable position. The book content was designed (s. below the subsection about Materials). The order of pages in the book was randomized. The experimental instruction for the mother was to "read" the whole book with the child and to look at each page at least once. There was no time limit for the reading. The reading situation always proceeded at the same place, so that our camera position always remained the same (see Figure 1 for an example of the experimental setting). The scenario was then videotaped and analyzed. Before analyzing, the data was transcribed using an XML-format program called MARTHA. This program was already used in some studies (Choi & Rohlfing 2010; Rohlfing 2011) and its customized structure makes the transcription process simple but appropriate for the analysis purpose. With this tool, mothers' verbal behavior was coded on four levels: lexicon, sentence reference, discourse and nonverbal behavior. The present article provides a report on the lexicon, sentence and the discourse coding. For the analysis, all words that the mother said were coded in word classes and counted via an automatic analysis program afterwards.

Figure 1. Picture of the experimental setting (left) with some examples of the early "nouns-book" and the early "relations-book"(right)

Additionally to the observation of the reading scenario, we asked caregivers to fulfill a questionnaire concerning the language development of their child. The "Elternfragebogen für die Früherkennung von Risikokindern" (ELFRA-1; Grimm & Doil 2000) measures early communicative skills of one-year-old children on 4 different scales: receptive and productive vocabulary, gesture and fine motor skills. This survey gives us data about the child's language abilities.

Participants

The participants of our study were mother-child dyads. The data that is reported below stems from a period that started when the children were 12 months old and lasted until they were 20 months old. During this time, each family was visited 6 times by our team, once every 6 weeks. All participants were recruited from local newspapers and public events for children in Bielefeld, Northern Germany. The following description of the study and its results will focus on the 1st, the 3rd and the 6th visit of the family, as they can be considered representative for important developmental phases.

Our sample was divided into two groups: 5 participants in the "nouns-group" (NG) and 5 participants in the "relations-group" (RG) (see the subsection about Materials for more details). In order to create an optimal match between both groups concerning personal variables, we asked the mothers to fulfill a questionnaire about demographic aspects, their status of education and the time mothers spent with the child per day. The status of education was comparable in both groups (1 PhD, 2 university degrees, 1 degree of the university of applied sciences and 1 high school diploma in NG and 2 PhD and 3 degrees of the university of applied sciences in RG). All mothers in both groups spent a minimum of 4 hours per day with their child, most of them the whole day.

Concerning the children, the sample matched satisfactorily, too. In the "nouns-group", we had 4 male and 1 female child, the range of their expressive vocabulary at 1 year was between 5 and 19 words. Three of these children were firstborn, 2 were siblings. In the "relations-group", 3 children were male, 2 were female, the range of their productive vocabulary at 1 year was between 8 and 26 words and 3 of them were firstborn, 2 were siblings. The nonparametric Mann-Whitney-U-Test for group differences (a statistical procedure) revealed that the mean age of all children did not differ at any point of time (1st visit: U[1] = 12.500, p = 1.0; 3rd visit: U = 12.500, p = 1.0; 6th visit: U = 10.000, p = 0.690). See Table 1 below for mean

1. U is the test value and p is the level of statistical significance.

age and its standard deviations[2]. None of the children was a preterm birth, and all children were healthy concerning visual and auditory capacities.

Thus, possible differences in the narrative discourse behavior of the observed mothers can be attributed to differences in the book contents on the basis of similar premises.

Table 1. Children's mean age and standard deviation at each data point; *M* = means, *SD* = standard deviations

data points	**"nouns-group"**		**"relations-group"**	
(every 6 weeks)	*M*	*SD*	*M*	*SD*
1. visit	12.8	0.48	12.8	0.48
3. visit	15.6	0.55	15.6	0.55
6. visit	19.6	0.55	19.8	0.48

Materials

Each book was self-created in order to fulfill the purpose of our study optimally and contained 12 or 14 pages, which showed a laminated photograph each.[3] The "nouns-book" (NB) depicted 14 different single objects and contained pictures of a table, a cup, a leg, a dinosaur, a spoon, a crown, a clothespin, a fridge, a sweater, a doll, a pencil, a sock, a shoe and a swing. See Figure 1 above for some photographs. This type of book is motivated by the early-concept books that Kümmerling-Meibauer and Meibauer (2005) refer to with their description of early picturebooks.

In contrast to the "nouns-book", the "relations-book" (BR) consisted of 12 pictures and showed two objects that were establishing a relation, like 'on'. The illustrations depicted a clothespin on a table, an eraser on a pencil, a lion sitting on a dinosaur, a necklace on a woman and a necklace on a foot, a spoon on a cup, a child swinging, a cup on a table, magnets on a fridge, a pair of shoes on a sofa, a fishing pole in a hand and a sweater on a clothesline (see Figure 1 for some examples).

By creating a relational picturebook, we pursued the goal to enhance the complexity of each picture of the early concept book. Yet, each page still depicts a scenario on its own without being related to the other pages with regard to contents. That might evoke more actions in the scenes by assigning particular roles to the objects.

2. The standard deviation measures the statistical spread of a variable around the mean value.

3. The different numbers of pages in both books were not intended, but caused by an experimental oversight.

As described in the listing of all pages in NB and RB, most of the objects of one book correspond to objects in the other book, e.g. a dinosaur in the "nouns-book" and a lion sitting on a dinosaur in the "relations-book".

Coding of verbal behavior

In our study, we were interested in the quantity and quality of maternal discoursive behavior depending on the book content. We therefore coded maternal talk as being a proto-narrative, when the mother talked about something that is perceptually not accessible on the pictures of our books.

Our way of operationalization of proto-narratives can best be illustrated by an example. The sentences (1) and (2) demonstrate maternal input about something that is perceptually perceivable on one picture. A cup with a spoon on it is exactly what one can see on the photograph. These two examples do not imply a proto-narrative. They consist of a simple demonstration of what is illustrated on the photograph. By contrast, Example (3) provides additional information that is brought into the reading scenario, to further comment on what can be seen on the picture. In this case, a story about an agent who acts on the cup and the spoon is created. This is what we call a proto-narrative.

(1) U:nd eine Tasse.
[and a cup.]

(2) Eine Tasse mit einem Löffel drauf.
[A cup with a spoon on it.]

(3) Wer hat den Löffel dadrauf gelegt? Wer macht denn sowas?
[Who put the spoon on it? Who does something like that?]

Along these lines of coding, we operationalized every sentence in the maternal input as being a proto-narrative, if any additional information is elicited to what is shown on a picture. In addition to the analysis of narratives, the quantity of elicited sentences and words was measured by the XML-format program MARTHA.

Results

The presentation of our results will be divided into two parts concerning a description of maternal use of sentences, words and word classes on the one hand and a quantitative and qualitative analysis of the use of proto-narratives on the other hand. As mentioned above, the following data stems the 1st, the 3rd and the 6th visit. We used the nonparametric Mann-Whitney-U-Test for independent samples to test whether mothers in both groups differed with respect to the variables of interest.

Analysis of elicited sentences and words

Before we come to the analysis of narratives in both conditions, we make a first step in comparing the two groups concerning the quantity of elicited sentences and words classes.

Considering the mean number of produced sentences of mothers in both groups, we find no apparent difference between conditions (1st visit: $U = 6.000$, $p = 0.222$; 3rd visit: $U = 9.000$, $p = 0.548$; 6th visit: $U = 7.000$, $p = 1.0$). Mothers in the "nouns-group" produce a mean number of sentences ranging from 73 ($SD = 41.5$) at the 1st visit to 90.2 ($SD = 42.19$) at the 3rd visit and 92.67 ($SD = 38.84$) on average at the 6th visit. The range of spoken sentences of mothers in the "relations-group" expands between 89 ($SD = 20.43$) at the 1st visit, 96.4 ($SD = 23.39$) at the 3rd visit and 76.8 on average ($SD = 20.54$) at the 6th visit. The data shows that, at each point in time, mothers produce a comparable amount of sentences. Additionally, there is no increase or developmental change observable over time.

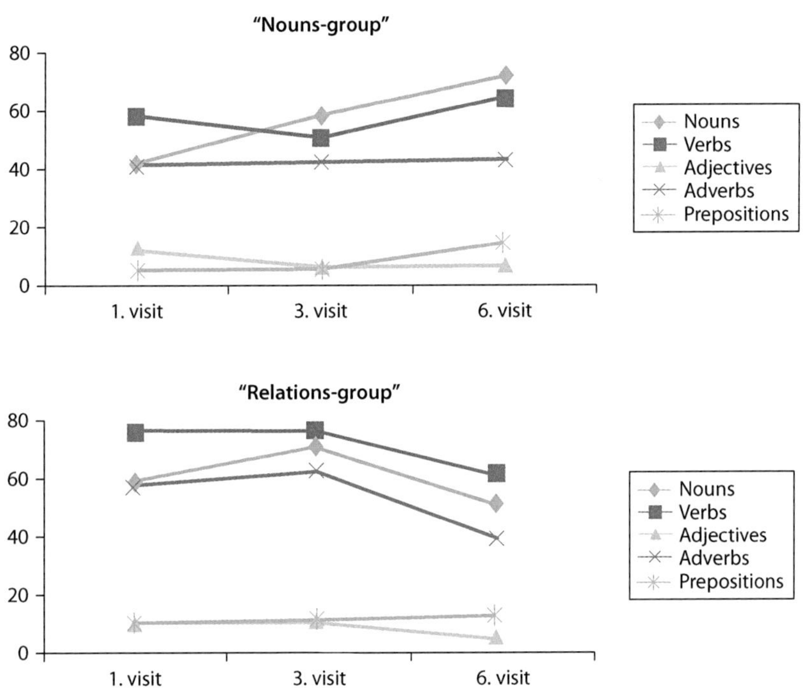

Figure 2. Mean number of produced nouns, verbs, adjectives, adverbs and prepositions in both conditions

Even if mothers produce approximately the same amount of sentences between the conditions and over the time, there might still be differences in their lexicon, i.e. the mean use of words. As in the case of sentences, our data does not point to a significant difference between both conditions at neither of the visits (the 1st visit: $U = 5.000$, $p = 0.151$; the 3rd visit: $U = 10.000$, $p = 0.690$ and the 6th visit: $U = 7.000$, $p = 1.0$). Both groups of mothers elicit a comparable amount of words (at the 1st visit NG: $M = 158$, $SD = 92.7$; RG: $M = 216.6$, $SD = 34.1$, at the 3rd visit NG: $M = 228.2$, $SD = 131.7$; RG: $M = 234.8$, $SD = 58.6$ and the 6th visit NG: $M = 200.3$, $SD = 113.9$; RG: $M = 178.4$, $SD = 33.9$).

By taking a closer look at the lexicon of the mothers, we analyzed their use of different word classes. We therefore counted nouns, verbs, adjectives, adverbs and prepositions of each participant at each visit. As can be seen in Figure 2, our analysis revealed no statistical difference in the use of nouns ($U = 7.000$, $p = 0.310$) in general, considering all three data points together. The analysis of the use of verbs ($U = 8.000$, $p = 0.421$), adjectives ($U = 10.500$, $p = 0.690$), adverbs ($U = 10.000$, $p = 0.690$) and prepositions ($U = 6.500$, $p = 0.222$) brought the same result, i.e. no significant difference between both conditions concerning all three data points together.

In summary, maternal behavior did not differ in the quantity of speech concerning syntax and lexicon during the reading scenario. Considering the amount of produced sentences, the amount of produced words and the amount of different word classes, there were no statistical differences between the two conditions. Thus, the content of a book does not seem to influence maternal input on the analyzed level of syntax and lexicon. To put it in other words, no matter what is in the book, the input seems to be stable and persist over the different time points.

Quantitative and qualitative analysis of proto-narratives

In order to investigate the production of proto-narratives in both groups, as a first step, we counted the amount of proto-narratives along our criteria (s. coding of verbal behavior) and conducted a statistical analysis for group differences concerning the quantity of stories at each visit.

Mothers in the "nouns-group" produced a mean number of 4.2 ($SD = 2.6$) narratives at the 1st visit, 12.2 ($SD = 2.9$) at the 3rd visit and 7.3 ($SD = 6.1$) at the 6th visit. As can be seen in Figure 3, the amount of elicited narratives in the "relations-condition" was consequently on a higher level than in the "nouns-group" at each visit (1st visit: $M = 9.6$, $SD = 5.5$; 3rd visit: $M = 15.4$, $SD = 12.8$; 6th visit: $M = 16.2$, $SD = 4.3$). A statistical analysis revealed a significant difference between these two groups at the 1st visit ($U = 2.500$, $p = 0.032$) and

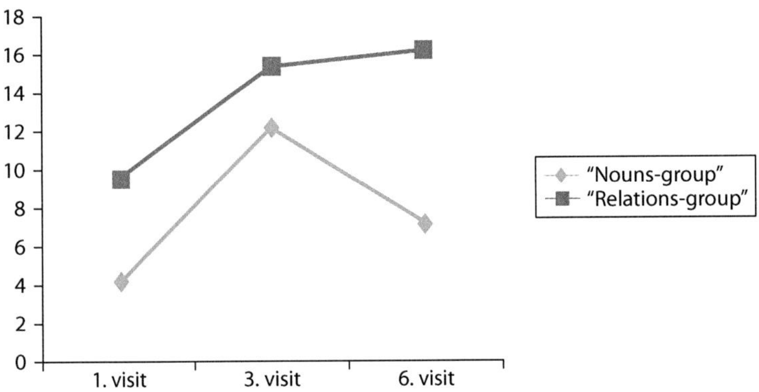

Figure 3. Presentation of mean number of elicited proto-narratives per visit

a statistical trend at the 6th visit (U = 1.000, p = 0.071), i.e. mothers in the "relations-group" elicited more narratives than mothers in the "nouns-group" at these two data points.

In our data, we found severe individual differences. In the "relations-group", some mothers produced very little (or no) proto-narratives, whereas some mothers in the "nouns-condition" produced many proto-narratives (e.g. 19 vs. 29 as the highest number of narratives in the "relations-condition"). Beyond that, the amount of mothers' proto-narratives varied from session to session (e.g. 5 proto-narratives at the 1st session and 23 at the 6th session in the "nouns-group").

During the qualitative analysis of our data, we observed different categories of proto-narrative expressions in general. On the basis of these findings, we further specify the concept of proto-narratives and postulate some strategies of how to build a proto-narrative in the following.

One way of creating a proto-narrative can be realized by making a direct reference and a comparison or a contrast to the child's body or what she/he is wearing, like in Sentence (1), or to objects in the surroundings (see Sentence (2)). Beyond that, a reference can be made to a place with a similar exemplar (see Example (3)), to own property (Example (4)) or to a canonical action (Example (5)).

(1) Füße. Deine Füße. Aber da sind Nackideifüße.
[Feet. Your feet. But these are bare feet.]

(2) Ein grü:ner Löffel. Guck' mal, der passt zu deinem Pulli.
[A green spoon. Look' it matches your sweater.]

(3) Eine Schaukel. Die hat Anna draußen.
[A swing. Anna has it outside.]

(4) Guck' mal, ein Kühlschrank! So einen haben wir auch.
[Look! A fridge! We have one like that.]

(5) Damit malen wir immer.
[We always use it for drawing.]

A further way of building a proto-narrative we noticed in our data implies that a story will be made up about something. This can be a story about an action (see Sentence (6)), about some involved objects (Sentence (7)) or about the whole situation (Sentence 8). Furthermore, a story can be told about an agent (Example (9)) or about a possible communication (Example (10)).

(6) Ein Kühlschrank? Mit bunten Teilen? Die am Kühlschrank kleben?
[A fridge? With colored parts? They stick to the fridge?]

(7) Ein Becher. Kann man trinken, ne.
[A cup. You can drink of, right?]

(8) Der Junge schaukelt hin und her.
[The boy swings back and forth.]

(9) Oh, guck' mal, da hat jemand die Tasse auf der Ecke vergessen.
[Oh look! Somebody forgot the cup on the edge.]

(10) Da geht das Löwenbaby auf dem Dinosaurier und sagt der. schneller, schneller, sagt das kleine Löwenbaby.
[The lion baby goes to the dinosaur and says faster, faster, says the little lion baby.]

Concerning the quality of elicited proto-narratives in our two conditions, we observed a general tendency of slight differences in both groups: Proto-narratives in the "nouns-group" more often include comparisons to own experience and concrete individual events (see Sentence (11)) than in the "relations-group". Oppositely, proto-narratives produced in the "relations-group" more often imply elaborations on events and elaborations on canonical functions of objects (see Example (12)).

(11) Guck'! Die Tasse, die hast du letztens zerschlagen.
[Look! A cup, you have broken it recently.]

(12) Da ist wieder das Kind auf der Schaukel. Guck' mal, eine Schaukel. Das kann schon ganz alleine Schaukeln da, ne? Braucht keinen Babybügel mehr.
[There is the child on a swing, again. Look' a swing. He can swing on his own, right? He doesn't need a protection bar any more.]

Discussion

The study we presented here was designed to investigate how caregivers, i.e. mothers in our case, structure their verbal input to their child in different book reading scenarios. The focus of interest was on maternal verbal behavior following the question whether different book contents influence the way mothers provide information to their children. Our study might be a first step to systematically explore and investigate maternal discourse behavior quantitatively as well as qualitatively in an interactional book reading setting with a child. We developed a particular method, i.e. self created pictures put together to one book, in order to optimally control for the book content and to create two comparable conditions that differ only with respect to the amount of depicted objects on the pictures. This study can thus be considered as additional to the existing research on early picturebooks.

As the results of our analysis reveal quite clearly, the content of an early picturebook has little influence on the linguistic structure, i.e. vocabulary and syntax, of the input to children: We found a similar amount of sentences, words and a similar distribution of different word classes in both conditions, the "nouns-group" and the "relations-group". This picture of the input remained stable across different time points of our investigation. Thus, concerning the linguistic structure, the input to children during a reading situation, is not only 'resistant' against the book content but seems also to persist stable over the course of development.

However, the lack of results concerning the input in the course of the children's development can be explained by two other factors. One caveat to our results might be that the fact that mothers were observed and their behavior was videotaped elicited a particular performance, to which the mothers get used with each visit. Thus, it is possible that at each visit, mothers recalled this behavior as a well-rehearsed procedure. In addition, mothers always read the same, familiar book that could help them even more to recall their performance at a previous visit. Taken together, these facts might be the reason for the static maternal input over the different time points in our investigation.

Furthermore, we introduced our notion of proto-narratives: An early form of narratives directed to infants who are on their way to develop language skills. Using 'proto-narratives', caregivers use background knowledge (about events or keywords) to help the child in understanding a present situation. Concerning the quality of input, we hypothesized that books containing events would elicit more proto-narratives than books depicting single objects. Our data shows that the content of an early picturebook can influence the discourse structure as early picturebooks containing events rather than static pictures of objects seem to elicit more proto-narratives in mothers talking to their children. In further studies, we need to consider greater samples of mothers and fathers coming from different socioeconomic background in order to draw representative conclusions about these effects we described above on developmental processes. For the time being, the results of our study can be considered as preliminary, because our sample was quite small and not representative concerning the status of education of the participating mothers. We think that the status is a relict of the practical and organizational aspects linked to a longitudinal study, for which the recruitment of participants is quite challenging.

Yet, considering the individual differences between mothers in both groups, we noticed that a good storyteller is able to elaborate on any book content. In this context, it seems to be important to have a good repertoire of strategies of how to build a proto-narrative. On the basis of our findings, we postulate some strategies of how to build proto-narratives that might be helpful for caregivers and educators to create a story during a reading situation. Though we did not take the effect of proto-narratives on the child's development into account in this study, our assumption of the importance of proto-narratives is consistent with other findings coming from memory development. Ornstein and his colleagues (2004) report about the benefit of "associative talk" for the memory development of children. The authors describe an elaborative style of speech of mothers that talk to their children while reminiscing about a past event and postulate the association of what a child already knows to something new as one aspect of this elaborative style of speech. As has been shown in many studies, children whose mothers use these elaborations remembered past events better and more detailed (Bauer & Wewerka 1995; Boland et al. 2001; Ornstein et al. 2004; McGuigan & Salmon 2006). This phenomenon resembles our idea of proto-narratives, because additional information is brought into a situation – in our case: a reading scenario – in order to help the child to incorporate the current perception of a picture in a book into her or his past experiences and thus to discern the relevance (and the meaning) of this perception. Thus, we assume that proto-narratives are helpful for the cognitive and linguistic development of a child (Rohlfing 2011), as they are brought-in a familiar event or object that a child can then associate with past experiences. These experiences evoke in the child concrete knowledge about this event or this object, e.g. how an object is handled, how it moves etc. This way, a concept can be activated that provides the child with information about the function, the role of an object in an event and the sequential organization of an event in the time. In this sense, concepts that the child has already formed contribute to a meaningful perception by being scaffolded by the sensitive caregivers. A picturebook that offers possibilities to make use of such conceptual knowledge is – in our view – a good tool for training mnemonic skills in children within a social context (Ornstein & Haden 2001). A further aim of our research is, therefore, to investigate in detail the role and effects of proto-narratives on learning and development. The associative character of proto-narratives, connecting past experiences and already existing knowledge of a child to something new might influence for example the lexical development and thus the semantic knowledge of an infant. These aspects form the basis of later literacy competencies and are, to our opinion, important to consider. Therefore, we are currently conducting a training study to pursue these open questions and hypotheses.

References

Bauer, P. J. & Wewerka, S. S. 1995. One-to two-year-olds'recall of events: The more expressed, the more impressed. *Journal of Experimental Child Psychology* 59(3): 475–496.

Boland, A. M., Haden, C. A. & Ornstein, P. A. 2003. Boosting children's memory by training mothers in the use of an elaborative conversational style as an event unfolds. *Journal of Cognition and Development* 4(1): 39–65.

Choi, S. & Rohlfing, K. J. 2010. Discourse and lexical patterns in mothers' speech during spatial tasks: What role do spatial words play? In *Japanese/Korean Linguistics*, Vol. 17, S. Iwasaki, H. Hoji, P. M. Clancy & S. O. Sohn (eds), 117–133. Stanford CA: CSLI.

Gee, J. P. 1991. Memory and myth: A perspective on narrative. In *Developing Narrative Structure*, A. McCabe & C. Peterson (eds), 1–25. Hillsdale NJ: Lawrence Erlbaum Associates.

Grimm, H. & Doil, H. 2000. *Fragebogen für die Früherkennung von Risikokindern (ELFRA-1)*. Göttingen: Hogrefe.

Kümmerling-Meibauer, B. & Meibauer, J. 2005. First pictures, early concepts: Early concept books. *The Lion and the Unicorn* 29: 324–347.

Labov, W. & Waletsky, J. 1967. Narrative analysis. In *Essays on the Verbal and Visual Arts*, J. Helm (ed.), 12–44. Seattle WA: University of Washington Press.

Labov, W. & Waletzky, J. 1973. Erzählanalyse: Mündliche Versionen persönlicher Erfahrung. In *Literaturwissenschaft und Linguistik. Eine Auswahl Texte zur Theorie der Literaturwissenschaft*, Vol. 2, J. Ihwe (ed.), 78–126. Frankfurt am Main: Athenäum Verlag.

Mandler, J. M. 2000. Perceptual and conceptual processes in infancy. *Journal of Cognition and Development* 1: 3–36.

Mandler, J. M. & McDonough, L. 1997. Nonverbal recall. In *Memory for Everyday and Emotional Events*, N. L. Stein, P. A. Ornstein, B. Tversky & C. Brainerd (eds), 141–164. Mahwah NJ: Lawrence Erlbaum Associates.

McGuigan, F. & Salmon, K. 2006. The influence of talking on showing and telling: Adult child talk and children's verbal and nonverbal event recall. *Applied Cognitive Psychology* 20(3): 365–381.

Nelson, K. 1974. Concept, word, and sentence: Interrelations in acquisition and development. *Psychological Review* 81 (4): 267–285.

Nelson, K. 1996. *Language in Cognitive Development: The Emergence of the Mediated Mind.* Cambridge: CUP.

Ornstein, P. A. & Haden, C. A. 2001. Memory development or the development of memory? *Current Directions in Psychological Science* 10(6): 202–205.

Ornstein, P. A., Haden, C. A. & Hedrick, A. M. 2004. Learning to remember: Social-communicative exchanges and the development of children's memory skills. *Developmental Review* 24: 374–395.

Reese, E., Haden, C. A. & Fivush, R. 1993. Mother-child conversations about the past: Relationships of style and memory over time. *Cognitive Development* 8: 403–430.

Rohlfing, K. J. 2011. Exploring "Associative Talk": When German Mothers Instruct their Two Year Olds about Spatial Tasks. *Dialogue and Discourse* 2(2): 1–18.

Schank, R. C. 2000. *Dynamic Memory – Revisited.* Cambridge: CUP.

Smith, L. B. 2005. Cognition as a dynamic system: Principles from embodiment. *Developmental Review* 25: 278–298.

Smith, L. B. & Thelen, E. 2003. Development as a dynamic system. *Trends in Cognitive Sciences* 7(8): 343–348.

CHAPTER 12

"Don't tell me all about it – just read it to me!"

Virginia Lowe

This paper describes two children from birth to their third birthdays in contact with books, and briefly their subsequent learning to read. The children's vocabulary acquisition, book handling skills and knowledge of print and reading, all happen without direct instruction or teaching. They are in control of the reading sessions. It recommends trusting the book to instruct and the child to reach understanding from repeated readings. It responds to Ezell and Justice's *Shared Storybook Reading* (2006), and builds on my work in *Stories, Pictures and Reality* (Lowe 2007).

The title is a plea from my daughter aged 2-7 (2 years seven months) to a grandparent talking about the pictures, and it sums up my attitude to reading aloud to young children. Trust the book.

Functional literacy, actually learning to read, is seen as the least important goal when very young children have joyous encounters with books. Recognition of pictures, enjoyment of narrative, awareness of language, a passion for books in all their "bookness" – all this comes first.

A Reading at two years eleven months

I will begin with a Reading Journal entry for my daughter, four days before her third birthday. We were reading Krasilovsky/Spier *The Cow Who Fell in the Canal* in the double bed.

> This morning, continuing the current phase of querying familiar stories, we read *The Cow Who Fell in the Canal* for the first time in a long while [three months, and infrequently for six months before that]. There were many queries and comments. The water-lilies were especially interesting, as we saw lots in a duck and moorhen pond yesterday – she commented on them at each opening. There were a lot of comments on the ducks and ducklings on the page where Hendrika falls in. To the last duckling "Why has he got his wings up?" V: "Perhaps he's hurrying

to catch up." R: "Or perhaps he's badly printed." (When have I ever said that I wonder, as an explanation? I can't remember, but certainly never to *The Cow* which is a Picture Puffin, and perfectly well printed). On the next page "That duckling is looking at Hendrika" (its head is turned to Hendrika – it certainly is watching.) V: "I guess it's surprised to see a cow in the water". R: "I can't see its eyebrows up" (This is synonymous with looking surprised, to her.) I just said "no it hasn't". Perhaps I should have launched into description of different creatures having different ways of expressing feelings, like [our cat] Pinkle Purr's ears, but I didn't. She counted ducks and ducklings on p. 14 [Figure 1]. Then she wanted to know why there were three mother ducks together – V: "Perhaps they're friends?" – then asked about the tulips which were mentioned in the text but were not pictured. So I looked back till I found a bed of them on an earlier opening, and she talked about their various colours.

"Why doesn't he fall into the water?" to the boy sitting on the end of a pier. I explain he's used to living next to the water and will be careful. Also he can certainly swim. To the barns, "that's where the horses live". [Incidentally on this page, she was only 1–3 when she could point out the "boy running" when asked. Our copy was an old Picture Puffin and small, so the detail was tiny.]

Figure 1. Image from *The Cow Who Fell in the Canal* by Phyllis Krasilovsky and Peter Spier. Harmondsworth: Penguin 1970

On the next opening she asked "what was in that tin?" (rubbish floating in the canal). V: "You tell me." R: "Chocolates!" (this was odd – we've never seen chocolates in tins). V: "Yes, or maybe peaches." She liked this idea, remarking that "The water has washed off the picture of peaches from the outside." Further on: "Why are the people running?" V: "They're trying to keep up with Hendrika. She's running fast." R: "I can't see her legs running" (picture is front-on – maybe the perspective is rather hard to make out. I can see why she'd query it, but never has before however.) "What is the cat looking at?" (I explained the fish bones, but should have said it was actually Hendrika.) "What does that say?" to the notice about the bicycles. I explained it was in Dutch and I couldn't really read it, but it probably says "bicycles to rent". I have a policy of reading only what the words actually say – so that when she's interested in trying to read them, she might be able to remember.

At the cheese market, I was pleased when she pointed to the nearest pile of cheeses (drawn biggest) and said "those are the closest" – she didn't remark on the *size* at all. Just lately we've been singing the *Sesame Street* song "That's about the size of it" – its basic point being "it looks big when you are closer, little back a bit". Also we've read *How Big is Big?* (Schneider) – a non-fiction book on the same theme, though much more involved – from suns to atomic particles. (She seemed to take it all in when it was read, though no comments.) Also at the cheese market (I can't remember the exact phrasing of the question) she asked how it was "painted", using that word. I tried to explain about painting the picture then printing.

On a coloured page, "Look at all the daisies in the grass" – these are just white and yellow dots in the green, but apparently recognisable. We have small white daisies through our lawn. And on the second last opening "What is the horse dropping?" I offered "oats". It is just dots below his nose bag.

This is an abridged version of the session. I have left out some of her comments and questions but these are representative. Look at the behaviours and abilities she exhibits before she turns three:

- She compares the book with her own experiences (waterlilies, daisies, the boy falling in)
- She expects a logical reason for the pictures to fit with the story (why are the people running?)
- She queries the written words in the illustration
- She counts ducks and names colours
- She shows she understands illustration conventions
  - notices the direction of regard of characters
  - perspective (the closest cheeses)
  - the missing parts convention (the label "washed off")
  - interprets dots as something falling from nose-bag
- She is interested in emotion and its representation (eyebrows up for surprise)
- She considers methods of production ("wrongly printed"; "how was it painted?")

There are no vocabulary queries. In fact this quantity of questioning occurred only because it was a completely familiar title – even though she had not heard it recently, she had owned it for almost two years. Rebecca never asked questions on the first few readings, only when a book was thoroughly familiar. I asked her no questions, nor probed her understanding (as could be seen from the full entry). All the queries came from her. Also, even when I was really impressed with something (her grasp of perspective) I certainly didn't praise her. She didn't do it for my approval. Now she had it clear it was not even worthy of comment. Praise would have sounded contrived and irritated her.

Parent-observer studies

I kept a record of my two children's book contacts and responses from birth until adolescence (6000 handwritten pages). It was kept daily until they could read at their interest level (at eight), sporadically from then on. I attempted to record, not only the actual reading sessions (of which there were usually several a day when there was no school), but also references and quotes in their conversation and games. They had a typical upbringing in a bookish middle-class Western family. The only difference from most children is the quantity of their book contacts, and the fact that their parents were observing these. The journal formed the basis of *Stories, Pictures and Reality: Two Children Tell* (2007).

As a family, our philosophy of reading to the children was different from what is usually recommended today, and needs description. John and I were both librarians. We considered picturebooks to be multi-modal works of art, with the words and the illustrations belonging together. Therefore we read the author's actual words, in full or slightly abridged. We did not worry about the children's understanding each word, or even the plot, as long as they were enjoying the experience. We assumed that they would ask if they really needed to know immediately, and would eventually understand with repeated readings. The joy of words for themselves, and the discovery of an explanation within the story or the illustrations, were more important to us. We never offered an explanation or definition unless it was requested. We did encourage discussion about concepts (as opposed to vocabulary or plot), such as the reality-status of the stories, but still only if they were instigated by the children. Basically we assumed that, even as infants, books would supply them with the enjoyment, comfort and knowledge they always had to us.

In the first of the parent-observer studies, *Books Before Five* (1954:2) White tells us that "The enjoyment of personal ownership was a fact of life more worth learning than how to look after this or that" so Carol's books from before two were torn and chewed and ultimately disintegrated. We, on the other hand, did not allow destruction of books, and in many cases they were library books anyway, so not even owned. Also we are chronically untidy – there were books on chairs and the floor as well as low shelves, all well within reach of a crawling baby. It seemed easier to teach respect for them, than to cure our untidiness.

Both parents used the performance style of reading (Reese and Cox 1999). We preferred not to break into the story unless it was absolutely essential, relying on the book itself to answer most questions. When a child asked the meaning of a word, if the reader could see the answer coming up, we would say "Wait, it will tell you". For instance Beatrix Potter with her famous "soporific" does this. "It is said that the effect of eating too much lettuce is 'soporific'. *I* have never felt sleepy after eating lettuces; but then *I* am not a rabbit" (*The Flopsy Bunnies*).

"Sharing" picturebooks

Ezell and Justice in *Shared Storybook Reading* (2005) advocate conversation during the reading, to enable language and literacy development. They do recommend that you break into the story no more than three times, to explain the point you are making – vocabulary, a grammatical point, or print awareness perhaps, because more interruptions will spoil the story. Their attitude towards reading aloud could not be more different from ours.

In an opening chapter they mention talking to children about concepts in the plot, problem solving, and illustrations, but these are never mentioned again. Nor do they mention, as a reason for the shared-reading activity, the pure pleasure it gives the child. They appear throughout to be interested only in the children learning language and literacy strategies. There is no discussion of the plot in any of the examples from actual reading sessions that are cited. For instance the title of a book called *Red Bear* is used only to identify and discuss the concept of a title, and colour, not what it might mean to the story, nor what colour bears actually are.

They deliberately use very short books – *Spot* (Hill) and *Dear Zoo* (Campbell) for instance. They do not give suggested ages, but the children they are aiming at appear to be older than two and a half, up to five (they do discuss the entrance year at school for instance). These books may be better for direct instruction, but Rebecca and Ralph would have found them extremely boring. Gradually listening to the longer and longer texts leads to better concentration, so that these two children were able to take in more complex concepts, vocabulary and character development. Before three both enjoyed chapters of *Winnie-the-Pooh* (A. A. Milne of course, not Disney) and long picturebook texts like the *Orlando the Marmalade Cat* series by Hale and the Beatrix Potter tales. Such stories led to understanding different personality types and logical problem solving, long complex imaginary games, and acquisition of delicious language. They needed challenge in length and complexity of story, though they enjoyed repetition as well, as the record of *The Cow who Fell in the Canal* demonstrates.

This concept of "shared reading" relates to the "labelling game" which is often the only contact between adult and child with a book, before the child turns two. This is the activity of naming, asking and pointing to the illustrations, constantly adjusting the difficulty to be within the child's zone of proximal development (Vygotsky 1978). Sometimes the story will be retold from the pictures in the adult's own words. How is the child to learn new and exciting vocabulary, if the book's words are not read? It is the family's everyday lexicon which is used in both "labelling" and telling the story from the pictures. (This process is described in great detail in Jones *Emerging Patterns of Literacy,* 1996).

It may also be that this form of interaction with the book does not encourage intense concentration. DeLoache remarks that "Since picture book reading sessions are most often terminated by the child's losing interest, a major part of the mother's role is trying to keep the interaction going" (1984: 18). This was certainly not so in our case. The children would always have listened to as many books (or later, chapters) as were offered. Occasionally they opted for something other than a book but normally they listened avidly. Of course they knew, as do all children, how best to get their parents' attention, and an interest in books was guaranteed to do so. Nevertheless Rebecca, even at twelve months, would sit for half an hour or more, while I did housework, looking at books alone; and both had three books put into their cots to look at quietly in the morning, from 1-0, which were subsequently read to them on getting up. At 1-6 they each had a book-word in their very limited vocabularies, and would chase us around the house carrying a book and demanding "Read! Read!" (Rebecca) or "Book! Book!" (Ralph).

Although we occasionally played the labelling game, it was not on our agenda to get the child to demonstrate mastery. Usually we could observe the learning and skills by their spontaneous responses to the words and pictures of the story, without quizzing them.

Words, spoken and printed

Rebecca, at age two, really enjoyed learning new words, words that were not in the family lexicon. She would take a word or phrase from a story: "tippet", "soporific", "elegant uncomfortable clothes", "mackintosh", "fortnight", "camomile tea" and say them to herself, not for the sense but for the enjoyment of the sounds, and the feel of them in her mouth. She might chant them, and even use them in pretend games for a couple of weeks before she would check back with us out of the context of the book: “What does fortnight mean?” Usually repeated renditions of the story would be enough for her to work out the meaning for herself.

We moved from a rural town to the city when Rebecca was just two. Many people we met commented on her “English accent”. John’s and mine are definitely just educated Australian, so this puzzled me, until one night I was listening to John reading to her, and realised that she had used the best language in her environment as her language model – the adult voice reading the words of her books. We used more colour in our speech, more emphasis, more variation in tone, and pronounced the words with more carefully as we read – and it was this she had chosen as her model.

Neither child was an early speaker. In Rebecca’s case, I put this down to her perfectionism. She refused to say anything that could not be understood by the listener, so the first body part in her spoken vocabulary (where she had been able to identify fifteen for the past five months, five of them for nine months) was “e-bow” 1-7. One presumes this was not because elbows were more important than mouths and eyes, but because she could say it and be understood at once. For instance when she was 1-4 (using fifteen words) I was occupied in the laundry when she came grizzling to me, obviously wanting her breakfast. I suggested “go and tell Daddy to get your bib” and she trotted off saying “bibibi” – a sound we had never heard her make before. John, not having heard the conversation, didn’t understand anyway, and had to bring her back to me to ask what she meant. She did not say the word “bib” again for about eight weeks, despite the fact that it was obviously within her ability to pronounce.

Her spoken language grew slowly. She still used only 35 words at 1-7, then suddenly there was a huge growth. Two months later I counted 350. She had well over 1000 (excluding names and inflected verbs) by 2-3 and by then it seemed that she could say any word in our lexicon or that of her books.

When she did start to speak in earnest, it tended to be in full sentences – in fact book language: “Yes, Daddy is coming now” for instance. Her first quote from a book took us by surprise. Sitting in her high chair (it was the day after her second birthday), she complained that her food was hot. I said “No, it’s warm”. “Warm and cosy” she countered. This was not a phrase we would use, especially as applied to food. Both John and I recognised it as a quote, but couldn’t remember from where. When asked she replied “Sayor” which we did not understand. Eventually she got down from the chair, and with great thumps, pushed all the books off her little table until she found *The Sailor* by Dick Bruna. Sure enough “The igloo was warm and cosy”. She could not only quote it, but knew exactly which book it was from – and it was not her fault that she couldn’t pronounce her /l/ sound as yet.

She was very aware of this failing however, although we never corrected her pronunciation. Eventually, five months later, she at last managed to pronounce "libry" instead of "yibry". Soon after, she was sitting in front of the heater with Pinkle Purr. It must have been the proximity of the cat which made her think of the quote. It is from *Benjamin Bunny* (Beatrix Potter) where Mr Rabbit is walking along the wall looking for his son, and sees the cat sitting on the basket. Rebecca began /l/. I can say /l/. When I was a little girl I had no opinion whatever of /l/. I took a tremendous jump off the top of the wall and onto the cat ..." then she petered out, as the rest of the quote was clearly irrelevant. (Text: "Old Mr Bunny had no opinion whatever of cats. He took a tremendous jump off the top of the wall onto the top of the cat...")

One month previously (2-3), she had come to me in the kitchen, hungry and saying "Banana!", then she stopped and realised with excitement – "Banana! I can say it with my tongue! Banana". Up to that moment she had pronounced it "wana". Without overt instruction she was very aware of her pronunciation. Her longest sentence at 2-1 concerned our new house: "In our garden there are birdies and snails on-a bricks", 10 or 11 words, with quite complicated syntax. Quotes were now common: "I saw a caravan. It was purple and very beautiful" she told us on a country trip at 2-2 (Gag's *Millions of Cats* says of one of the kittens: "It was black and very beautiful").

An interesting example of her awareness of words occurred at 3-7 – outside my chosen age boundary, but worth the telling. She was playing a book-based game, collecting "blueberries" and "bottling them for next winter" with clover from the lawn as blueberries (*Blueberries for Sal* – McCloskey). I was sitting on the ground "minding" her jars, and she felt baby Ralph, on my lap, to be in the way. I joked "I'm bottling Ralphs for next winter". Her reply – "You can't. Ralph's a little boy. You can't eat boys!" Then she paused for thought. "Ralph's a boy's *name*. You can't bottle *names*!"

A second child has a quite different experience. The quantity of language in the house is vastly increased with a talkative older sibling, and much of it is not addressed to the younger child. The only time Rebecca used jargon was when she pretended to read a handwritten letter – which she would have heard read aloud from adult to adult with no concession to the understanding of small ears. Consequently she heard and repeated it as garbled nonsense. Other language was addressed specifically to her, or else carefully within her ability to understand.

But Ralph heard a lot of language that was not addressed to him, and consequently he used jargon for speech for quite a long time. He spoke earlier than his sister, beginning at 0-11. It happened that I counted 14 words for both, he at 1-1 and she a month older. By 1-4 he had 29 words in use, and he went from 68 at 1-9 to 203 in three months. This was the traditional big jump from 50 words, but nothing like Rebecca's explosion. For him, language was mainly for socialising. The understanding of the recipient was not important. For Rebecca it was all about communication, and if the recipient did not understand immediately there was no point in saying it at all.

Ralph did not go through the period of intense quotation, as Rebecca had, which may be why his language development was slower. On the other hand, he asked many more questions to books. This may be because most books were heard with Rebecca as well, and as they would have been simple, familiar ones to her, she would be asking questions to them (as she only did with familiar titles) – a model for her little brother.

He also had some different book experiences. In *Lucy and Tom's Day* (Hughes) which Rebecca had had since 2-4, Lucy "shows him the pictures", sharing books with her younger brother. Rebecca interpreted this as talking about the pictures rather than attempted reading or recitation, and had for months, with other friends' babies, amused them by "showing the pictures". She saw this as the duty of an elder sister, and began immediately with baby Ralph. This was essentially the labelling game, clearly distinguished in her mind from "reading". We had not played this often with her, consequently Ralph received more of the standard book sharing experience than she had. She would often climb into his cot and talk about the books with him, and sometimes report his responses back to me, knowing that I was interested in book-behaviour.

Whatever the reason, Ralph's awareness of print and words seemed to be more sophisticated than Rebecca's. For instance, when he was only 1-1, I was reading *Dear Teddy Robinson* (Robinson) to Rebecca, a book with one black and white sketch per chapter. We were reading a story where Teddy Robinson has a conversation with a bird. "Bir" was one of Ralph's few words – he had about ten at the time. He crossed the room to see the picture of a bird, but there was none on that page, so he pointed to the writing and said "bir" firmly, not even as a question. It was certainly as if he knew that "bird" was in the print.

Later that day, Rebecca was spending time with him, showing him the pictures in *Lucy and Tom's Day*. At the picture of them in the park, he pointed to the block truck and said "bu" for "bus" – his word for any wheeled vehicle. Rebecca did the good big sister act of praising him "Yes, it's a bus!" Even this amused her (knowing it wasn't in fact a bus), then she moved on to other things in the picture, first the other wheeled toys, then a ball, a tree, and when she asked him "what's that Ralphie?" he replied "bu" to her great amusement, and her careful "a bus is it? Yes, it's a bus!". She whispered to me, with delight, "He says everything I ask him is a bus!" It had clearly become a game for him, to amuse the most important person in his life. I was just wondering how a second child actually learns anything and whether I should step in, when he solved the problem himself. With careful deliberation he pointed back to the block truck again and said "bu" – he knew all the time. Her hilarity showed he was making errors, and he continued it deliberately.

His awareness of words and the reading process continued to develop. At 2-5 I noted that he often pointed to a word and asked "What does that say?" He remarked to me, as John was reading to Rebecca: "Daddy read 'crash'!" (2-5). In *Hop on Pop*, Dr Seuss asks "A fish in a tree! How can that be?" and he replied to it, as a considered serious answer, "It's just a word" (2-6). After a drawing session at 2-7, I was labelling the pictures at his dictation, and he requested "more words" at the one of his grandfather. At the same age, in Alderson/Oxenbury's *Cakes and Custard*, he wanted to know where the cat and the fiddle were in "Hey diddle diddle". I said they were just not in the picture, and he countered "But the words say it!" At 2-9 he received his first *Meg and Mog* book (Nicoll/Pienkowski), and was inspired to pick out the print shown as unusual graphics integrated into the pictures – especially as they were mainly the onomatopoeic ones – "Crash" "Tinkle" and "Downstairs" coming down the stairs.

Many children think that it is the pictures that hold the story (which may be an effect of not hearing the author's actual words.) My children knew about authors, and had several author's names before they were three – mainly ones whose books were identifiable in matching series, Dick Bruna and Beatrix Potter. Ralph also recognized Richard Scarry (whose books were not uniform). He referred to his favourite *Best Word Book Ever* as "That big Scarry" and told an adult friend at 2-11 "We've got a new Scarry, John!" The previous month on first hearing the title page of *Meg's Car*, when the adult read "by Helen Nicoll and Jan Pienkowski" he exclaimed with delight "like the others" (by then he knew several in the series). By three the children certainly understood the concept, talking about "The lady who wrote it" (Rebecca) and "The man who draw-ed it" (Ralph). Ralph had forgotten the word "author" at 4-0 when I read a condescending question "Can you see the brown bear?" and he replied with scorn "A'course I can, read-maker". He clearly understood the author's role, even if he felt belittled by the question.

Book-handling skills, letters and learning to read

Ezell and Justice are keen that children are taught book handling skills also. Again, here is a small selection of my children's skill, learned without any direct instruction.

Rebecca regularly had a big nursery rhyme book on the floor among her play things (Eve's *Mother Goose*), and looked at it often, sometimes crawling around it to look at it the other way up. I felt she was positioning herself so that the picture was the correct way up, but I wasn't completely sure. However at 1-2 I had proof of this ability. We had a set of coloured stacking beakers with raised line sketches on the base. The blue one had a bear sitting down. I had never pointed them out to her. Sitting on the floor, at 1-2, she discovered the picture and was staring at it intently. I told her it was a bear, and she began to turn the beaker round and round in her hands, finally stopping. I looked over her shoulder and yes, she was holding it correctly. Soon she could correctly orient the other animal pictures on the beakers, though not the car, house, train and pram.

Here the second child's experiences differ markedly. Ralph often came as I was reading to his sister, and stood at my knee, hence looking at the book upside down – an experience which would never have happened with the older child. Nor did he spend the same long periods looking at books alone that she did – there was always something more amusing to look at, with Rebecca in the house. Books were a social activity for him. Consequently Ralph was 1-8 before he consistently looked at them the correct way up – six months older than his sister had been.

Rebecca understood about definitions. Occasionally she would perceive a gap in the English language, and invent a word to fill it: "I'm chambering – that means turning over the pages sideways" she told me at 2-10, also demonstrating in words that she knew exactly how a book should be orientated. The previous year, if she had forgotten the words when singing a nursery rhyme, she would make up a word, then reassure me that she knew it wasn't a real word – "Funny song" (1-11).

I am not sure that I would have demonstrated directionality, because learning letters and reading were something we kept apart from the actual story reading process. We did not want the joy of language and story to be spoilt by didacticism. Nevertheless, we talked about letters quite often with Rebecca. I was interested in the process of learning to read. All the books at the time assured me that, read to extensively, children would pick up reading for themselves early and easily. It did not happen so in the case of either child. Possibly it was because we did not do the deliberate instruction using simple books, that they had so much trouble – but I do not regret it. They acquired a love of words and narrative, which has stood them in good stead as adults. We felt they may not have if the book was made into a reading lesson, with the accompanying testing and praise.

Rebecca took an interest in print, asking about and locating letters and numbers for herself. She was excited to discover "her" letter, a minuscule "R", raised in glass on the side of a milk bottle at 1-7. I had read Doman's book *Teach your Baby to Read*, where he recommends making letters about ten centimetres high and coloured red, so the child can recognise and remember them more easily. I was dubious about the necessity of this, and felt justified by Rebecca's discovery of this transparent one, only about three millimetres high. By 2-0 she could name 18 uppercase letters.

We had trade alphabet books, so she had the concept of a letter standing for something pictured. However they did not satisfy me, because many of the pictures were of things that were foreign to her – fine for a book, but not as useful for learning the alphabet. So I made her a scrap book with an opening for each letter, and many objects she recognised on the page. Some I actually drew so she could also name her favourite dolls and toys ("Fido" on the "F" page, for instance). We had the usual magnetic letters on the refrigerator. By 2-3 she could name all 26 letters (uppercase) and knew most of their sounds. One day at a friend's place, where she had seen Seuss's *Fox in Socks* and heard it read only once, she remarked "Fox and box rhyme because they've both got an X". There were occasional other comments about how things were spelt. Both could also read the figures (useful in counting books), being able to name 1 to 9 by age 2-3.

Their acquisition of reading may be of interest, despite it being well outside the age range. Rebecca had a sight vocabulary of thirty words by the time she started school, but unfortunately they used the ITA[1] method, so she was effectively cut off from the print she knew so well, and she found the whole process frustrating and disheartening. She did not learn to read at her interest level until she was 7-6.

Ralph had less intensive instruction at an alternative school. He usually listened with Rebecca, so had heard much longer stories (such as chapters of *The Lion the Witch and the Wardrobe*, Lewis, at 3-1 and the complete *Moominland Midwinter*, Jansson, at 4-2) so there was even less incentive to try to make out the words. Clearly these texts were beyond his possible reading ability. He was eight before he read at his interest level.

Both children could recite many book-texts. Rebecca playing alone, without the book present, at 2-3 recited half of *Peter Rabbit* almost word-for-word (Beatrix Potter). However she never attempted to read the words even of books she knew by heart – perhaps because she knew we would always read to her when asked.

One aspect of learning to read which is not considered by Ezell and Justice, is being able to recognise pictures. When my children were small, commentators were still saying that children could not recognise anything in a picture until they were 1-6. These commentators were clearly not parents, or had never spent time observing their children and books, because it is perfectly clear that all children can understand pictures well before their first birthday. I will now relate almost the first encounters of the children with books, demonstrating a nascent ability to recognise pictures. My record of babies is almost unique amongst the four other parent-observer diaries of children with books. Butler in *Cushla and her Books* (1979) has a few references, as do the Cragos in *Prelude to Literacy* (1983),

1. The Initial Teaching Alphabet has 44 symbols for the 44 English phonemes, thus avoiding English's eccentric spelling while the child is learning to read.

but no specific details. The others (White *Books Before Five* 1954, and Wolf and Heath *The Braid of Literature* 1992) begin at age two. (It is of note also that mine is the only record to include a male child, and to look at the siblings in the same detail.) Jones *Emerging Patterns of Literacy* (1996) is a record of two children with books from 0-9 to 2-3, but it is more of a linguistic study, and largely analyses the adult's language and how it changes over the period. These parents use "labelling" (which they term "picture book reading" and retelling the stories (termed "storybook reading"). They rarely read the author's words, but concentrate on the child's understanding of both the vocabulary and the plot. They also have to work quite hard to keep the child's interest. This is an excellent description of the more common way of sharing books with young children. However it denies them the joy of discovery for themselves, and of encountering unusual words.

Infant picture recognition

Here are my two children's encounters with Bruna's *B is for Bear*, their first or second book. They had the first edition, which has a larger format than the present one, and has white rather than coloured backgrounds. Also Ralph's Eskimo has now been replaced with an Elephant. Even at this age, there would have been little excited pointing and exclaiming on my part. I wanted them to concentrate on the book, not on me.

B is for Bear (Bruna)

Figure 2. Image from *B is for Bear* by Dick Bruna

This journal entry is of Ralph at 16 weeks. (See Figure 2).

> In bed [again the double bed] this morning, after his feed, I showed Bruna's *B is for Bear* to him. He was lying beside me, so I could see him easily in profile and watch his eye movements. We went through the apple, bear, castle and duck with minimal interest. He was lying still, with a glance at the picture and then away to another section of the page or right off the book altogether. I was just telling myself that he and Rebecca are two different children [her record is below], and comparisons are odious, when we reached the Eskimo. This time the reaction was completely different. He stared and stared at it, with his eyes going from the feet up to the face over and over again. I didn't count how many times this happened, but certainly more than ten. After about six of these, he started vocalising to it, making three or four cheerful "ah"s, and began to move his arms excitedly, too. At first it was generalised arm waving and kicking, but gradually his left arm waved closer and closer to the book, until it was right on the picture, hitting it quite hard with his fist. He also smiled at it several times. He seemed completely fascinated. I've never seen him smile at any object before, only people. After a long time – at least several minutes – his concentration was not broken, but I wanted to see if the same interest was apparent on other pages. His waving continued during the fish and the grapes, and he grasped the bottom of the book with his left hand several times, but not the same concentrated looking. He used the bottom-to-top eye sweep again on the fish once or twice, so it may be an automatic picture scanning reaction, but then looked right off the book. At the Hammer he made an unhappy sound, so I turned back to the Eskimo and he was excited again and repeated his happy noise. This time he looked steadily but only for several seconds, then away, so I continued. We got to the Owl, when he grizzled again. I returned to the Eskimo, but there was minimal interest, and I assumed he had had enough "reading" for one day.

Figure 3. Image from *B is for Bear* by Dick Bruna

Rebecca had first encountered the book at 13 weeks. Her great love, and it was so for at least the next six months, was the lion (Figure 3). I had assumed it was the bright yellow colour and the spiky black outlines which so attracted her (she looked at it the longest, with arm waving and some vocalisation, as well as hitting it enthusiastically – though none of these at 13 weeks). I imagined that these were the aspects that would attract all children, but as we have seen, infant Ralph showed no interest in it at all. His Eskimo has several colours rather than a block of bright yellow, and no spiky outline. It seems certain now that he responded to the Eskimo as a representation of a person, just as she responded to the animal as a cat-like animal (she loved our Pinkle Purr). They have continued to be a person person and an animal person (speaking very broadly of course).

Recognising illustration of specific characters is a skill not unlike recognising photos of actual people. Rebecca and Ralph demonstrated this ability with photographs at ages 8 and 6 months respectively. A number of experiments have shown conclusively that infants are able to recognise and respond to images of faces as early as 3 months However it appears the picture-book critics were unaware of these studies, because they frequently used to imply that children cannot recognise anything in pictures until they are about one and a half years old. This was why Rebecca's first recognition of pictured faces at eight months surprised me. At ten months, she would react to pictures of babies exactly as she did to real babies seen down the street. At the same age, her visiting grandmother taught her a game – "eyes, nose, mouth, hair!" – pointing to the features on all large pictures of faces. She had learned to point to the correct features herself by 11 months.

Baby Ralph provided the youngest clear example of an infant recognising a picture at 6 months old, when he attempted to insert his forefinger into the mouth of a pictured baby, just as was his wont to do with actual people. He did not complain when the pictured mouth would not allow access, as he did with real mouths, however.

I have described these encounters at some length, because being able to "read" pictures is a first step to being able to "read" writing. There are many steps in between, but none of them need specific instruction. The difference between our reading style and that advocated by Ezell and Justice, is that in their reading sessions the adult has all the power, makes all the decisions – chooses the book (as good for demonstrating the particular skill the child needs to learn), initiates the session, asks the questions, and praises the "turn taking" conversation and attempts at answering.

In our reading sessions, the child was in control. They would choose a specific book, and often demand emphatically to hear it read. Sometimes I chose one I wanted to try out with them, but would not persist if they did not enjoy it. We did not ask leading questions, expecting that the text itself would supply what was needed and disliking the testing implicit in the questions and answers Ezell and Justice recommend. And as for praise, it would have never occurred to us. It would be like saying "You've done an excellent job eating that ice-cream!" Praise for something the child very much wants to do is contrived and pointless.

This is an account of reading aloud practices totally without the "sharing" (conversation and instruction) advocated by Ezell and Justice. These two children learned about the bookness of books, about language and print, about the joy of plot and character (all part of "literacy") and they learned to read as well, without this form of scaffolding. The "sharing" may be essential for children with problems, but for pleasure in the narrative and language, the book can speak for itself. As Rebecca told Granny "Just read it to me!"

Children's books cited

Alderson, B. & Oxenbury, H. 1974. *Cakes and Custard.* London: Heinemann.
Bruna, D. 1966. *The Sailor.* London: Methuen.
Bruna, D. 1967. *B is for Bear: An ABC.* London: Methuen.
Campbell, R. 1985. *Dear Zoo.* Harmondsworth: Penguin.
Eve, E. 1958. *Mother Goose Nursery Rhymes.* London: Pearl Press.
Hill, E. 1983. *Spot's First Walk.* Harmondsworth: Picture Puffin, and others.
Hughes, S. 1973. *Lucy and Tom's Day.* Harmondsworth: Puffin.
Jansson, T. 1971. *Moominland Midwinter.* Harmondsworth: Puffin.
Krasilovsky, P. & Spier, P. 1970. *The Cow Who Fell in the Canal.* Harmondsworth: Penguin.
Lewis, C. S. 1959. *The Lion, the Witch and the Wardrobe.* Harmondsworth: Penguin.
McCloskey, R. 1967. *Blueberries for Sal.* London: Angus & Robertson.
Milne, A. A. 1926. *Winnie-the-Pooh.* London: Methuen.
Nicoll, H. & Pienkowski, J. 1976. *Meg and Mog.* Harmondsworth: Puffin.
Nicoll, H. & Pienkowski, J. 1978. *Meg's Car.* Harmondsworth: Puffin.
Potter, B. [1903]. *The Tale of Peter Rabbit.* London: Warne.
Potter, B. [1904]. *The Tale of Benjamin Bunny.* London: Warne.
Potter. B. [1909]. *The Tale of the Flopsy Bunnies.* London: Warne.
Robinson, J. G. 1966. *Dear Teddy Robinson.* Harmondsworth: Puffin.
Scarry, R. 1964. *Richard Scarry's Best Word Book Ever.* London: Hamlyn.
Schneider, H. & N. 1959. *How Big is Big?* Leicester: Brockhampton.
Seuss, *Dr.* 1964. *Hop on Pop.* London: Collins & Harvill.
Seuss, *Dr.* 1966. *Fox in Socks.* London: Collins & Harvill.
Tison, A. & Taylor, T. 1974. *Barbapapa's Ark.* London: Warne.

References

Butler, D. 1979. *Cushla and her Books.* Auckland: Hodder & Stoughton.

Crago, M. & Crago, H. 1983. *Prelude to Literacy: A Preschool Child's Encounter with Picture and Story.* Carbondale IL: Southern Illinois University Press.

DeLoache, J. 1984. What's this? Maternal questions in joint picture book reading with toddlers. ERIC ED 251 176.

Doman, G. 1965. *Teach your Baby to Read.* London: Cape.

Ezell, H. K. & Justice, L. M. 2005. *Shared Storybook Reading: Building Young Children's Language & Emergent Literacy Skills.* Baltimore MD: Brookes.

Jones, R. 1996. *Emerging Patterns of Literacy: A Multidisciplinary Perspective.* London: Routledge.

Lowe, V. 2007. *Stories, Pictures and Reality: Two Children Tell.* London: Routledge.

Reese, E. & Cox, A. 1999. Quality of adult book reading affects children's emergent literacy. *Developmental Psychology* 35(1): 20–28.

Vygotsky, L. 1978. *Mind in Society: The Development of Higher Psychological Processes.* Cambridge MA: Harvard University Press.

White, D. 1954. *Books Before Five.* Wellington: N.Z. Council for Educational Research.

Wolf, S. A. & Heath, S. B. 1992. *The Braid of Literature: Children's Worlds of Reading.* Cambridge MA: Harvard University Press.

CHAPTER 13

"This is me"

Developing literacy and a sense of self through play, talk and stories

Janet Evans

This chapter focuses on 3 and 4 year old children; their interactions with picturebook read alouds, their repeated requests to have favourite books read over and over again, their developing concept of identity and their growing ability to respond to the books. As the children had picturebooks read *to* and shared *with* them, they were able to identify a sense of self mirrored in the content of some of the books and these were the ones they chose to read and re-read, making informed choices about their favourites.
The children identified themselves in the storybook narratives and went on to record their responses in a variety of differing modes some of which led to them becoming real authors as they made their own books to be read, re-read and enjoyed.

Figure 1. "This is me and that is my name. It says Kelly."

3 year old Kelly pointed to her picture and her emergent writing as she described what it said. Her work was chosen as the cover for the first book some 3 year old children, several of whom were from non literate home backgrounds, created as part of a bookmaking project. The resulting zigzag book was based on *Faces* (1986) by Jan Pienkowski and *Funny Face* (2006) by Nicola Smee.

Both of these simple picturebooks provided the stimulus which helped the children to begin thinking of themselves as 3-year-old emergent readers and writers. In depicting faces of youngsters exhibiting different moods and emotions the books allowed the children to see themselves represented both physically and symbolically. In the case of *Funny Face*, which includes a mirror for children to see their own reflection, they were able to see themselves positioned in the book thereby giving them a real sense of self as an emergent reader.

The ten 3-year-old children involved in this study represented all of the children in the morning group of a nursery school in the North West of England, they were all white working class and had been attending nursery for just three months. Their routine included a daily read aloud and the two mentioned books had been read and re-read on several different occasions. Both depicted children's faces reacting to different moods and emotional states such as happy, sad, tired, cheeky and scared. The simplicity of the books and their subject matter helped the children to see characters like themselves represented in the books. It also helped to establish the children as authors in their first book making activity, thereby affording them a positive self image and sense of self. None of the children could read and yet they were all keen to interact with the books. They talked about the different expressions prior to looking at themselves in a mirror, drawing their own face and writing their name. Each child's work became a page in the book, *This is Me* (see Figure 1).

Young precocious readers

Whilst working with these young children I began to consider:

- Why is it that some children learn to read very young when others do not?
- What exactly is "in place" or "special" about certain children that enables them to become readers at a young age?
- Does a highly developed "sense of self" play a part?
- What about the important role that talk and play linked to picturebook texts have to play?

Being in the company of these children and seeing the books they created provided the practical examples that illustrated the background rationale and theoretical constructs I had been considering.

Literate home backgrounds

Research looking at pre-school children's ability to interact with and make sense out of print has been showing, for over three decades, that children from literate home backgrounds who have exposure to supportive, positive role models willing to share the process of reading, using good quality texts, are the children who are best able to cope with the demands of learning about literacy and the transition from home to school. (Bissex 1980; Butler 1980; Campbell 1999; Clark 1976; Martens 1998; Shickendanz 1990).

These literate home backgrounds are very often middle income families. It has been suggested that children from these families are regularly provided with a great deal of support for literacy learning. Vandermaas-Peeler, Nelson, Bumpass and Sassine (2009) found that highly educated parents seem to privilege storybook reading and play, seeing these two activities as necessary to prepare their children for their educational and occupational future. However they also found that, during reading and play activities, "*...regardless of income and education, parents provided high levels of support to sustain the children's interest and engagement...*" (2009: 311).

A literate home background is evidently a very important, indeed crucial factor for children of all ages; it provides most of the following opportunities:

- Lots of talk and reasons to talk
- Lots of play and reasons to play
- Exposure and access to good quality, relevant and stimulating texts which make children want to read
- Exposure and access to patterned, predictable texts
- Exposure to positive role models who will read and re-read the same texts
- Adults reading **to** children
- Children sharing reading **with** adults
- Children looking at books and reading **by** themselves
- Opportunities to sing, say and chant nursery rhymes and jingles
- Exposure to mark making materials, for example paint, pens, pencils, crayons, paper, cards, postcards, and encouragement to use them
- Lots of encouragement and the chance to develop positive self images, a positive sense of self – children need to know that they **can** read and that they **are** readers.

Reading aloud and re-reading books

"Read it again, read it again", was 3 year old Olivia's response to the reading of *We're Going On A Bear Hunt* (1989) by Michael Rosen with illustrations by Helen Oxenbury. It is a typical response from a child reading and re-reading a favourite book.

Young children love listening to stories read aloud. Having repeat readings of them means they often get to know and recognise many of the words and they also grow to know and understand the differing narratives (Spreadbury 1998). This reading and re-reading of books is not to be underestimated and is an essential part in the process of forming young fluent readers as observed by Margaret Clark as early as 1976. Many readers begin to memorise substantial parts of a text and instantly recognise if any pages or parts of pages are missed during a storybook read aloud, demanding that all parts of the book be read at each and every read. For some emergent readers it is the illustrations in picturebooks which help them to make sense of the text (Evans 1998).

One might expect repeat readings of the same text to provide similar responses; however Parkes (1998) noted that repeat readings of a text never came out the same and each new reading allowed the children to discover something different about the book. Parkes described these repeat interactions as "a perpetual firstness" whereby the picturebooks become,

> "meaning potentials and meaning is created through interactions involving the reader's prior knowledge and experience with the book, the reader's purpose for returning to the book and the sign complex formed by print and illustrations." (1998:45)

In a study looking at children's favourite books, Wilkinson (2003) felt that what they choose to read for themselves might define what literacy and literature mean to them, the beginnings of the development of a "sense of self" reflected in the reader/text relationship. In a similar vein Calinescu (1993) suggested that books are re-read for many different reasons to include, finding out what attracts them to us, rediscovering aspects of a previously read text, and noting how books can be seen to reinvent themselves when re-read.

In his book, *Reading with Alice: Literacy from Home to School,* Robin Campbell commented on one of the picturebooks which Alice, his granddaughter, returned to time and time again, *Good-Night Owl* by Pat Hutchins. Campbell (1999:70) noted that at the age of 3 Alice had almost entirely memorised the book and when they read it together Alice contributed significantly to the text, indeed she contributed more than he did as he guided her through the text:

Gf: *Owl*
A: *tried to sleep.*
Gf: *The*
A: *bees buzzed,*
buzz, buzz,
and owl tried to sleep.
Gf: *The squirrel*
A: *cracked nuts, crunch crunch,*
and owl tried to sleep.

Over a period of time Alice had many books read to her and shared with her and these read alouds gave her tremendous confidence (Campbell 2001), indeed by the time Alice was five Campbell had noted she was emerging as a competent reader and what previously had been, "*Reading with Alice had increasingly become reading by Alice.*" Campbell (1999: 141). In a longitudinal study of her two children, Virginia Lowe (2007) emphasised this same point and demonstrated that reading and re-reading helped her children, Ralph and Rebecca access the patterned language of many texts.

The reading environment that a child is exposed to has a crucial part to play in their growing ability to read. Aidan Chambers (1991) stated that emergent readers must have many books read to them in their first five years in order that they can effectively benefit from learning to read in the formal school setting. Many of these books do not have to be "new reads" but can be re-readings of previously read books. It is during the repeated readings of books that children start to pick out rhythm and rhyme, similar and same initial letters, the existence of capital letters that represent the beginning of their own names and whole words etc. The importance of re-reading books cannot be stressed highly enough.

Margaret Mooney (1990) noted that children who have a series of picture-books read *to* and shared *with* them, are more able to move on to reading *by* themselves, especially if the books are patterned, predictable texts with strong picture/text relationships. Mooney designed a continuum (see Table 1) to describe the move from the child as a potential literacy user having books read *to* him/her, through the stage of reading books *with* a supportive, expert reader, progressing onto the child as a developing independent reader able to read books *by* him/herself.

In looking at children's choice of books, Wilkinson (2003) asked why children choose to read and re-read the same book time and time again and why they choose certain books in particular. Her study found that although parents obviously affected their children's choices, the children themselves chose books that held great personal meaning and gave them much pleasure. Also, their favourite books,

> "were those that were embedded in the private context of each child's world. Their status as "favourite books" was defined by this personal meaning and displayed in each child's idiosyncratic and emotional response." (2003: 296)

This choice can be seen when children choose books with photographs of very young children involved in everyday activities that represent their lives in relation to significant others; their awareness of self as represented in books is more than evident.

Table 1.

The "To", "With" and "By" continuum in relation to reading *and* writing

At every stage in a child's journey to be literate, adults need to provide different levels of support depending on the supports and challenges in the texts.

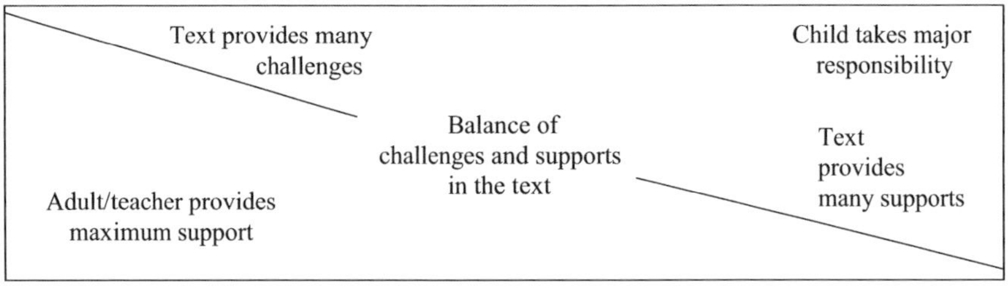

TO	WITH		BY
Reading to Children	Shared Reading	Guided Reading	Independent Reading
Modelled Writing	Shared Writing	Guided Writing	Independent Writing

Adapted from Mooney, M. (1990) *Reading To, With, and By Children*. New York: Richard Owen

Literacy learning through play

Just as children often choose books featuring images of youngsters like themselves, their play also mirrors this choice and is frequently very egocentric in the early stages. *"Play is the work of children"* is a phrase which has been used many times by adults who work with and observe young children going about their everyday activities. Vivian Paley (2004) talks about the first time she heard this phrase in 1949 and in so doing talks about the language of play and children learning through play. Paley's research is part of many well documented links between children's play and their literacy development (Campbell 1998; Hall 1987; Hall & Abbott 1991; Hall & Robinson 2003).

As part of a recent critical review of research considering some of the links between play and literacy, Roskos and Christie (2001:59) noted that the studies showed,

> "play can serve literacy by: (a) providing settings that promote literacy activity, skills and strategies; (b) serving as a language experience that can build connections between oral and written modes of expression: and (c) providing opportunities to teach and learn literacy."

They went on to say that children's practical experiences with language and literacy set in meaningful, everyday social activities, "*give rise to the internal mental processes that are needed to do the intellectual work of reading and writing activity*" (2001:59). Play provides opportunities for children to use language in meaningful ways and when the play is linked to book-related narratives the play-related talk is often modelled on the language of the book.

In a further critical review of research, this time looking at the relationship between play and literacy development over a 30 year period, Roskos, Christie, Widman and Holding (2010) found that the focus of research had often been too narrow, the pace too "uneven and discontinuous" and the measures of literacy outcomes inconsistent. They did find however that individual studies point very conclusively to the positive gains to be made by linking children's play, talk and stories and it is evident that play and literacy share common areas in the young child's mind.

Literacy learning through play and stories

Books provide a rich source of imaginary world situations and play scenarios; they help to develop the inner self in relation to the outer world. They also allow children the opportunity to endow toys and other objects with life and feelings, providing children with play scenarios that they can act out using small world toys. After being exposed to picturebooks many children can be seen acting out characters such as: the big, bad giant, Bob the Builder, the wicked witch, the princess or some other book related character from traditional and popular culture stories. It is often the language from the books, especially the repetitive language from patterned, predictable texts, which enriches the child's personal language allowing them to "*talk about many virtual experiences and think by means of verbal analogies*" (Whitehead 2002:285).

Whitehead studied her grandson's interactions with picturebooks in his first three years. In a longitudinal case study, which shows many similarities with Campbell's research, she found that for Dylan,

> "Books actually miniaturize the world of creatures and objects.......We observed an interesting pattern of shock and fear in Dylan's first "real" encounters with the very real animals and machines he loved as familiar picture book characters. At 18 months he was noticeably upset by his first encounter with the dinosaurs and large stuffed animals at the London Natural History Museum and, not surprisingly, by a live shark in an aquarium. He clung to his carers, hid his face and desperately waved "bye-bye" to these monsters he knew so well from his books."
>
> (Whitehead 2002:284)

This same scenario happened with some horses and other animals he saw on a visit to a farm and Whitehead noted that Dylan was clearly alarmed at the size of the animals which up to this point had only occurred for him as small characters in his picturebooks. Whitehead recounted how Dylan became preoccupied by "playing out" horses as if to come to terms with the shock he had received.

Literacy learning through play, talk and stories

When children enjoy what they do they are more likely to benefit and learn from the experience. Play activity linked to books being read and enjoyed provides exactly this kind of experience. Children learn through talk, through involvement with stories being focussed on, and through the different kinds of play: pretend play, role play, dramatic play and small world play that bring together aspects of the stories and talk about the stories.

For young children, books often provide a bridge between the real world and the world of make believe and there are genuine links to be observed between their play, their talk and the stories they have been reading or are currently reading with expert readers. This "bridge" still exists with slightly older children and can be clearly seen with Hal, a young boy who has always had exposure to books which in turn have linked to his play. Mills (2010) considers Hal, who at the age of 8 years is still linking his imaginary play to the books he is reading. He is currently preoccupied with wars and battles and this links closely to his favourite book of the moment, *Astrosaurs, Day of the Dino-Droids* (2006) which depicts pterodactyls with machine guns and other such weapons. The fantasy fighting from his favourite book is closely re-enacted in his fantasy play and shows how his play and talk are very much linked to the story even as he grows older and matures.

In making links between his book and his play Hal shows us that young children's reading competencies often develop most effectively when there is a whole language approach to literacy and learning, whereby children's engagement with oral language and reading is situated in real, meaningful experiences. Therefore children develop their early literacy abilities through the inextricable links between:

- playing,
- talking and
- listening to stories (see Figure 2)

Figure 2. Play, talk, and stories

What comes first? Is it listening to and reading stories; playing linked to the stories; or, talking related to the play and the stories? There are obvious links between all three aspects but which comes first? Do we know? Indeed, does it matter? As can be seen with the experiences of Dylan and Hal, it was the books that influenced their play activities. Their talk was then related partly to the book narratives and partly to the type of play activity, the associated resources and the other people present, that is, the social context. The story provided the ideas which influenced the children's play and this, along with the accompanying talk, led to new ideas which often influenced their literacy responses. However the children's previous real life experiences are subconsciously drawn upon as are references to previous books they have read and shared and their ongoing social talk.

Talking about books as they are being read and re-read to children has a crucial part to play. In her reader response research into the importance of talking about books, Evans stated, "*It isn't enough just to read a book, one must talk about it as well*" (2009: 3). She went on to say, "*...just reading the book itself is hardly ever enough! It is the shared oral responses and the ensuing discussions that allow fuller and maybe differing understandings to take place*" (2009: 5).

Talk around and about stories

Talk is ongoing and takes place for many different reasons. It is well documented that we learn through talk and it was Halliday (1984) who stated that we need to give children opportunities to learn language, to learn about language and to learn through language. There are major differences between oral and written language and in engaging children in literacy learning through playing and talking about books the links between these two communication forms are made easier for them. Certainly the ability to benefit from the written language of books is augmented through book talk and book related play:

- Talk is very much linked to the "here and now"; the scene is already in place for the participants. **It is context bound.**
- Written language is not necessarily linked to the "here and now", it is usually written by someone else and dictates that the reader must set his/her own scene, often in another time and place. It is context free.
- In order to fully understand written language and book narratives the reader must develop an ability to abstract, symbolize, imagine and gain meaning from the text. Children who have developed these abilities are very often able to benefit from the school situation and the language of school.

Children who have listened to, then talked about stories are better able to:

- *Imagine characters in stories*
- *Empathise with the characters*
- *Set the scene*
- *Retell the story in their own words*
- *Sequence the story parts – beginning, middle, end, and ...*
- *Think abstractly*

Hence they are able to benefit from the world of story more easily than children who have not had stories read to them and shared with them (see Figure 3).

Developing a sense of self through books

Texts play an important part in teaching what young literacy learners learn (Meek 1988) and in helping them to realise who they are in terms of self. Young readers need to be able to see themselves reflected in the text and to be able to respond meaningfully, consequently books need to represent characters from many different cultural and social backgrounds. Children who have many books read to them begin to develop a sense of self reflected in the content of the book. They will often choose books about babies and toddlers, relishing in looking at what they eat, drink, play with, talk about etc. These books, showing images of youngsters like themselves, are often the ones they choose to re-read, indicating their evident ability to make informed choices about their favourites. They see themselves mirrored in the books and with the help of expert role models they read and interact with the characters, setting, time, events and endings thereby developing a sense of self and of place through the text.

In a thought provoking study which fore-grounded the development of self in literacy development prior to conventional reading, Lysaker (2006) looked at the development of the "self that reads" in young children and proposed a continuum of self development as it relates to the young reader's developing ability to read. Lysaker worked with 18 children who were at various stages on the reading development continuum – some were nearer to, and still on, the beginner stage, whilst some were on the emergent stage. She proposed five "self positions" which the young children in her study, all at different stages as beginning and emergent readers, went through in their responses to a wordless picturebook:

1. Reactor
2. Observer
3. Emerging narrator
4. Developing narrator
5. Established narrator

The children's responses ranged from simple reactions to the text characterised by the use of labels to single pictures in the Reactor stage, through to the much more complex, "richly developed" responses to the story overall in the Established Narrator stage.

Lysaker questioned some of the conventions that have to be in place before children begin to read and stated that it is not enough just to know *about print*. In successful reading the reader demonstrates the capacity to enter into the world of the text and to make sense of it through a personal experience with the text itself. This was what Louise Rosenblatt (1978) called a transaction. Children need to know the text and to have an awareness of self in relation to the text to bring about understanding; they also need to be able to see themselves in the text and to position themselves as one of the characters in the narrative. As Lysaker puts it, "*such an experience involves linking self to text and representing one's experience through text.*" (2006:36).

Wilheim (1997) calls this, "being the book" and the successful understanding of stories by young children is based on their ability to participate in them as an event of self.

The language encounters which help us to construct a sense of self take place within the self as well as in the social world; Lysaker makes an observation in relation to precocious young readers that ties in with the points relating to the importance of literate home backgrounds,

> "It seems likely that children with particular kinds of language and literacy backgrounds would have more opportunity to develop capacities of "self as reader". That is to say, children whose early years provided not only for frequent storybook reading events, but also for opportunities in which they were able to take on the roles of make believe characters in symbolic play, would have more opportunities to develop capacities necessary for reading." (2006: 51)

This is a crucially important point as we are increasingly seeing young children in school who are able to decode but fail to develop a full understanding of texts. Lysaker states that,

> "The current focus on print related knowledge and the reduction of curricular activities involving story telling and play may work to inhibit the ontological work of early childhood that leads to literacy learning." (2006: 53)

Moving from play, talk and stories to writing … portrayal of self in multimodal book making activities

The 3 year old nursery children with whom I was working were beginning to develop this sense of self through their class based play, talk and stories. They were being exposed to good quality, stimulating books on a daily basis and this exposure continued into their first year in school. They gradually developed the ability to recognise children like themselves in the books, children involved in everyday activities that they could relate to. Following this they were able to write themselves into their narratives as main characters in the personally authored books. Their developing sense of "self" was helping them to read and write.

After drawing, writing and creating *This is Me*, the children went on to create three more books, two in nursery when they were still 3 years old and one in reception class when they were 4 years old. All four books showed their abilities to *read* themselves in the books they chose, then to *write* themselves into their book-making activities, that is, they were able to "import" representations of themselves in their own text innovations (Elster 1995).

I worked with the children for half a day a week over a period of four weeks. A format similar to the first session as previously described was used; the children read and re-read the books, talked about the storylines, identified characters like themselves in the narratives and went on to record their responses in a variety of differing modes. As they created their own books to be read and re-read the main character from each stimulus book was replaced by them, in so doing they were placing their own personality at the centre of each newly created story.

Look Through the Window

The children's second book, which they called, *Look Through the Window,* was based on two books, *Who's in the Shed*? (1986) by Brenda Parkes and *Through My Window* (1986) by Tony Bradman & Eileen Browne. In the first, a patterned, predictable book, the narrator draws the reader into the story by repeatedly asking the question, "Who's in the Shed?" Using the many cueing systems to be found in the book (picture cues, rhyming verse and words and previous knowledge etc.) the reader is helped to "read" and make sense of the book, and to "solve" the problem posed on each page.

The second book depicts a little girl who is unwell looking out of her window to see various people and things over the period of a day. After reading, re-reading and drawing on the ideas from the two books the children were encouraged to think about what they might see if they looked out of one of the windows in their house, that is, if they pulled the curtains back what might they see? The children used the language of the book as a model for their writing and started to ask the question, *Look through the window what can you see*? By repeatedly asking this question the text for the book was formed and in answering the question the children placed themselves at the centre of their response. The repetitive storyline was created! Some unusual responses were given; these children obviously lived in streets where unusual things took place:

> *Look through the window what can you see?*
> *Abbey can see a car.*
> *Kelly can see two pussy cats.*
> *Sinead can see three people.*
> *Rebecca can see a squiggly picture.*
> (see Figure 3)

Look through the window.

What can you see?

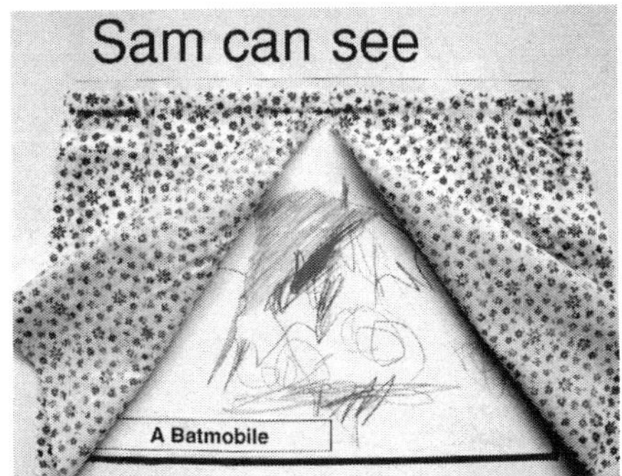

Figure 3. *Look through the window what can you see? Sam can see a batmobile*

Hide and Seek

The third book originated from reading a selection of hide and seek, flip-the-flap books by Eric Hill and by singing the traditional finger rhyme, *Tommy Thumb, Tommy Thumb, Where are you? Here I am. Here I am. How do you do?* The children loved the hide and seek aspect of trying to find things under the flaps and after acting out the story and the rhyme using finger puppets they created their next book, *Hide and Seek* by asking the question, *Where are you?*. To answer the question the children drew themselves with a speech bubble response. Some interesting responses were devised:

> *Where are you Abbey? Here I am, in the toy box.*
> *Where are you Rebecca? Here I am, under the bed.*
> *Where are you Kelly? Here I am, behind the door.*
> (see Figure 4)

Children's drawings enable them to represent their feelings and emotions and to communicate some of the ways in which they see themselves (Anning & Ring 2004; Kendrick & McKay 2004). They also allow the children to identify a sense of self and to place themselves at the centre of their narratives.

Where are you Abbey?

Here I am, in the toy box.

Figure 4. *Where are you Abbey? Here I am, in the toy box*

Children, Children, What Do You See?

One year on these children were still reading, playing and talking! They were now well on the way to being confident literacy users, both readers and writers, and in their play they were using puppets as resources to act out *Brown Bear, Brown Bear What Do You See*? (1984), a classic patterned predictable text by Bill Martin Jr. with illustrations by Eric Carle. Their sense of self was once again evident as they substituted themselves instead of the creatures in their text innovation entitled, *Children, Children What Do You See?* (see Figure 5).

Children, Children, What do you see?

Figure 5. *Jonathan, Jonathan, what do you see? I see an astronaut*

Conclusion

The children in this study created four unique books which showed their developing sense of self and their ability to relate their play and talk linked to books. As they read their own contributions in the finished books it was evident that in seeing themselves at the centre of their bookmaking process they were able to make sense out of print, that is, they were reading for meaning.

Nearly thirty years ago, Frank Smith (1984) was of the opinion that in order to learn to read and write, children's learning must be meaningful, useful, continual and effortless, incidental, collaborative, various and no-risk. Since this time Smith, in considering how children learn to read and write, has been convinced that they write what they read and they learn from the company they keep. In stating "*we learn from the company we keep*" (1992: 432) Smith refers not just to the company of expert readers and writers who share the books with children but also to the company of the books themselves. The children in this bookmaking project had a variety of books read and re-read to them on a daily basis, they were also given opportunities to act out the storylines in different play settings and to talk about the books. In their group bookmaking activities they were also given the chance to use talk to:

- Work collaboratively
- Make decisions
- Promote logical thought
- Solve problems
- Explore self and others
- Role play
- Sequence stories in different ways

It was the books which provided a stimulus for the children's play and subsequent talk and Margaret Meek in her seminal text, *How Texts Teach What Readers Learn* (Meek 1988) was in agreement with Smith when she noted the crucial importance of keeping company with books.

The practical and theoretical observations made during this bookmaking project with very young children show the value of giving them the chance to develop an awareness of self and to link this awareness to play, talk and stories. These links, if focussed on, will almost certainly point the way to effective literacy learning.

Children's books cited

Bradman, T. & Browne, E. 1986. *Through My Window.* London: Methuen Books.

Cole, S. 2006. *Astrosaur. Day of the Dino-Droids.* London: Red Fox.

Hutchins, P. 1972. *Good-Night Owl.* London: The Bodley Head.

Martin Jr, B. & Carle, E. 1984. *Brown Bear, Brown Bear What Do You See?* London: Collins Picture Lions.

Parkes, B. 1986. *Who's in the Shed?* Melbourne: Methuen Australia.

Pienkowski, J. 1986. *Faces.* London: Puffin Books.

Rosen, M. & Oxenbury, H. 1989. *We're Going On A Bear Hunt.* London: Walker Books.

Smee, N. 2006. *Funny Faces.* London: Bloomsbury Publishing.

References

Anning, A. & Ring, K. 2004. *Making Sense of Children's Drawings*. Berkshire: Open University Press.

Bissex, G. 1980. *Gnys at wrk: A Child Learns to Read and Write*. Cambridge MA: Harvard University Press.

Butler, D. 1980. *Babies Need Books*. London: Penguin Books.

Calinescu, M. 1993. *Rereading*. New Haven CT: Yale University Press.

Campbell, R. 1999. *Literacy from Home to School: Reading with Alice*. Staffordshire: Trentham Books.

Campbell R. 2001. *Read-Alouds with Young Children*. Newark DL: International Reading Association.

Campbell, R. (ed.). 1998. *Facilitating Pre-school Literacy*. Newark NJ: International Reading Association.

Chambers, A. 1991. *The Reading Environment: How Adults Help Children Enjoy Books*. Stroud: Thimble Press.

Clark, M. 1976. *Young Fluent Readers*. London: Heinemann.

Elster, C. 1995. Importations in pre-schoolers' emergent readings. *Journal of Reading Behaviour* 27(1): 65–85.

Evans, J. (ed.). 1998. *What's in the Picture?: Responding to Illustrations in Picturebooks*. London: Paul Chapman Publishers.

Evans, J. (ed.). 2009. *Talking Beyond the Page: Reading and Responding to Picturebooks*. London: Routledge Farmer.

Hall, N. 1987. *The Emergence of Literacy*. London: Hodder & Stoughton.

Hall, N. & Abbott, L. (eds). 1991. *Play in the Primary Curriculum*. London: Hodder & Stoughton.

Hall, N. & Robinson, A. (eds). 2003. *Exploring Writing and Play in the Early Years*. London: David Fulton.

Halliday, M. A. K. 1984. Three aspects of children's language development: Learning language, learning about language, learning through language. Paper presented at The Ohio State University.

Kendrick, M. & McKay, R. 2004. Drawings as an alternative way of understanding young children's constructions of literacy. *Journal of Early Childhood Literacy* 4(1): 109–128.

Lowe, V. 2007. *Stories, Pictures and Reality: Two Children Tell*. London: Routledge.

Lysaker, J. 2006. Young children's readings of wordless picturebooks: What's self got to do with it? *Journal of Early Childhood Literacy* 6(1): 33–55.

Martens, P. 1998. Growing as a reader and writer: Sarah's inquiry into literacy. In *Facilitating Pre-school Literacy*, R. Campbell (ed.), 51–68. Newark NJ: International Reading Association.

Meek, M. 1988. *How Texts Teach What Readers Learn*. Stroud: Thimble Press.

Mills, R. 2010. Hal's reading diary. *Books for Keeps* 181 (March): 13.

Mooney, M. 1990. *Reading To, With and By Children*. New York NY: Richard Owen.

Paley, F. G. 2004. *A Child's Work: The Importance of Fantasy Play*. Chicago IL: University of Chicago Press.

Parkes, B. 1998. Nursery children using illustrations in shared readings and rereadings. In *What's in the Picture?: Responding to Illustrations in Picture Books*, J. Evans (ed.), 44–57. London: Paul Chapman.

Rosenblatt, L. 1978. *The Reader, the Text, the Poem: The Transactional Theory of the Literary Work*. Carbondale IL: Southern Illinois University Press.

Roskos, K. & Christie, J. 2001. Examining the play-literacy interface: A critical review and future developments. *Journal of Early Childhood Literacy* 1(1): 59–89.

Roskos, K., Christie, J., Widman, S. & Holding, A. 2010. Three decades in: Priming for meta-analysis in play-literacy research. *Journal of Early Childhood Literacy* 10(1): 55–96.

Shickendanz, J. 1990. *Adam's Righting Revolutions*. Portsmouth NH: Heinemann.

Sipe, L. 2008. *Storytime: Young Children's Literary Understanding in the Classroom*. New York NY: Teachers' College Press.

Smith, F. 1984. *Joining the Literacy Club*. Reading: Centre for the Teaching of Reading.

Smith, F. 1992. Learning to read: The never-ending debate. *The Phi Delta Kappan* 73(6): 432–435, 438–441.

Spreadbury, J. 1998. Reading – It's a natural: Reading aloud to children in the home. In *Facilitating Pre-school Literacy*, R. Campbell (ed.), 30–39. Newark NJ: International Reading Association.

Vandermaas-Peeler, M., Nelson, J., Bumpass, C. & Sassine, B. 2009. Social contexts of development: Parent-child interactions during reading and play. *Journal of Early Childhood Literacy* 9(3): 295–317.

Whitehead, M. 2002. Dylan's routes to literacy: The first three years with picturebooks. *Journal of Early Childhood Literacy* 2(3): 269–289.

Wilheim, J. D. 1997. '*You Gotta be the Book*': *Teaching Engaged and Reflective Reading with Adolescents*. New York NY: Teachers College Press.

Wilkinson, K. 2003. Children's favourite books. *Journal of Early Childhood Literacy* 1(3): 275–301.

CHAPTER 14

How responses to picturebooks reflect and support the emotional development of young bilingual children

Evelyn Arizpe and Jane Blatt

This chapter is based on events recorded through the videos, audio-tapes and diary kept by Evelyn Arizpe to record her daughters' bilingual language development and their relationship to books. While there have been case studies on the linguistic progress of young bilingual children and case studies of monolingual children's developing literacy and relationship with literature through books, illustrations and stories, there have been no detailed observations of similar development in a bilingual household. The case study highlights how the children's responses to the complex interweaving of two languages through a trail of books and stories within a highly literate household supported and reflected their emotional development in the first 3 years of life.

This chapter is based on events recorded through the videos, audio-tapes and diary kept by Evelyn to record her daughters' bilingual language development and their relationship to books from their birth until Isabel was nearly 6 and Flora was just over 3 years old. The extracts have been selected to highlight how the complex interweaving of two languages through a trail of picturebooks and stories within a highly literate household, supported and reflected the children's emotional development in the first 3 years of life. As we examine the talk, play and performance that took place around books in both English and Spanish, we note the ways in which physicality; visuality and intertextuality were intrinsic parts of their bi-cultural responses. In addition, by looking at these responses against the background of the children's developing emotional life, we provide a unique view of the way in which normal anxieties around separation and sibling rivalry; their pleasures in sharing as well as their preference for independent learning; and their growing inner world, can be traced through the bilingual nature of their responses to picturebooks (see Figure 1).

Figure 1. Isabel (3.1) practices picturebook sharing on Flora (1.4)
Reprinted by permission of Evelyn Arizpe

There are many parent-observer case studies on the linguistic progress of young bilingual children (Leopold 1939–1949; Totten 1960; de Houwer 1990) but the variety of factors that impact on bilingual language learning makes generalizations difficult. It is accepted, however, that 'bilingual children move in different cognitive worlds, experience different linguistic environments, and are challenged to communicate using different resources, remaining sensitive to different abstract dimensions' (Bialystok 2001: 88). The research on the literacy acquisition of bilingual children tends to focus on these differences when it comes to reading and writing, but there are few parental case studies; most studies consider groups of children in pre-school or in early school years (e.g. Kenner 2000; Drury 2007; Gregory 2008). Although there is some research on bilinguals' storytelling ability (Herman 1996), there seems to be a gap in the research on bilingualism when it comes to interaction with books and literature in a pre-literate stage.[1]

A description of this type of interaction does appear in several case studies of monolingual children. The most detailed studies in English are those by

1. Carme Durán and Martina Fittipaldi (2010 forthcoming) do provide insights into the contrast between first and second language learning, of a three and a half year old boy, in their observation of the mediating role of the mother in the experience of reading and literacy learning.

Dorothy White (1954), Hugh and Maureen Crago (1983), Shelby Wolf and Shirley Brice Heath (1992), and Virginia Lowe (2007).[2] Admittedly, as in the case we describe below, most of these studies took place in white, middle-class households in which parents or carers (most of them academics who were aware of literature on the subject) created print-rich environments. Two other studies, Baghban (1984) and Robinson and Turnbull (2005), do describe bilingual households however, the research focus was not so much on bilingualism as on emergent literacy. Although these studies touch on the emotional impact of books and literature, providing evidence as to how children use their reading to explore a wide range of emotions, the only account that focuses on socio-emotional development is that of Roger Mills, a psychologist who looks at his son Hal's responses in terms of issues such as security, predictability and the development of self-consciousness (Mills 2002–2004). Our study looks at early biliteracy *and* emotional development and although we take into account the children's supportive social background, our starting point is the child's making sense of, and acquiring ownership of, the 'book' experience for themselves in their first three years.

There also seems to be a gap in research on bilingualism and its effect on emotional development and early learning at a pre-literate stage. Most fears about the negative effects of bilingualism (confusion, retarded development) have been overturned by research (Hakuta 1986; Bialystok 2001). Although bilingual children can lag slightly behind monolingual children in early language acquisition, this gap soon closes. On the other hand, recent cognitive research has revealed important benefits of bilingualism for communicative skills such as an early understanding of the communication needs of others (including those who speak foreign languages); increased metalinguistic insight and the ability to consider two possible interpretations at the same time (Nicoladis, Charbonnier & Popescu 2006).[3]

The background to this study

Evelyn's own simultaneous bilingual upbringing in Mexico had a significant impact on the language context in which Isabel and Flora grew up. Her family were fluent English speakers; she read mainly in English and attended bilingual

2. A more detailed synthesis of these studies, including methodological issues, can be found in Arizpe and Styles (2011). In Spanish, Angeles Molina Iturrondo (1998 and 2001) has analyzed the independent retellings and dialogic story reading of her young daughter.

3. This applies to pre-school children or early school years, 'below the range most often considered critical in learning a second language' (Nicoladis, Charbonnier & Popescu 2006: 1).

schools. When she was a doctoral student at the University of Cambridge she met her Scottish husband, Nigel. When the children were born, they decided to raise them bilingually: Evelyn would speak to them in Spanish and Nigel would speak to them in his native English.

Initially Evelyn read in Spanish to the children even if the books were in English, but she soon realized that when the text involved rhyme, such as *Each Peach Pear Plum* (1986) and *Peepo* (1983), both by Janet and Allan Ahlberg, it was necessary to read them in English to share the pleasure of the poetry and word games. This also applied to nursery rhymes and songs in English. Therefore Evelyn broke the consistency rule when reading English text but continued to comment on the books and pictures in Spanish.[4] When the girls began to speak and pointed to objects in the pictures and said the names in English, Evelyn reinforced the English but also provided the name in Spanish. Nigel read exclusively in English and enjoyed sharing art books (i.e. books with pictures) more than children's picturebooks. As the girls matured they preferred the English texts and responded to them in English. However, in their first three years of life books were closely associated with either English or Spanish.

Evelyn began to record her observations of the children's language development and responses to books from their birth. Written entries were made on an average of once per week while audiotapes and videos were used less consistently, about every three to four months. In a similar way to Bryce Heath who provided a perspective on Wolf's observations (1992) the collaboration with Jane (a specialist in Early Childhood Education and infant development) offers a new understanding of the data in terms of how the children's responses to books correspond to their stage of emotional development.[5]

Isabel – Early exposure to books from birth through first year

For the first 6 months Isabel explored books in a physical manner, as most babies do, shaking them, putting them in her mouth, using her fingers and even toes to play with the pages. Here she was learning about the "bookness" of books.

4. Most books on raising bilingual children advise parents to be consistent in order to be successful: either one parent/one language, language in the home or particular times/days for one language (Tokuhama-Espinosa 2001). While this formula no doubt tends to work, for a parent speaking a minority language without the support of family, community and sufficient resources (as in Evelyn's case) it is difficult to be consistent.

5. We are aware that in the recording of parental observations there are issues of objectivity and reliability; Jane's more objective perspective in the analysis helps to counteract this.

She had a variety of books to explore – cardboard, linen, paper, plastic for the bath, some with flaps, others with animal noises, and some with mirrors or rustly sounds. The books changed depending on which way up or down they were held, whether they were good to make hats or houses or seats or how much floor space they could cover. Over time Isabel learnt that her parents liked to 'play' with them too, with her, in a special way, sitting close, talking to her and focussing her attention on a part of a book which might disappear and then could reappear again. Isabel was learning about anticipating events and repeating experiences, all of which gave her intrinsic pleasure and is a pre-requisite for intentionality. Developmentally, the ability to sequence comes later in a child's general learning so a story being narrated through the turning of pages in an ordered manner feels like a mystery for the baby. We see this with Isabel (aged 10 months) who patiently tries to refocus her mother on the pictures, turning the pages backwards and forwards even though it is clear to the observer that her mother wants to move forward to tell the story.

The first book Isabel took a particular interest in was *Peek-a-boo!* by Jan Ormerod (1997). On every page of this simple but engaging picturebook, against a different coloured background, there is a baby, usually sitting up and one small object such as a toy car or duck. The baby's face is hidden by a flap picturing a bib, a towel or a teddy bear. Instead of reading the English words, as she turned the pages, Evelyn would ask, "¿Dónde está el bebé?" [Where's the baby?] before lowering the flap. She would then usually add comments like "¡Mira qué lindo bebé!" [Look at that lovely baby!] or "Es como tú con tu toalla cuando sales del baño." [Just like you with your towel when you come out of the bath] and she would point to the other object in the picture. By 5 months Isabel was responding excitedly with her whole body when the baby's face was revealed: smiling, moving her mouth, making little exclamations like 'eh eh', waving her arms, bending over and touching or 'stroking' the pages. At 7 months her gaze centred on the place where the baby's face was hidden, expecting the baby to appear when the flap was lowered. This response coincided with her understanding and playing 'Peek-a-boo' with cloths and towels that Evelyn would put on her head saying, "¿Dónde está Isabel?" [Where is Isabel?] Isabel would pull it off and laugh. By 8 months, as she was being tucked into bed, Isabel herself was pulling up her cot sheet over her head and pulling it down suddenly. This sort of game, which children generally play around this age, reflects their growing awareness and comes when they are physically able to move away from their parents and are becoming more emotionally independent. All this change makes for unsettling times and usually results in a separation/stranger anxiety that can last a few months. It is as if the babies fear abandonment, even though it is them crawling away from their caregivers.

At 9 months the video diary shows one of Evelyn's colleagues, Florence, reading *Peek-a-boo!* to Isabel, whom she had not met before. Rather than taking Isabel into her lap, Florence sits on the floor, facing her and reading the book in English. Evelyn is behind the camera, focusing on Isabel's reaction. Although Isabel smiles on cue when the baby is revealed, she is clearly uneasy. At one point, she tries to hold the book herself, to turn the pages and move the flap and when she can't manage, she shows frustration. Her favourite book which has delighted her with the expected 'surprise' of hiding and finding has turned into something puzzling and less secure: her mother is in fact 'hiding' behind the camera; the visitor is too present facing her and Spanish sounds and words in her mother's tongue have been replaced by English coming from a stranger. Isabel tries to find comfort by playing with her book herself, cutting out the stranger using English, but she can't quite do it on her own. Isabel's responses confirm how language and reading routines, including physical contact and familiar 'baby talk' can provide the security that babies need at this crucial stage.[6]

Isabel – The emotional pull of the 'mother tongue' from 1 to 2 years

Isabel celebrated her first birthday in Mexico where the family was living for four months during Nigel's sabbatical. Books were important in Isabel's transition from England to Mexico as was the routine bedtime reading.[7] *Goodnight Moon* by Margaret Wise Brown (1991) was one of the favourite books she chose to take with her although in Mexico she found new favourites such as a version of 'The Little Red Hen'. It is fitting that Isabel's first words which were in Spanish, 'agua' [water] and 'jugo' [juice], reflected the special stage she had reached around orality and being weaned. Her pleasure in eating is reflected in her responses to the sight of food in her well loved picturebooks. For example when Isabel saw the 'bowl of mush' in *Goodnight Moon* or the 'pan' [bread] being eaten by the Red Hen and her chicks, she would smack her lips.

Back in Cambridge at 15 months, Isabel's vocabulary increased dramatically both in English and Spanish, as she began going to crèche for three mornings a week but also to a Spanish playgroup. There was much mixing of languages in songs,

6. At 14 months, Mills notes the 'safety' that the social act of reading (Hal wanting to read with his mother) provides during the stage of 'separation anxiety' when Hal becomes mobile.

7. In Cambridge, Isabel spent at least an hour a day reading books with Evelyn; with Nigel, she read most evenings before bed. This routine continued in Mexico. Mills notes the way that being read to (the routine and the re-reading of favourite books) makes a child feel the world is a safe and predictable place, particularly when they experience a significant change of context.

made up words and pretend play. There is also a growing pleasure in stories, in the skills of manipulating books, identifying objects in the pictures and in the use of dialogic interaction with the reader. Her favourite book became *The Baby's Catalogue* by the Ahlbergs (1984), particularly the 'Accidents' page, where she would say 'oh oh' and point to the spilt juice, the baby that peed on a little girl's knee and the baby that's fallen into the toilet. This corresponds to her emerging awareness of bodily functions. She also loved the image of the swings. Swings connected her two worlds, her grandparent's house in Mexico and the play park in Cambridge, as well as providing links between books and between her two languages. This example shows how picturebook reading becomes doubly significant within a bilingual context.

A video session, back in Cambridge of Isabel at 16 months shows her to be in complete control, not only of the books themselves –turning the pages, lifting the flaps and finding her favourite pictures, but also of her choice of books. She refuses the offer of books she does not want, wriggles off Evelyn's lap and even turns her back to her slightly – she is clearly determined to show she can do all this without Mum. Her interest in *The Baby's Catalogue* is still mainly divided between the swings and the 'accidents' and as she looks she repeats words like 'papá' [daddy], 'pipí' [pee], '[m]ira' [look] and 'cayó' [it fell]. At the last picture, with the sleeping babies, she lowers her voice and whispers 'bebé' [baby]. At this stage she is moving away from identifying with the baby to wanting to be the mummy who puts the baby to bed. However, despite her new independence, the language link with Evelyn is still very strong and Spanish continues to be the language of favourite books. At 20 months she started to contribute to family conversations, recounting what happened during the day using a mixture of her languages. As new words, pictures and stories added to an emerging awareness of narrative and of audience, they helped her to become a more active participant in the communications around her.

Isabel – Changes in the family and her use of language from 2 to 3 years

In the six months before Flora was born Isabel, now 2 years old, developed an awareness of the two languages and began to separate them according to the person she was with. There was also an awareness of impending change. In the months before her sister was born Isabel's favourite picturebooks dealt with two themes that were preoccupying her: 'being naughty' such as the classic *Where the Wild Things Are* by Maurice Sendak (1992) and 'babies', such as *Rosie's Babies* by Martin Waddell (1990).

English and Spanish were used for everyday practical interactions. In addition they had their own function in supporting psychological developments. This is exemplified by the following observation when Isabel was 2.2 and Evelyn was six months pregnant.

Observation. Sunday morning. 5 December 1999.
Nigel and I had finished breakfast. Nigel had gone into the garden with a book and Isabel was playing in the living room. She had taken some dolls for a "walk" and had put them on a beanbag covered with a tea towel to go to sleep, following the schedule at her nursery. She asked me to come and see. On the beanbag were little Teletubby dolls, Dipsy and Po; in front of them, on a plastic blue child's chair was a big Po doll.[8]

Isabel: Look, Mami. Mamá silla. Cuento. [Mother chair. Story]
Me: ¿La mamá les está contando un cuento antes de dormir? [Is mother telling them a story before going to bed?]
Isabel: Sí. Cinderella.
Me: ¿Y cómo va el cuento de Cinderella? [and how does the story of Cinderella go?]
Isabel: [hesitates]
Me: Cuéntame el cuento de Cinderella. [Tell me the story of Cinderella]
Isabel: Teddy Bear. ¡GRANDE! [BIG] *makes face of big bear, wide eyes, loud voice*
Me: ¿Había un oso grande? [Was there a big bear?]
Isabel: Cinderella. ¡Es my casa! [It's my house]
Me: ¿Y qué dijo la mama oso? [And what did mother bear say?]
Isabel: ??? *not clear*
Me: ¿Y el bebé oso? [and baby bear?]
Isabel: Ayayayay *noise of baby bear*
Me: Ah sí.
Isabel: And Cinderella said… ??? *not clear but adopts storytelling voice*

I go upstairs. When I return, Isabel is telling a story to the dolls.

Isabel: Un día un príncipe [one day a prince] … said… ??? … frightened "oh" Giant ??? … bye bye said Giant… frightened the Giant ???

Isabel plays with dolls on beanbag.

Isabel: Shhhhhh

She cuddles them.

Isabel: ???… tomorrow… bed

Isabel puts cushion on beanbag and dolls on it.

Isabel: Sleep.

Removes cushion puts it on her head then back on the sofa.

Isabel: [to dolls] Look, watch. Yes. Up. I climb. Watch.

She gets on armchair.

8. Dipsy and Po are two of the Teletubby creatures (who walk, talk and act like toddlers) that appeared in a British children's television programme which was very popular at the time.

Isabel: Mami come watch. Everyone. Plum pie sun. Wait.
Me: Cuéntales el cuento de los tres ositos. [tell them the story of the three bears]
Isabel: Cuento de príncipe. Cuento de príncipe. ??? Teddy bears. ??? House.

Isabel puts dolls on armchair with her.

Isabel: We doing a picnic Mami.
Me: I see.
Isabel: Yummy yummy. We doing a picnic. Open the mouth. Dipsy. Open the mouth… sit up! Sandwiches. [9]

Nigel comes back into the room.

Isabel: Daddy, we're doing a picnic *repeats several times until Nigel pays attention to her*
Nigel: Where?
Isabel: Lunch.
Nigel: Very nice. [To Evelyn] I'm going up to the computer.
Isabel: To computer?
Nigel: Yes.

She continued playing with dolls. Big Po gives a hug to little one.

Isabel: Teddy Mami?

She went upstairs and brought down her favourite teddy bear. She put one little teletubby on big Po and one on Teddy Bear.

Isabel: Mami, Daddy, big hug!

Isabel was drawing on various resources including languages, stories and familiar picturebooks and what these represented to her in order to help her work through the upcoming changes in her life. She knew that her mother had a baby in her tummy. She also identified with her mother and her nurturing role in her play. In this particular play scene her fantasies about where babies come from and unconscious fears about being displaced by a new baby are beautifully shown. The play incorporates performance (acting out), use of story and song and important choices in her use of language. [10] If we look at how Isabel uses the two languages we can see that she is on the cusp of moving from Spanish to English. On the one side is Spanish, her mother's tongue, which in Isabel's mind represents her mother and suggests the baby part of herself. The actual words in Spanish (fewer than English) relate to experiences she associates with her mother's early storytelling, 'Once Upon a Time', and are indeed in her past. There is some confusion in her

9. 'Open the mouth' is a direct grammatical translation from the Spanish: 'Abre *la* boca'.

10. In *Each Peach Pear Plum* various fairytale characters like Cinderella and the three bears enjoy a picnic together. There are also references to the song her father sings to her about Teddy Bears having a picnic in the woods.

mind between Cinderella (who has a bad Daddy) which elides into the story of The Three Bears (also a reference to her father's favourite song). "It's My House!" is heartfelt and could represent her mother's womb which is not hers anymore.

On the other side of the divide (in the oedipal sense too) stands Isabel's 'father tongue' or in other words, her father. For Isabel, her father represents her more mature side, the 'not' baby side (Blatt 2007) and the opening out of her world. It represents her fantasies about having a different and exciting relationship in which she wants to take her mother's place. In English she stands up to the giant (she is strong like her Daddy) and then plays with a cushion which in her mind could represent her own enlarged tummy like her mother's. Towards the end of the play she acts out the Teddy Bears' Picnic song which she loves to sing with her father and adds the picnic scene which is very familiar to her from *Each Peach Pear Plum*. She gives both toy parents a baby each and instructs the mummy and daddy to hug, just as the four Teletubbies do on the TV programme. For the present, it is as if her father has helped to redress the balance in her ambivalent mind to enable her to include the possibility of a new baby in her life where she is protected by her father.

Isabel and Flora – The impact of the new arrival

Flora was born in March 2000. The congratulatory cards received by the family all mysteriously disappeared after a few days and were later found by Evelyn hidden under a book. It was pretty clear who the culprit had been. Isabel found her sister's arrival very difficult for the first weeks, refusing to eat and do as she was told. She finally told it straight: "I don't want my sister, I want to do *cosas bonitas con Mami* [nice things with Mummy] and Winnie the Pooh (her favourite soft toy)' and broke into tears. Here her use of Spanish emphasizes her anxiety about not being loved as she had been by her mother.

Isabel regularly translated for Nigel. If Evelyn said to her, 'Está caliente la sopa', she'd turn to her father and say, 'It's hot, Daddy'. With the exception of a few words, Isabel spoke to Flora in English. Sometimes she would ask Evelyn to 'tell Flora' in Spanish (as if Flora didn't understand English) 'these are my new shoes and she's too small to wear them' or 'I can make that puzzle by myself' or 'I don't want the horrible foxes to eat her'. These are wonderful examples of Isabel using her bilingual self to grapple with her ambivalence around the arrival of her sister. She clearly wants Flora to be relegated to only understanding Spanish. She wants to split off from this baby and to outline her boundaries. Then, in the more literary example of the foxes (a reference to various other picturebooks with foxes as characters), Isabel is showing us how she rather likes the powerful feeling that she might be the bad fox who could attack and eat her sister up (a reference to *Where the Wild Things Are*) but that at the same time she is able to show her friendlier side. Perhaps there is a growing part of her which is learning to accommodate her small sister who can't do very much yet, can't wear shoes or do a puzzle and needs someone big like herself to protect her from the foxes. She is trying out the idea that maybe her sister is not quite such a threat after all.

A vignette with Isabel and her father follows where she is using language to define roles and relationships and understand the dual nature of her family. When Flora was 4 months and Isabel 2.10, Evelyn's parents came for a month-long visit and as a consequence there was more Spanish spoken in the house. One night, as Isabel was looking at *The Art Book* (Phaidon 1994) with Nigel, she asked who God was. When Nigel replied that He was 'Jesus' Daddy', Isabel asked 'Does God speak to Jesus in Spanish?' In the same period, after a trip to Scotland with her grandparents, Isabel had the following exchange (in English) where language is used as an identifier and a way of understanding her own dual identity:

Isabel to Nigel: You speak like Scottish.
Nigel: How do you speak?
Isabel: I speak Spanish.
Evelyn: How do I speak?
Isabel: You speak Spanish.
Evelyn: What does Flora speak?
Isabel : No, she doesn't, only a little she speaks. [*A few minutes later to Nigel*] I'm half Scottish and half Mexican.

Flora starts her journey with picturebooks

Flora went through similar stages to Isabel as a baby, exploring books with hands, mouth and feet; looking at pictures with intensity and babbling as she did, before the age of 1. She became fascinated by books and concentrated on them for even longer than her sister (see Figure 2). At 12 months she was demanding to be read to, pushing books into people's hands and climbing onto their laps, including her sister's. Although she was exposed to more English than Isabel at that age – through her sister, books and videos – her Spanish was still strong and linked to time spent with Evelyn and the Spanish playgroup. Her first words were 'gato' [cat], 'pato' [duck], 'ibo' [libro – book], all of them associated with images in books. At 16 months, her favourite books were those with strong rhythm, rhyme and wordplay but she also loved looking at babies in various art books.[11]

11. Flora's responses to *Peepo*, which have to do with her increasing engagement with the world around her, have been described in *Children Reading Pictures* (Arizpe and Styles 2003: 32–33).

Figure 2. The Book Encampment: Flora (2.1) tells her own picturebook story
Reprinted by permission of Evelyn Arizpe

Flora – Interlinguality, intertextuality and humour from 2 to 3 years

In what follows, we focus on the complex emotional and bilingual relationship she was developing with books between her second and third year. At this stage Flora was at the language 'mixing' stage, using bilingual compound words like 'washamanos' [wash hands]. There was an intermingling of life and text, such as in the pretend 'eating' from images in books (moving her hand to the page and then to her mouth and pretending to chew) or saying 'como princesa' [like princess] when sitting on the potty (a reference to Tony Ross's book, *I want my Potty* (1986)). A significant part of Flora's world was put together by books, linked by intertextuality. For example, one day when she was reading Crockett Johnson's *Harold and the Purple Crayon* (1983) with Evelyn, Flora spontaneously said, 'como Bear' [like Bear], meaning the bear character from Anthony Browne's *Bear Hunt* who, like Harold, uses a pencil to draw himself out of dangerous situations; here Flora has made a sophisticated link between the two books based on her understanding of the character's actions.

The following extract of a reading of *Meg and Mog* with Evelyn, illustrates how this intertextuality works in both English and Spanish and includes song, gesture and performance. Here humour plays an important part.

Reading with Flora [age 2.1] Meg and Mog.
Flora has seen this book several times before and it's a favourite.

Evelyn reads: *At 1 o'clock she got her broomstick her cauldron and a spider*
Flora starts singing 'Incy Wincy Spider'.
Evelyn: ¡Bravo!
[...]
Evelyn reads: *They landed on a hill in the moonlight to make a spell*
Flora immediately notices fire under cauldron: Fire!
Evelyn: Fire!
Flora sings 'London's burning', Evelyn joins in and they finish singing
Evelyn reads: *This is what they put in*
Flora: Cro cro.
Evelyn: Una rana. [A frog]
[laughter...]
[Next page]
//Evelyn reads: *and they all stirred the cauldron frog in a bog*
//Flora points at large letters in speech bubble: RRAAAAA
Evelyn points at letters: AAAA ...
Evelyn reads: *ABRACADABRA*!
[Next page]
//Evelyn reads: BOOM!
//Flora: RRAAAAA! BOOM!
Evelyn reads: *Something has gone wrong.*
Evelyn: Pero, ¿qué hay aquí? [But what have we here?]
[Pause] ¡Un ratón! [A mouse!]
Flora immediately starts singing and clapping: 'A ton ton ton ton, a tin tin tin [sings 'El botón de Martin' about a mouse under a button]
Evelyn: ¡Bravo! Se acabó. [It's finished.]
Flora: More!
[Pause]
Flora: ¡Más! [More!]

The extract reflects that special enjoyment that Flora derived from text. There is much laughter on Flora's part at the sounds of rhyming words, such as the witches' names. The images –spider, fire and mouse- are immediately linked to songs in which they play a main part in both English and Spanish. The songs become part of the reading event and there is a shared understanding as they sing in both languages. There is also a pleasure in the onomatopoetic words which Flora anticipates and in a real sense is reading, supported by the visual effects and enlarged font. 'ABRACADABRA' and 'BOOM' come to life for her. As Evelyn comments on the pictures and praises Flora in Spanish, this language is confirmed as a language specific not only to books but to an added layer of reading, an almost critical running commentary which provides the space for questions and making links between texts and life. At the end of the extract, Flora asks for 'more' and, not getting an immediate reply, cries 'más', strengthening her demand by using a word that might have more influence on Evelyn –which it does, as they continue to read the next 'story' in the picturebook.

Flora – The pleasures of two languages or of words in two languages

The following extract from the audio tapes again illustrates Flora's sense of humour, love of word play and nonsense. Evelyn's willingness to adapt to Flora's play allowed Flora to extend her metalinguistic abilities. Their interaction is based on a complex understanding of the humour that occurs when there is an incongruity between the signifier and the signified and took place when they were looking at a book called *La Guacamaya* [The Macaw] by Catalina Fernández Mata:

Reading La Gucamaya with Flora [age 2.1]
Flora has seen it a few times before. The illustrations show a colourful parrot in its native landscape. The text is based on a traditional Mexican song.

Evelyn: Vamos a ver *La guacamaya* [let's look at *The Guacamaya*]
Flora: Guacamaya
[...]
Evelyn: *Estaba la guacamaya parada en un platanar* [the guacamaya was standing on a banana tree]
Flora: Here macaguaya
Evelyn: Sí, ahí está una guacamaya [yes, there's the guacamaya] *arreglándose las alas para salir a volar* [arranging its wings to fly]
[...]
Flora: [points at a cloud] Esa macaguaya! [that's a guacamaya!]
Evelyn: Esa no es guacamaya. [that's not a guacamaya]
Flora: [points at cloud, laughing] Esa es macaguaya! [that's a guacamaya!]
Evelyn: [entering the game] Esa no es guacamaya, esa es un nube! [that's not a guacamaya, that's a cloud!]
[...]
Flora: [points at the flower] Esa macaguaya!
Evelyn: Esa no es una macaguaya, esa es una flor! [that's not a guacamaya, that's a flower!]
Flora: Esa macaguaya!
Evelyn: No es macaguaya!
[The game continues until Nigel interrupts, says something in English to Evelyn]

Flora [continues on her own, pointing at other objects in the pictures]: Macaguaya! Esa es macaguaya!
[Evelyn replies to Nigel]
Flora [continues on her own and demands Evelyn's attention back]: Macaguaya! Esa macaguaya! Esa macaguaya Mami! Esa macaguaya! Esa macaguaya Mami!

Flora was evidently enjoying saying an unusual word like 'guacamaya' but was playing with the sounds and converting it to 'macaguaya'. She was not interested in the story and therefore subverts the reading by interrupting to point at objects in the picture such as a cloud, a pigeon, a flower, and calling them all 'macaguaya'. Evelyn at first corrects her and then realizes the 'mistake' was intentional and reacts as Flora wants her to, by pretending surprise and shock. The game of subverting signifier and signified goes back and forth until it reaches a crescendo which is interrupted by Nigel. Flora expresses her desire to continue the game and the fun and tries to get her mother's attention back. She ignores her father, just as he ignores her. He is not part of this game which requires both players to know both the text and the language. There is therefore also a sense of exclusivity here and pleasure which this entails. This example highlights how the understanding that there can be two words for one thing – one of the consequences of bilingualism – leads to creative play with picturebooks.

Flora – Keeping up with big sister

Another episode on the video tape shows Flora at 2.7 pretending to play a toy violin. Isabel, who had just started violin lessons, is practising a tune with a music book open in front of her on the music stand. Flora is sitting on a small trampoline, legs crossed, with a picturebook on her lap. With the violin under her chin, she alternates between turning the page and making 'playing' motions with the bow, as if she were reading music from the picturebook. The book takes on an intermedial role both as a picturebook and a music book. This particular picturebook was *Pájaros en la cabeza* by Laura Fernández, about a little girl who wakes up one morning with three little birds on her head who stay there throughout the day, joining in all her activities. It has nothing in particular to do with music, although the little birds occasionally chirp and sing but perhaps there is something about the choice of book which represents something in Flora's mind. After all, the girl in the story carries a burden on her head, pleasant at times but intrusive at others. Flora is trying to imitate Isabel who is playing the violin. The intensity with which she plays at playing is very strong and we feel this as we view the video. Then Flora is asked by Isabel if she wants to play a piece together, which they do, both looking intently at the music sheet before them. It is like a burden for Flora to want to be like her older sister all day, every day, but then there are benefits: if she practices hard enough she might be asked to play a duet with her!

From the age of 2.5 Flora enjoyed imitating her sister and parents by pre-writing motions on paper. On one bit of video Flora makes marks on a piece of paper and then tears this bit of paper off. She continues this until she has six or seven bits of paper with marks on them around her. It is as if she is making her own story, building up a "picturebook", thought by thought and mark by mark. At this time, she was tutored by Isabel (aged 4.8) while they 'played school' and they communicated almost entirely in English. Yet like Isabel, Flora was very interested in the fact that she had two languages; it somehow empowered her in a place where she might have felt slightly anxious. When a young Argentinian student came to do some childminding for Flora, Flora announced to her, in English, 'I speak Spanish'.

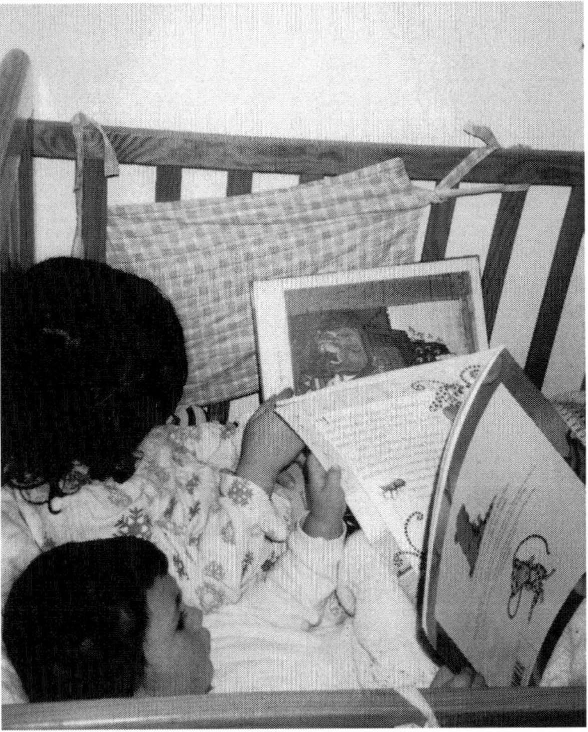

Figure 3. Isabel (4.2) and Flora (1.8) sharing a quiet independent moment in Flora's cot
Reprinted by permission of Evelyn Arizpe

The two girl's different personalities reflect the quality of their interaction with books (see Figure 3). The particularly supportive experience that Flora derived from picturebooks can be seen throughout her first three years. Unlike her sister, who had a strong desire to communicate through language from an early age and was mainly interested in narrating (and singing) stories, Flora's priority was to immerse herself in long periods of mainly silent looking: spoken language was not necessary. Her mute offering of books was her way of communicating and developing relationships with others. She also developed a fine-tuned responsiveness to what books had to offer through the pictures and through both languages. In addition stories and pictures provided (and continue to provide even ten years later) a safe space for retreating to when the outer world becomes too complex or threatening.

Discussion

In attempting a triadic analysis of the relationship between early "book learning" through responding to picturebooks; bilingualism and emotional development, we were confronted by the difficulties of untangling these three strands, intertwined threads, in each child's complex and unique tapestry of development. At times, as we teased them out, we found ourselves with more questions than answers but also with possibilities for viewing data from different perspectives.

Despite the questions that remain, some of our findings clearly add to the evidence from previous case studies. Analysis of the first 'thread' confirms the significant link between early contact with books and literacy development. The benefits of reading aloud to children from an early age have been well documented for some time but our study also indicated the importance of children learning about books on their own, selecting and exploring them with their body and mind as part of their sensory motor stage, without adult interference. The sorting, identifying, comparing, mixing and organizing that is involved in book learning are all important tasks for cognitive development.

Analysis of the second 'thread' revealed the benefits of early contact with books for emotional development. We saw how the intentional and 'accidental' choices as well as the rejection of certain books fulfilled the girls's particular needs at different stages. These choices were particularly poignant around the separation from mother and, for the purposes of this study, the 'mother's tongue'. We also saw how the situation and language of certain reading events loaded the books with particular emotional charges. *Peek-a-boo!* is a good example: when Isabel meets the book with a stranger, plus an altered language and context, the book becomes a slight threat.

Apart from the obvious advantages of learning another language and the implications for developing biliteracy, the role of the third 'thread', bilingualism, was harder to identify. However, if we start from the fact that being bilingual implies that there are *two* parents or carers involved in the nurturing of the child, with the concomitant advantages this provides, we begin to understand why bilingualism *does* make a difference in the children's responses and emotional development. We know that the mother is usually the primary driving force in instilling bilingualism within the family and the roots of that 'mother tongue' in the relationship between parents and children grow deep.[12] Equally, we know that fathers "contribute a different though complementary role to mothers" (Stroh et al. 2008: 158) and their 'father tongue' (usually the 'second' language), as we have seen, takes on its own significance over time.

Summary

Babies and young children from 0–3 years of age show us how they feel and think through their behaviours. At this stage, much of their general learning develops independently against the background of nurturing adults. As the child's language develops this adds a special dimension not only to their ability to communicate but to their understanding of the world around them. Like the ongoing exploration of language, the exploration of books involves sorting, sounding out, playing with and understanding what fits with what else, including feelings and relationships. Although these discoveries will be different for each child, the books are linked to particular developmental stages and we have seen over time that the young child's responses to picturebooks and books with pictures reflect their growing personality. In addition, the understanding of linguistic, literacy, social and cultural conventions supports the bilingual child in moving forward, 'leaving' baby books and baby language behind. Finally, we hope that the language, stories and images, and the pleasures of sharing them in two languages with both parents in these important first three years, will continue to provide support in their emotional life, as they learn to weave their own tapestry for themselves.

12. At least for the first three years. Tokuhama-Espinosa (2001: 191) provides a table which provides evidence for the mother's tongue usually being the child's first language.

Children's books cited

Ahlberg, J. & Ahlberg, A. 1986. *Each Peach Pear Plum.* Harmondsworth: Puffin Books.
Ahlberg, J. & Alberg, A. 1984. *The Baby's Catalogue.* Harmondsworth: Puffin Books.
Ahlberg, J. & Ahlberg, A. 1983. *Peepo.* Harmondsworth: Puffin Books.
Browne, A. 1994. *Bear Hunt.* Harmondsworth: Puffin Books.
Fernández Mata, C. & Gómez, C. 1996. *La guacamaya.* México DF: CONAFE.
Fernández, L. 1983. *Pájaros en la cabeza,* México DF: Trillas.
Johnson, C. 1983. *Harold and the Purple Crayon.* London: HarperCollins.
Nicoll, H. & Pieńkowski, J. 2001. *Meg and Mog.* St. Helens: The Book People.
Ormerod, J. 1997. *Peek-a-boo!* London: The Bodley Head.
Phaidon Press Editors. 1994. *The Art Book.* London: Phaidon Press.
Ross, T. 1986. *I want my Potty.* London: Andersen Press.
Sendak, M. 1992. *Where the Wild Things Are.* London: HarperCollins.
Waddell, M. & Dale, P. 1990. *Rosie's Babies.* London: Walker.
Wise Brown, M. & Hurd, C. 1991. *Goodnight Moon.* London: HarperCollins.

References

Arizpe, E. & Styles, M. 2003. *Children Reading Pictures.* London: Routledge.
Arizpe, E. & Styles, M. 2011. Children reading at home: An historical overview. In *The Handbook of Research on Children's and Young Adult Literature,* S. A. Wolf, K. Coats, P. Enciso & C. A. Jenkins (eds), 2–43. New York: Taylor & Francis.
Baghban, M. 1984. *Our Daughter Learns to Read and Write.* Newark DL: International Reading Association.
Bialystok, E. 2001. *Bilingualism in Development.* Cambridge: CUP.
Blatt, J. 2007. A father's role in supporting his son's developing awareness of self. *Infant Observation* 10(2): 173–182.
Crago, M. & Crago, H. 1983. *Prelude to Literacy.* Carbondale IL: Southern Illinois University Press.
De Houwer, A. 1990. *The Acquisition of Two Languages from Birth: A Case Study.* Cambridge: CUP.
Drury, R. 2007. *Young Bilingual Learners at Home and School.* Stoke-on-Trent: Trentham.
Durán, C. & Fittipaldi, M. 2010. Entre En Joan y El Drac: La literatura como experiencia compartida. *Lectura y Vida* 31(3): 20–28.
Gregory, E. 2008. *Learning to Read in a New Language.* London: Sage.
Hakuta, K. 1986. *Mirror of Language: The debate on bilingualism.* New York NY: Basic Books.
Herman, J. 1996. "Grenouille, where are you?" Crosslinguistic Transfer in Bilingual Kindergartners Learning to Read. PhD dissertation, Harvard University.
Kenner, C. 2000. *Home Page – Literacy Links for Bilingual Children.* Stoke-on-Trent: Trentham.
Leopold, W. 1939–1949. *Speech Development of a Bilingual Child,* 4 Vols. Evanston IL : Northwestern University Press.
Lowe, V. 2007. *Stories, Pictures and Reality. Two Children Tell.* London: Routledge.

Mills, R. 2002–2004. Hall's reading diary. *Books for Keeps* 133–144. <http://www.booksforkeeps.co.uk/member/roger-mills> (8 April 2010).

Molina Iturrondo, A. 1998. Adriana y los recuentos independientes de sus cuentos favoritos. *Lectura y Vida* 19(4): 5–12.

Molina Iturrondo, A. 2001. Leer y conversar sobre los cuentos favoritos: La lectura dialógica en la alfabetización temprana. *Lectura y Vida* 22(1): 40–46.

Nicoladis, E., Charbonnier, M. & Popescu, A. 2006. Second language/bilingualism at an early age with an emphasis on its impact on early socio-cognitive and socio-emotional development. In *Encyclopedia on Early Childhood Development* (online), R. E. Tremblay, R. G. Barr & R. De V. Peters (eds), 1–6. Montreal, Quebec: Centre of Excellence for Early Childhood Development. <http://www.enfant-encyclopedie.com/documents/Nicoladis-Charbonnier-PopescuANGxp.pdf> (8 April 2010).

Robinson, M. & Turnbull, B. 2005. Veronica. An asset model of becoming literate. In *Popular Culture, New Media and Digital Literacy in Early Childhood*, J. Marsh (ed.), 51–72. London: Routledge Falmer.

Stroh, K., Robinson, T. & Proctor, A. 2008. *Every Child Can Learn*. London: Sage.

Tokuhama-Espinosa, T. 2001. *Raising Multilingual Children*. London: Bergin & Garvey.

Totten, G. O. 1960. Bringing up children bilingually. *American Scandinavian Review* 48: 42–50.

White, D. N. 1954. *Books Before Five*. Oxford: OUP.

Wolf, S. A. & Heath, S. B. 1992. *The Braid of Literature: Children's Worlds of Reading*. Cambridge MA: Harvard University Press.

About the editor and contributors

Kathleen Ahrens is Professor and Head of the Language Center at Hong Kong Baptist University. She received her Ph.D. in linguistics from UC San Diego and has published extensively in academic journals on issues surrounding meaning and metaphor. She is also a writer and translator of children's books. She serves on the board of the Society of Children's Book Writers and Illustrators as the International Regional Advisor Chairperson. She has been invited to talk in Taiwan, Italy, Germany, and Hong Kong on topics relating to language in children's picturebooks, picturebook evaluation, and the creation of literature for children.

Evelyn Arizpe is a Lecturer at the School of Education, University of Glasgow. She has taught and published in the areas of literacies, reader-response to picturebooks and children's literature. She is co-author, with Morag Styles, of *Children Reading Pictures: Interpreting visual texts* (Routledge 2003) and *Reading Lessons from the Eighteenth Century: Mothers, Children and Texts* (Pied Piper Press 2006). Also with Styles, she co-edited *Acts of Reading. Teachers, Texts and Childhood* (Trentham 2009). She has a special interest in Mexican children's books and children's literature about Latin America. She is project leader for Visual Journeys, an international project based on research in Spain, Australia and the US which involves immigrant children reading wordless picturebooks.

Jane Blatt has worked for over 30 years as a teacher with young children, including preschool, primary bilingual learners and children with special needs. She has a Diploma in Therapeutic Skills with Children and Young Adults (Scottish Institute of Human Relations 2006). She is the author of the article 'A Father's Role in supporting his Son's Developing Awareness of Self' (*Infant Observation* 2007, 10 (2): 173–182). In her Language and Literacy work both in schools and in her private work, she has a special interest in supporting all children to create their own books and has an impressive array of self made books of her work with her children through the years.

Martin Roman Deppner is Professor of Media Theory and Dean of the Faculty of Design at Bielefeld University of Applied Studies. He was visiting professor of cultural science, media and for the graduate program "Jewish Studies" at the University of Oldenburg and at the Pentiment international summer academy at the Hamburg College of Applied Sciences. He is advisor for the "Kunst aktuell" column of the magazine "Kunst und Unterricht" and was involved in exhibition projects with the Museum of Art (Hamburg), the Jewish Museum (Berlin), Museum of History (Bielefeld), among others. His main research areas cover the presentation of Jewish identity in the media and fine modern arts, picturebook research, perspectives of design in the digital era, the aesthetic of feature films, paradigms of photography, and medial aspects of art and their interaction with other contemporary media.

Janet Evans is a Senior Lecturer in Education at Liverpool Hope University and Literacy and Educational Consultant. Formerly a primary school teacher, she has written nine books on language, literacy and maths education. Her latest edited book, *Talking Beyond the Page: Reading and Responding to Picturebooks.* Routledge (2009) focuses on a reader response approach to responding orally to picturebooks. Her ongoing research interests include an exploration of strange, ambiguous and unconventional picturebooks, critical literacy and interactive writing linked to popular culture. She has taught in India, Nigeria, Australia, America, Canada, Chile and Spain and was awarded two research scholarships which enabled her to work and study in the USA. In 2010 she was awarded a research scholarship to study at the International Youth Library in Munich. She has presented papers at many international conferences and is currently doing part time freelance consultancy.

Bettina Kümmerling-Meibauer is Professor in the German Department at the University of Tübingen. In spring 2010 she held the position of guest-professor in memory of Astrid Lindgren at Linnaeus-University Växjö/Kalmar in Sweden, and in winter 2010/11 she was guest-professor at the University of Vienna. Among her recent works are a two-volume encyclopedia on international children's classics (Metzler 1999); a monograph on the relationship between children's literature, canon formation and literary evaluation (Metzler 2003), and three essay collections on children's and youth films (co-edited with Thomas Koebner, Reclam 2010), *New Directions in Picturebook Research* (co-edited with Teresa Colomer and Cecilia Silva-Díaz, Routledge 2010) and Astrid Lindgren (co-edited with Astrid Surmatz, Routledge 2011). She was one of the advisory editors for *The Oxford Encylopedia of Children's Literature* (2006). She is chair of the project "Children's Literature and European Avant-Garde", funded by the European Science Foundation.

Lesley Lancaster is Reader in Multimodal Literacy in the Education and Social Research Institute at Manchester Metropolitan University, and is a member of the Communication, Discourse, and Learning research group. Her current research interests include children's early symbolic learning, writing in early childhood, distributed cognition, and multimodal analysis, with recent publications and conference papers reflecting these interests. She was Director of the ESRC funded project *Grammaticisation in Early Mark Making*, and a member of the UK national *Early Language and Communication Project*. She is currently writing a book, to be published by Routledge, about the study reported on in this volume. She is an active member of BAAL, and jointly co-ordinates the Multimodal Communication special interest group, and is on the editorial board of the *Journal of Early Childhood Literacy*. She teaches in the field of Applied Linguistics at undergraduate and doctoral levels, and in the past she has worked as a member of a literacy advisory team, a researcher at the National Foundation for Educational Research, and as a teacher.

Virginia Lowe is the author of *Stories, Pictures and Reality: Two Children Tell* (Routledge 2007), which is based on the parent-observer record she kept of her son and daughter's responses to books for over thirteen years, beginning at birth (6000 handwritten pages). She has lectured at universities and is an Adjunct Research Associate of Monash University, from which she received her doctorate. She has been a public and school librarian and Victorian Judge for the Children's Book Council of Australia's Book of the Year Awards. She has conducted a manuscript assessment agency, Create a Kids' Book, for fourteen years. www.createakidsbook.com.au.

Jörg Meibauer is Professor for German Linguistics at the Johannes Gutenberg University Mainz (Germany) and Affiliated Professor at the University of Stockholm. His academic stations include Cologne, Brighton, Lund, Tübingen, and Dresden. Among his recent publications are monographs on rhetorical questions (1986), modal particles (1994), pragmatics (1999) and German linguistics (co-authored 2002, 2007); in addition, he edited collections on sentence mood (1987), lexical acquisition (with M. Rothweiler 1999), quotation (with E. Brendel and M. Steinbach 2007), experimental pragmatics and semantics (with M. Steinbach 2010) and language acquisition and children's literature (with W. Klein 2001). His main research interests lie in the grammar-pragmatics interface, in word formation, and in language acquisition. He is currently working on a book-length study on lying, deception, and bullshit.

Kerstin Nachtigäller is a member of the Emergentist Semantics Group (Center of Excellence, Cognitive Interaction Technology) at the Bielefeld University. 2008 she received her diploma in Psychology at the Bielefeld University. Her Ph.D. project takes place within the Dilthey Fellowship to Dr. Katharina Rohlfing and is supported by the Volkswagen Foundation. The project is concerned with the acquisition of semantics in early lexical children. Fast and slow mapping mechanisms of word learning as well as child-directed input are particularly considered as important factors of influence.

Marie Luise Rau does research on picturebooks as a free scholar with support from Johann Gutenberg-University in Mainz. She studied English, classical languages and educational sciences at the universities of Marburg and Cologne and wrote her thesis in English linguistics at Mainz University. After teaching languages at a German Gymnasium she intensified her studies of first-language acquisition with a view to picturebooks. Publication: *Literacy. Vom ersten Bilderbuch zum Erzählen, Lesen und Schreiben* (*Literacy. From the first picturebook to storytelling, reading, and writing.*). Bern, Stuttgart, Wien: Haupt 2007/second revised edition 2009.

Cornelia Rémi earned her MA and PhD in German literature at Ludwig-Maximilians-Universität, Munich, where she currently holds a post-doctoral position. Her research focuses on transformation processes between different eras in the history of literature, on interferences of poetry and spirituality, intermediality, erudite communication and strategies of poetic self-reflection. She has published book-length studies on Friedrich Spee and Clemens Brentano and essays on (amongst other subjects) the composition of early modern devotional texts, King Solomon as an ambiguous literary authority, Albrecht von Haller's theology and the Swedish reception of *Anne of Green Gables*. Her dedication to sharing her enthusiasm for literature with others resulted in her leading several workshops in creative writing at the Bücherpiraten Festival for Children's and Young Adult Literature in Lübeck.

Katharina Rohlfing received the Masters degree in Linguistics, Philosophy and Media Studies from the University of Paderborn, Germany, in 1997. From 1999 to 2002 she was a member of the Graduate Program Task Oriented Communication. She received the Ph.D. degree in Linguistics from the Bielefeld University, Germany, in 2002. Her postdoctoral work at the San Diego State University, the University of Chicago and Northwestern University was supported by a fellowship within the Postdoc-program of the German Academic Exchange Service (DAAD) and by the Emmy Noether-Program of the German Research Foundation (DFG). 2006 she became a Dilthey-Fellow (Funding initiative "Focus on the Humanities"), and her research project on the "Symbiosis of Language and Action" is supported by the Volkswagen Foundation since May 2008. She is head of the Emergentist Semantics Group within the Center of Excellence "Cognitive Interaction Technology", Bielefeld University. Katharina Rohlfing is interested in learning processes. In her research, she is investigating the interface between early stages of language acquisition and conceptual development.

Carole Scott is Professor Emeritus of English and former Dean of Undergraduate Studies at San Diego State University, California and serves on the board of its National Center for the Study of Children's Literature. She has worked on the boards of the Children's Literature Association (ChLA), International Research Society for Children's Literature (IRSCL), and was a Senior Scholar on the Nordic Children's Literature Network (NorChiLNet). She is co-author with Maria Nikolajeva of *How Picturebooks Work* (Garland 2001), shared editorial responsibility with Muriel Lenz for *His Dark Materials Illuminated* (Wayne State Univ. Press 2005), has articles and chapters in a variety of journals and essay collections specializing in children's literature, and acts as a reviewer for several journals.

Kyoko Takashi Wilkerson received her Ph.D in Linguistics at Georgetown University in 1990. She is currently Professor at Nagoya University of Foreign Studies, teaching courses in sociolinguistics and comparative linguistics. Her primary research interests include studying how "power" and "solidarity" are expressed in various types of discourse, such as narratives written by men and women, child caregivers' reports, and advertising. In doing so, she has examined reference terms for husbands in Japanese, code-switching in advertising, and style shifts and schema shifts in narratives, and published the results in "A Sociolinguistic Analysis of English Borrowings in Japanese Advertising Texts" (1990); "Language and Desired Identity: The case of contemporary Japan" (1992); "A Study of Speaker's Subjectivity in Causal Expressions" (1997); "Reference Terms for Husbands in Japanese" (1997); "Rethinking Power and Solidarity in Japanese Discourse" (1999); "When Power and Solidarity Collide: New Politeness Strategies in Japanese" (2000); and "Emotivity in Narrative Discourse: Cross-cultural and Cross-Gender Perspectives" (2005).

Annette Werner studied Biology at the Free University Berlin, and in 1990 completed her Ph.D. in Zoology and Neurobiology. Between 1990 and 1995 she worked at universities in Germany and abroad, including Munich (Germany), Hong Kong (China), and New York (USA), covering research areas in Neurology, Physiology, Psychology, Computer Sciences and Optometry. After a period of maternity leave between the 1998 and 2001, she moved with her family to Tübingen in 2002. Here, she is heading the *Colour Research Group* at the University Centre for Ophthalmology, which investigates human and animal color vision, using psychophysical methods. She is a member of the Werner Reichardt Centre for Integrative Neuroscience (CIN) and the Bernstein Centre for Computational Neuroscience Tübingen.

Douglas Wilkerson is Professor in the Department of Japanese Studies at Nagoya University of Foreign Studies. His research interests include cultural and socio-linguistic aspects of Japanese discourse and language use. He has written about the spiritual dimensions of social activities in contemporary Japan, and how this dimension influences and is incorporated into both formal (ritual) and informal discourse; how cultural identity, especially domestic identity, is created and manipulated through and in Japanese travel advertising; and the cultural limitations of metaphorical conception, ways in which metaphors must be altered for adaptation in different cultural contexts, and the constraining parameters for such adaptation.

Index